8

LONGMAN

e-world

Computers: Basics and Applications

Anshu Kumar
Shweta Malik

PEARSON

This book is printed on ECF card and ECF environment-friendly paper manufactured from unconventional and other raw materials sourced from sustainable and identified sources.

ISBN 978-81-317-5667-6

10 9 8 7 6 5 4

Published by Dorling Kindersley (India) Pvt. Ltd., licensees of Pearson Education in South Asia.

Head Office: 7th Floor, Knowledge Boulevard, A-8(A) Sector 62, NOIDA 201309, UP, India.
Registered Office: 11 Community Centre, Panchsheel Park, New Delhi 110 017, India.

Typeset by HT Burda Media Ltd.

Printed in India by Manipal Technologies Ltd.

PREFACE

Small children operating gadgets effortlessly is a common sight these days. Be it the remote control of TV sets, keys of cell phones or gaming consoles—kids can navigate through them all with amazing ease and dexterity. The reach and penetration of computers in our day-to-day lives has gone up tremendously and have aided in the development of children's familiarity with gadgets and computers at an early age. The formal learning of Computer Science can be made more interesting and easy if the scope of the subject and knowledge are imparted in a student-friendly and innovative manner.

e-world, a series of eight books, is our humble effort to provide comprehensive learning and understanding of basic concepts and applications of computers. Based on the National Curriculum Framework (2005) and the CCE approach, the books have been written keeping in mind the feedback received during our decade of experience in teaching and interacting with the students. Interspersed with illustrations, tips and interesting facts, we have tried to present the concepts in a lucid and student-friendly manner.

The focus of books for classes 1 to 5 is on learning basics of computers, Microsoft Office 2003 and skills of programming through LOGO. The books for classes 6 to 8 take the students to a different realm where they are encouraged to explore and experiment with software such as Macromedia Flash, Windows Movie Maker and Adobe Photoshop. The foundations of programming are further strengthened through chapters on QBASIC and Visual Basic. Great care has been taken to provide a smooth transition of topics across all books in the series. Posters and Stickers provided at the end of books for classes 1 and 2 make learning more fun.

Some of the key features of the books are:

- **Adorable Characters** Aladini, Anjali and Aryan introduce the topics that will be learnt in each chapter
- **Quick Questions** and **Check Your Progress** questions interspersed within the text for quick self-testing help in the formative assessment
- **Quick Fact** provides interesting tidbits of information related to the topic at hand
- **Quick Tip** presents useful alternative options/shortcuts for performing operations
- **Recap Time** at the end of each chapter for quick and easy recapitulation
- **Assessment Time** contains carefully graded exercises to test the knowledge of concepts learnt. Besides, these can also be used for summative assessment.
- **Activity Time** for practical hands-on exercises to strengthen the understanding and to hone computer skills
- **Notes for the Teacher** contain suggestions on how to introduce the various topics
- **Project Work,** sample **Olympiad Questions** and **Tech Terms** have been included at the end of the books

We sincerely hope that each book in this series will be enjoyed by students and teachers alike. We welcome feedback and suggestions for improving the books.

Anshu Kumar
Shweta Malik

IN THIS SERIES

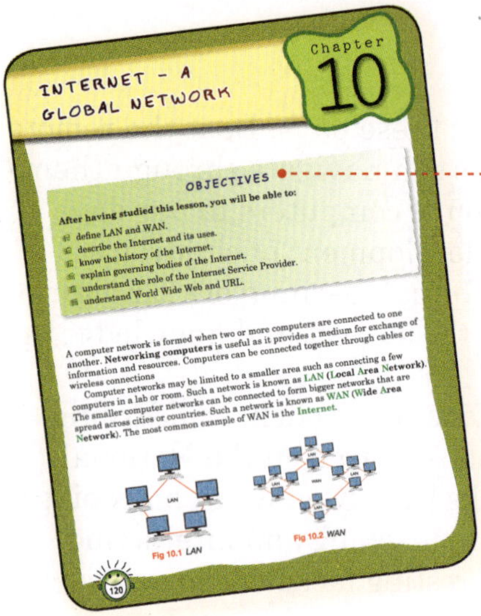

INTERNET – A GLOBAL NETWORK

Chapter 10

OBJECTIVES

After having studied this lesson, you will be able to:

- define LAN and WAN.
- describe the Internet and its uses.
- know the history of the Internet.
- explain governing bodies of the Internet.
- understand the role of the Internet Service Provider.
- understand World Wide Web and URL.

A computer network is formed when two or more computers are connected to one another. **Networking computers** is useful as it provides a medium for exchange of information and resources. Computers can be connected together through cables or wireless connections.

Computer networks may be limited to a smaller area such as connecting a few computers in a lab or room. Such a network is known as LAN (**Local Area Network**). The smaller computer networks can be connected to form bigger networks that are spread across cities or countries. Such a network is known as WAN (**Wide Area Network**). The most common example of WAN is the **Internet**.

Fig 10.1 LAN

Fig 10.2 WAN

120

Objectives outline the topics that will be taught within a chapter.

Quick Question and **Check Your Progress** questions interspersed with the text for quick self-testing help in the formative assessment.

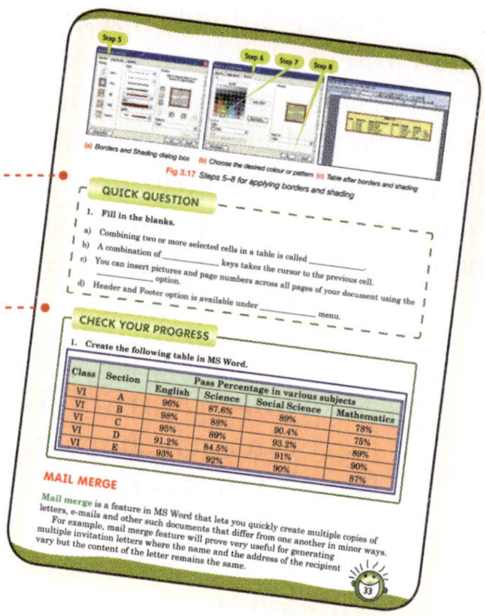

(a) Borders and Shading dialog box (b) Choose the desired colour or pattern (c) Table after borders and shading

Fig 3.17 Steps 5–8 for applying borders and shading

QUICK QUESTION

1. Fill in the blanks.
   a) Combining two or more selected cells in a table is called ________.
   b) A combination of ________ keys takes the cursor to the previous cell.
   c) You can insert pictures and page numbers across all pages of your document using the ________ option.
   d) Header and Footer option is available under ________ menu.

CHECK YOUR PROGRESS

1. Create the following table in MS Word.

Class	Section	Pass Percentage in various subjects			
		English	Science	Social Science	Mathematics
VI	A	96%	87.6%	89%	78%
VI	B	98%	88%	90.4%	75%
VI	C	95%	89%	93.2%	89%
VI	D	91.2%	84.5%	91%	90%
VI	E	93%	92%	90%	87%

MAIL MERGE

Mail merge is a feature in MS Word that lets you quickly create multiple copies of letters, e-mails and other such documents that differ from one another in minor ways.

For example, mail merge feature will prove very useful for generating multiple invitation letters where the name and the address of the recipient vary but the content of the letter remains the same.

33

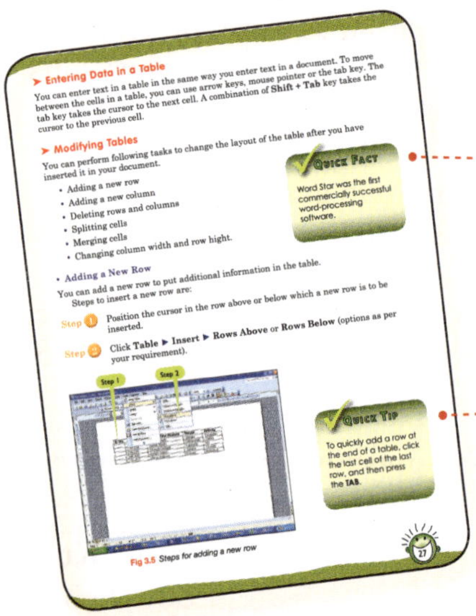

➤ Entering Data in a Table

You can enter text in a table in the same way you enter text in a document. To move between the cells in a table, you can use arrow keys, mouse pointer or the tab key. The tab key takes the cursor to the next cell. A combination of **Shift + Tab** key takes the cursor to the previous cell.

➤ Modifying Tables

You can perform following tasks to change the layout of the table after you have inserted it in your document.

- Adding a new row
- Adding a new column
- Deleting rows and columns
- Splitting cells
- Merging cells
- Changing column width and row hight.

QUICK FACT

Word Star was the first commercially successful word-processing software.

- **Adding a New Row**

You can add a new row to put additional information in the table.

Steps to insert a new row are:

Step 1 Position the cursor in the row above or below which a new row is to be inserted.

Step 2 Click **Table ▶ Insert ▶ Rows Above** or **Rows Below** (options as per your requirement).

QUICK TIP

To quickly add a row at the end of a table, click the last cell of the last row, and then press the TAB.

Fig 3.5 Steps for adding a new row

27

Quick Fact provides interesting tidbits of information related to the topic at hand.

Quick Tip presents useful alternative options/shortcuts for performing operations.

Recap Time at the end of each chapter for quick and easy recapitulation.

Assessment Time contains carefully graded exercises to test the knowledge of concepts learnt. Besides, these can also be used for summative assessment.

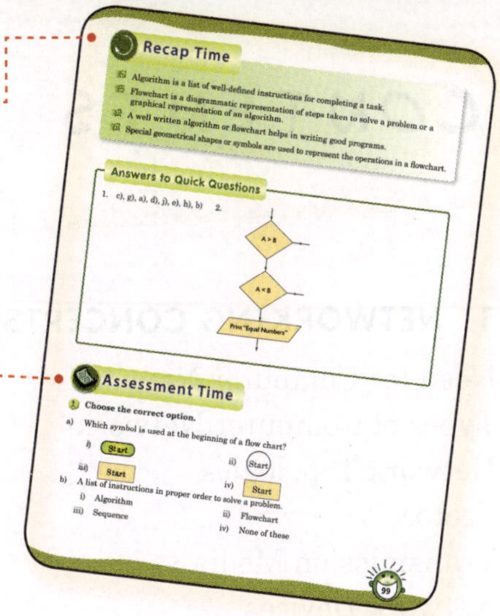

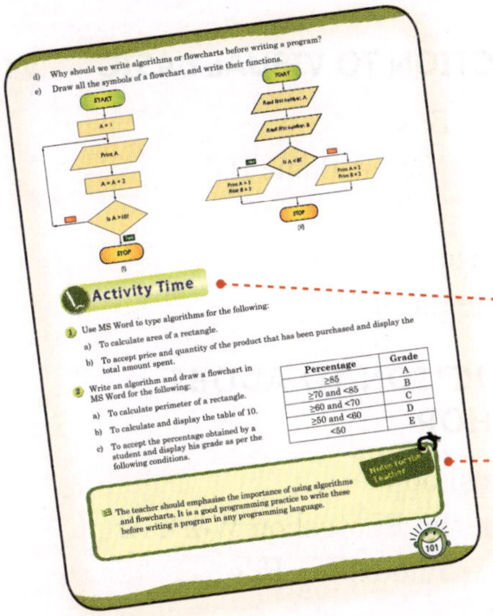

Activity Time for practical hands-on exercises to strengthen the understanding to hone computer skills.

Notes for the Teacher contain suggestions for the teacher to introduce the various topics.

Project Time, **Sample Olympiad Questions** and **Tech Terms** have been included at the end of the books.

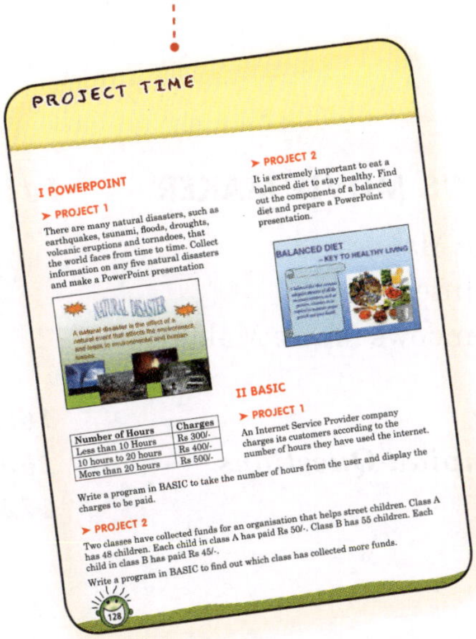

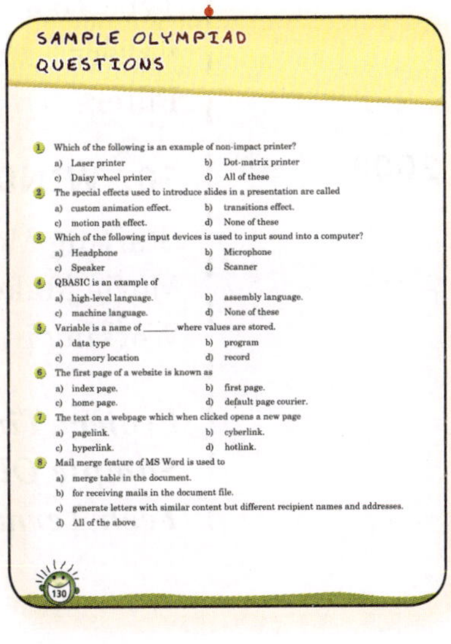

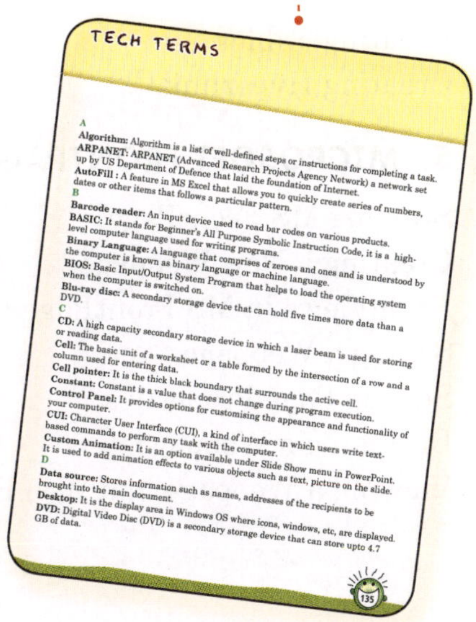

CONTENTS

NETWORKING CONCEPTS

Chapter 1

OBJECTIVES

After having studied this lesson, you will be able to:

- understand the need for computer networks.
- describe the types of computer networks.
- illustrate the different network topologies.
- define protocols—HTML and TCP/IP.
- identify the different types of transmission media used for a computer network.
- describe the uses of various network devices.
- state the need for network security.

These days, computers are used at almost every place such as offices, shops and homes. The computer networks have extended the power of a computer beyond the expanse of a room. With the progress in technology, these computer networks form the core of communication. The Internet is an example of world wide network of computers that is growing at a rapid rate.

A **computer network** consists of two or more computers that are linked in order to share resources such as printers, exchange files and allow communication.

Let us learn more about computer networks.

NEED FOR COMPUTER NETWORKS

Nowadays computer networks are a vital part of any organisation. Some of the advantages of computer networks are:

- **Resource Sharing.** All computers in a network can share resources such as printers, fax machines, modems and scanners.
- **File Sharing and Remote Database Access.** A computer network allows sharing of files and access to remote database. You can easily access the files stored on various computers on a network. Also, networking allows many people to work simultaneously on the data stored in a database.

- **Ease of Communication.** Computer networks allow people to communicate through e-mails and instant messaging facilities. This makes the transmission of information easier, more efficient and less expensive.

TYPES OF COMPUTER NETWORKS

Depending on the geographical area covered by a network, there are three types of computer networks (**Fig. 1.1**). They are:

- **Local Area Network (LAN).** A LAN is a computer network that is limited to a local area such as a laboratory, a school or an office building.
- **Metropolitan Area Network (MAN).** A MAN is a computer network that usually covers a larger area than a LAN. For example, a network that connects two offices in a city, a neighborhood area, etc.
- **Wide Area Network (WAN).** A WAN is a computer network that spans a wide geographical area. A WAN may be spread across cities, countries and continents. A WAN is formed by connecting various LANs and MANs. The Internet is considered to be the largest WAN.

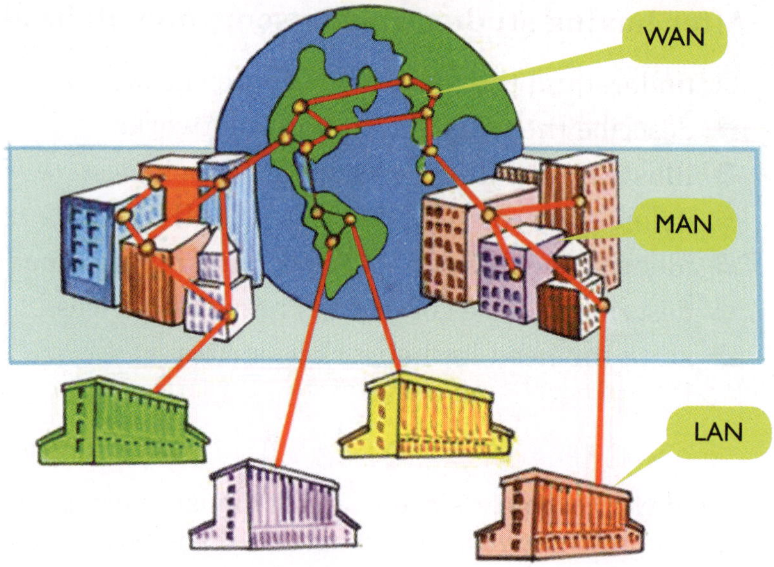

Fig 1.1 *Types of computer networks based on the geographical areas covered*

NETWORK TOPOLOGIES

Topology refers to the layout pattern in which various computers are connected to one another to form a network. The computers on a network are also referred to as **nodes**. There are four main types of topologies. They are:

- **Bus Topology.** In bus topology, all the computers are connected to a single cable called the bus (**Fig. 1.2**). The transmission of data from any computer travels through the length of the bus in both the directions and can be received by all other computers on the network. If the address of a computer is that of the intended recipient, it accepts the data; otherwise the data is rejected. The advantage of the bus topology is that it is quite easy to set up. However, a network cannot function if there are breaks in the bus.

Fig 1.2 *Bus topology*

- **Ring Topology.** In ring topology, each computer is connected to two other computers so as to form a closed ring-like structure (**Fig. 1.3**). In this topology, data is transmitted in one direction only. The disadvantage of ring network is that the breakdown of any one computer on a ring can disable the entire system or network.

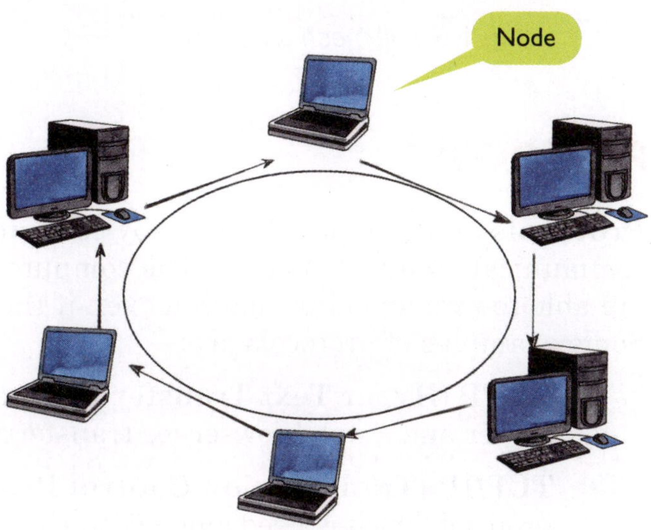

Fig 1.3 *Ring topology*

- **Star Topology.** In star topology, all the computers are connected to a central computer or a central node (**Fig. 1.4**). The data to be exchanged between any two computers passes through the central node. The central node controls all the activities of the nodes. More computers can be easily added to the network. The breakdown of computers, except the central node, does not affect the functioning of network. However, failure of the central node disables the communication across the entire network.

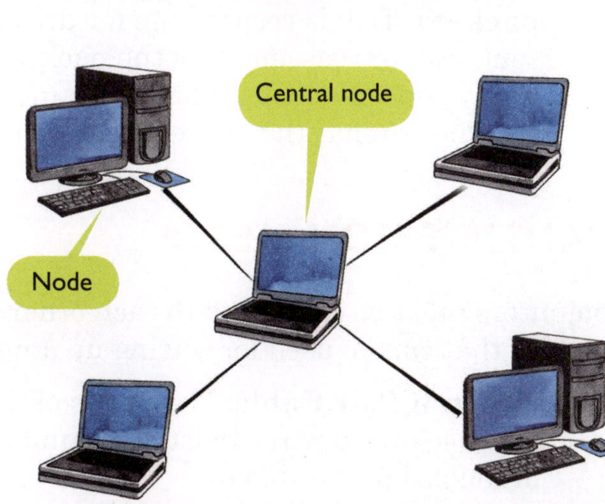

Fig 1.4 *Star topology*

- **Mesh topology.** In mesh topology, every computer is connected to every other computer on the network. Full mesh topology is very expensive to implement. Normally partial mesh topology is implemented in which a computer is connected to few other computers in the network (**Fig. 1.5** and **Fig. 1.6**).

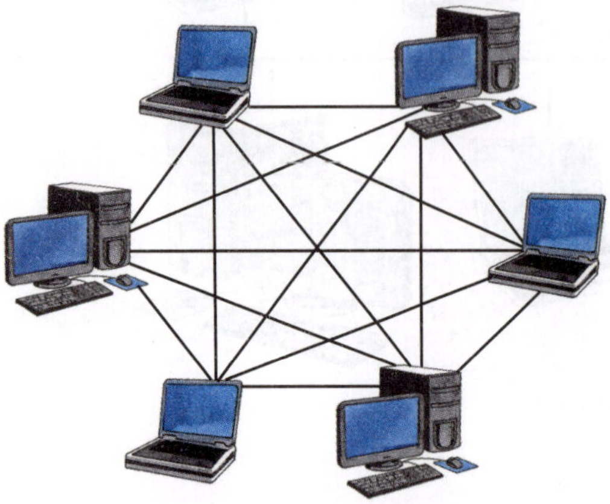

Fig 1.5 *Full mesh topology*

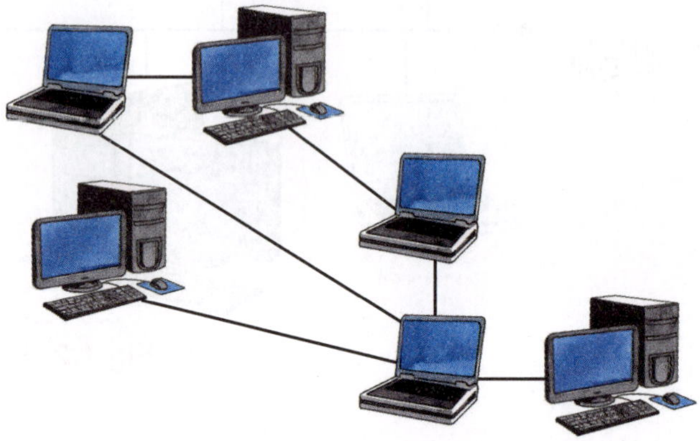

Fig 1.6 *Partial mesh topology*

PROTOCOLS

Protocols are a set of rules used by computers on a computer network to communicate with each other. The computers that follow the same rules or protocols are able to exchange information even if they have different operating systems. Some examples of protocols are:

- **HTTP (Hyper Text Transfer Protocol).** It is a protocol used between a web server and a web browser for transferring HTML pages.
- **TCP/IP (Transmission Control Protocol/Internet Protocol).** TCP is a protocol which is used along with the IP to send data over the Internet. The information is transmitted across the Internet in the form of bundles called **packets**. TCP is responsible for dividing the data into packets before they are sent and for reassembling the packets when they arrive at the destination. IP is a set of specifications that determines the best route for the packets across the Internet so that the packets reach their destination address.

TRANSMISSION MEDIA

Computers must be connected to each other to form a network. There are various types of cables that can be used for setting up a network. Some of them are discussed here.

- **Twisted Pair Cable.** It consists of a pair of insulated wires twisted together. The use of two wires twisted around each other helps to reduce any disturbance and noise in the signals.

Twisted pair is often used in two or more pairs, all within a single cable. Twisted pair cabling comes in two varieties—shielded (**Shielded Twisted Pair** or **STP**) and unshielded (**Unshielded Twisted Pair** or **UTP**). UTP cable is the most common cable used in computer networking.

Fig 1.7 *Shielded twisted pair cable*

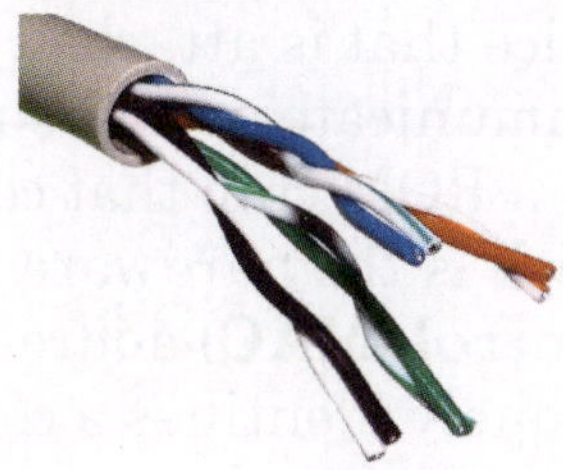

Fig 1.8 *Unshielded twisted pair cable*

- **Coaxial Cable (coax).** It is an electrical cable with a conductor at its centre. The inner conductor is surrounded by a tubular insulating layer. The insulating layer is surrounded by a conductive layer called the **shield** which is finally covered with a thin insulating layer on the outside.

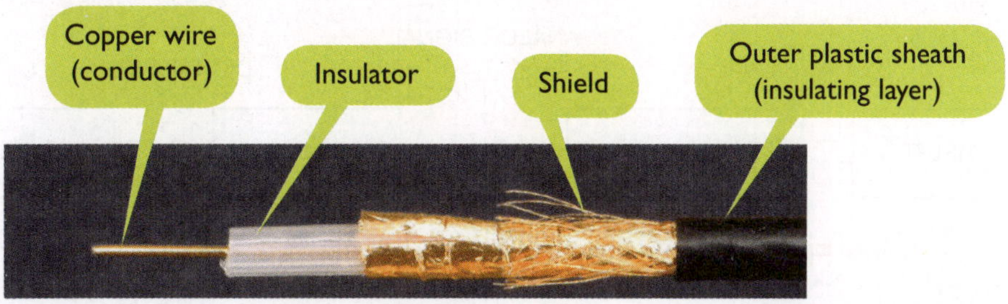

Fig 1.9 *Coaxial wire*

- **Optical Fiber Cable.** It consists of a centre glass core surrounded by several layers of protective material (**Fig. 1.10**). It transmits data in the form of light rather than electronic signals, thus eliminating the problem of electrical interference.

  Fiber optic cable is expensive as compared to coaxial and twisted pair cable but can transmit signals over much longer distances. It also has the capability to carry data at a very high speed.

Fig 1.10 *Optical fiber cable*

QUICK FACT

- A LAN can be set without using wires or cables. A wireless LAN uses high-frequency radio waves to communicate between the different computers.
- Optical Fibers use the principle of total internal reflection of light for the propagation of light signals.

NETWORK DEVICES

Various devices are used for setting up a computer network. Let us discuss a few devices that play a crucial role in a computer network.

- **NIC (Network Interface Card).** It is a hardware device that is attached to a computer to enable it to communicate over the network (**Fig. 1.11**). The NIC has a ROM chip that contains a unique number which is the hardware address or **Media Access Control (MAC)** address. This hardware address uniquely identifies a computer on the network.

Fig 1.11 *Network Interface Card*

- **Modem** (short for **modulator-demodulator).** It is an electronic device that converts the digital signals of a computer into analog form so that they can travel over a telephone line (**Fig. 1.12**). At the destination, the receiving modem converts the analog signals back into their digital form so that the destination computer understands them.

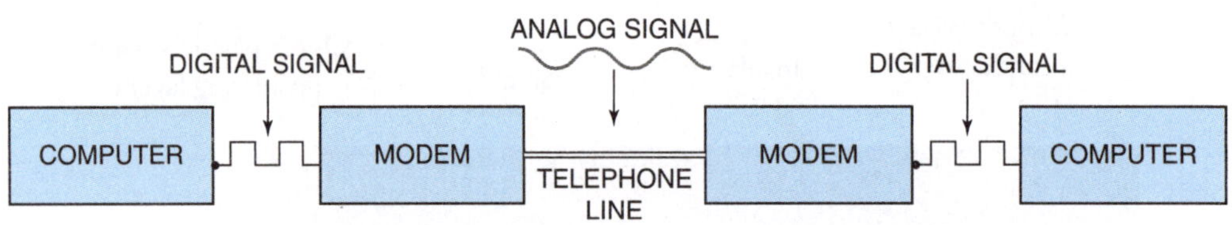

Fig 1.12 *Transmission of signals through modem*

Modems are used for connecting computers to the Internet. Modems are connected to a computer and a telephone line (**Fig. 1.14**).

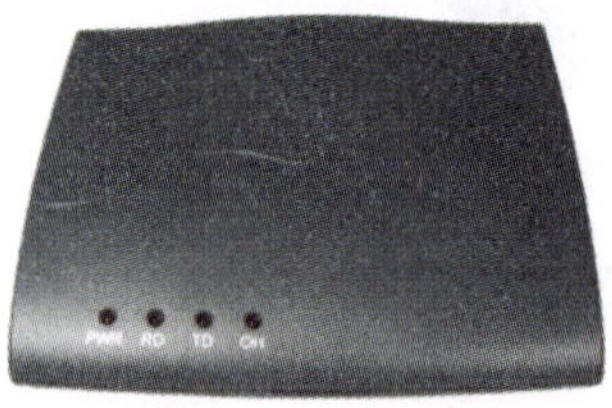

Fig 1.13 *Modem*

Fig 1.14 *Connection of modem*

- **Hub.** A **hub** is a device that is used to connect computers in a network. In a hub, when one computer sends data on the network, the hub simply forwards the packets to all the other computers connected to it. Each computer is responsible for determining which packets are destined for it while ignoring the others.

Fig 1.15 *Hub*

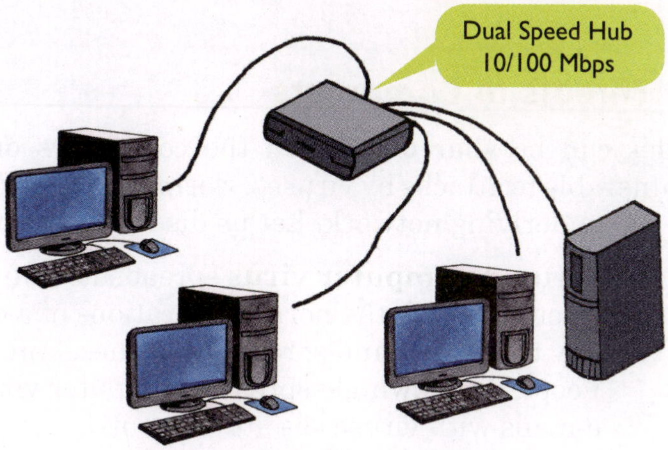

Fig 1.16 *Networking using a hub*

- **Switch.** A **switch** is a device that is also used to connect computers in a network (Fig. 1.17). However, a switch is a more intelligent device than a hub. Unlike a hub, a switch sends the incoming data to the desired destination only. It records the addresses of all the computers connected to it. Thus, when a packet is received, the switch reads the information about the destination address to determine if the destination device is connected to it or not. If the destination device is connected, the switch forwards the packet only to the destination device. In this way, the other computers do not have to read and deal with data that is not meant for them.

Fig 1.17 *Switch*

QUICK QUESTION

1. **Fill in the blanks.**

a) A network that is limited to a small geographical area such as a room is known as ______________.

b) The Internet is an example of ______________.

c) Central node dependency problem arises in networks with ______________ topology.

d) A device that can convert digital signals into analog form and vice versa is known as ______________.

e) A device that is used to connect computers in a network is called ______________.

f) A transmission medium that transmits data in the form of light signals is referred to as ______________.

g) The data is transmitted across the Internet in the form of little bundles are called ______________.

NETWORK SECURITY

A computer on a network can be accessed by many users. Security measures have to be taken to protect networks from unauthorised access and prevent data or information theft.

➤ Threats to Computers

Files can be shared between the computers on a network. This makes a computer vulnerable to attacks by viruses, worms, Trojan horses, etc, that can easily spread because of the underlying network. Let us discuss some of the common threats to computers.

- **Virus.** A **computer virus** spreads itself from one computer to another and interferes with the normal operations of a computer. Viruses attach themselves to any type of file and spread when these infected files are copied to other computers. People unknowingly spread a computer virus by sharing infected files or sending e-mails with viruses as attachments.
- **Worm.** A **worm** is a computer program that uses computer networks to send copies of itself to other computers on a network. A virus requires human action such as transferring of an infected file to spread itself but a worm can spread without any human action. A worm replicates itself without the knowledge of user. Worms can cause severe harm to computer network such as blocking the network and reducing the speed of the network.
- **Trojan Horse.** A computer program that appears to be a useful software but actually causes damage once installed or executed on your computer system is known as **Trojan horse** or **Trojan**. After getting installed, it allows unauthorised access to the computer. Trojan horses are very dangerous as they allow your computer to be remotely controlled by someone else and cause loss of personal and confidential information (**Fig. 1.18**).

Fig 1.18 *People can install Trojans onto your computer or send it via e-mail attachments*

Viruses, worms and Trojan horses may harm the data or affect the performance and speed of the computer.

- **Data Theft.** It is a very serious problem for computer networks. People break into computer networks to either disrupt their functioning or to steal confidential information. **Hackers** are the people who are computer experts and break into computer systems and networks. There are two types of hackers—white hackers and black hackers.

  White hackers study and break into networks to find and fix security loopholes. They offer their services to corporations, public organisations and educational institutions to make their networks more secure.

  Black hackers or **crackers** have a criminal intention. Some examples are—cracking bank accounts in order to transfer money to their own accounts, stealing confidential information, attacking the computer network of an organisation for money, etc.

Quick Fact

Malware (malicious software) is a term used to describe all types of unwanted software such as computer viruses, worms, Trojan horses and spyware.

➤ Computer Security

- **Antivirus Software.** Every computer on a computer network must have antivirus software installed that is updated on a regular basis. Antivirus software can be used to protect the computer from various types of malware. Antivirus software can detect viruses, worms, etc, and warn you of their presence in your computer. It can also deactivate and clean the computer of different types of malicious software. There are various types of antivirus software such as AVG, Avira, Norton and McAfee.

Fig 1.19 *Logos of some antivirus software*

- **Firewall.** A **firewall** is used to prevent unauthorised access to a computer network. A firewall can be implemented as software, hardware or a combination of both. All data or messages entering or leaving a computer network pass through a firewall. A firewall examines each message and blocks those that do not meet the specified security criteria.

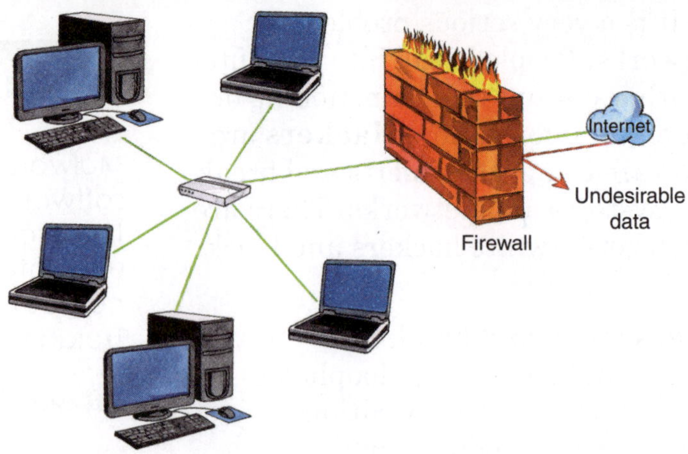

Fig 1.20 *Firewall (visual representation)*

Recap Time

- A computer network consists of two or more computers that are linked in order to share resources such as printers and exchange files and allow electronic communication.
- Based on the geographical area covered, computer networks can be of three types— LAN, MAN and WAN.
- Topology refers to the layout pattern in which various computers are connected to one another to form a network. For example, bus, star, ring and mesh topology.
- Protocols are a set of rules used by computers on the network to communicate with each other.
- Various types of cables such as twister pair, coaxial and fibre optic cable are used for connecting computers in a network.
- A Network Interface Card is a hardware device that stores the hardware address of a computer and enables it to communicate over the network.
- Modem is an electronic device that converts the digital signals of a computer into analog form and vice versa, so that the signals can travel over a telephone line.
- Switch and hub are devices that connect computers in a network.
- A computer virus is a computer program that can spread itself from one computer to another and interferes with the normal operations of the computer.
- A worm is a computer program that uses computer networks to send copies of itself to other computers on the network.
- Trojan horse is a computer program that appears to be a useful software but actually causes damage once installed or run on a computer.
- Antivirus software can be used to protect the computer from different types of malware such as viruses and worms.
- A firewall is used to prevent unauthorised access to the computer network.

Answers to Quick Questions

1. a) LAN or Local Area Network b) WAN or Wide Area Network c) Star d) Modem e) Hub or Switch f) Optical fiber g) Packets

Assessment Time

1 Choose the correct answer.

a) What is the importance of a computer network?

i) It allows sharing of resources.

ii) It is an effective communication medium.

iii) It lets users share files.

iv) All of these.

b) A network that spans countries and continents is known as

i) LAN. ii) MAN.

iii) WAN. iv) None of these

c) A device used to connect computers in a network is referred to as

i) firewall. ii) CPU.

iii) HTTP. iv) switch.

d) A topology in which every computer is connected to every other computer is called

i) ring topology. ii) mesh topology.

iii) star topology. iv) bus topology.

2 Fill in the blanks using the words given below.

MAN	TCP/IP	Topology	Firewall	Ring	Modulator-demodulator	Protocols

a) ______________ refers to the layout pattern in which the computers are connected to each other in a network.

b) A ______________ is formed when the computers are connected in a neighborhood area.

c) A ______________ is used to prevent unauthorised access to a network.

d) Modem stands for ____________________________.

e) ______________ are a set of rules used by computers on the network to communicate with each other.

f) _______________ protocol is used to send data in the form of packets on the Internet.

g) In _______________ topology, each computer is connected to two other computers so as to form a closed structure and the breakdown of any one computer can disable the entire system.

3 Answer the following questions.

a) Define the term 'computer network'. What are its advantages?

b) State the three types of computer networks. Now arrange them in the order of increasing geographical area covered by them.

c) Write a note on twisted pair and coaxial cables.

d) Give the advantages of optical fiber cables.

e) What is a bus topology?

f) How is a hub different from a switch?

g) Discuss some common threats to network security.

h) What is a firewall?

Activity Time

1. Study the computer network used in your school computer lab and find information about the following:
   a) the cable used for setting up the network
   b) the topology of the network
   c) the hub or switch used in the network

2. Find out the names of two companies that manufacture switches and modems.

3. A company has two offices in adjacent buildings. The computers in the two offices need to be connected to one another for a very high speed connectivity.
   a) What cable should be used to connect the computers in these two offices?
   b) What type of network is formed when the computers in the two offices are connected to form a network?

Notes for the Teacher

- The teacher can discuss the evolution of networks in the class.
- The teacher can show the transmission cables and other network devices being used in the computer lab.

INTRODUCTION TO MS ACCESS 2003

Chapter 2

OBJECTIVES

After having studied this lesson, you will be able to:

- define database and DBMS.
- state the advantages of a database.
- start MS Access.
- create a database in MS Access.
- name and state the purpose of various objects in MS Access.
- define components of a table in MS Access.
- create tables in MS Access.
- explain different views of a table—Design view and Datasheet view.
- add and delete records in a table.
- set and remove a primary key in a table.
- modify the table design.

Supermarkets use computers for storing lists of items, their prices, quantities available and quantities sold. Have you ever wondered how do they store, manage and quickly retrieve data about so many products?

Your father can book railway tickets online. Where is the data about trains, their timings and seat allocation stored? How is it that when he books a ticket, the reserved and the available seats are automatically shown?

If a person is asked to memorise such records, it will be an almost impossible task. To deal with such problems, data is stored and managed in a computer using **databases**. These days, large amounts of data are required to be stored at all the places such as hotels, hospitals, supermarkets, railway stations, airports and offices. In this chapter, we will learn more about database and its related terminologies.

DATABASE AND DBMS

A **database** is an organised collection of related data so that it can be easily accessed, managed and updated.

A **Database Management System (DBMS)** is a software program that enables you to create, modify and extract data from a database. DBMS can be based on different data models such as network, hierarchical and relational.

A DBMS based on the relational data model stores data in the form of tables and is called **Relational Database Management System (RDBMS)**. In this chapter, you will learn about MS Access, which is an example of RDBMS. Some other examples of RDBMS are Oracle and Microsoft SQL Server.

➤ Advantages of a Database

Some of the advantages of storing data in a database as compared to files are listed here.

- **Reduced Data Redundancy.** The duplication of data is referred to as **data redundancy**. In contrast to non-database systems which maintain multiple copies of the same data at different locations, DBMS stores data at a central place and does not require you to maintain multiple copies of the same data. Thus, DBMS prevents data duplication.
- **Reduced Updating Errors and Increased Consistency.** When the data is stored at multiple locations, there are chances that modifications are not carried out at all the places. Multiple-mismatching copies of the same data are known as **data inconsistency**. DBMS ensures data consistency by storing data at one place and ensuring that there is no duplication of data.
- **Improved Data Access to Users.** A DBMS stores data at a centralised location and facilitates sharing of data among multiple users according to their requirements. For example, users from all over the country access the database for booking railway tickets.
- **Improved Data Security.** One of the most important advantages of DBMS is data security. In DBMS, user IDs can be created with various levels of security. All the users have some rights and permissions. Only authorised users can access the data, some may have the privilege of changing the data while others can only view the data.
- **Maintaining Standards.** A DBMS ensures that the stored data follows the organisation's own standards or national/international standards. This ensures greater data integrity. This also aids in sharing data between different systems.

Quick Fact

- The relational data model was invented by E F (Ted) Codd in the year 1970.
- A language called SQL (Structured Query Language) can be used to work on any RDBMS.

MS ACCESS 2003

MS Access is the most popular RDBMS that comes as a part of the Microsoft Office suite. MS Access provides a graphical user interface for managing data. The databases created in MS Access are saved with the extension **.mdb**. Let us learn to create a database in MS Access.

➤ Starting MS Access

To start MS Access, click **Start ▶ Programs ▶ Microsoft Office ▶ Microsoft Office Access 2003** (Fig. 2.1). The Microsoft Access window opens as shown in Fig. 2.2.

Fig 2.1 *Starting MS Access*

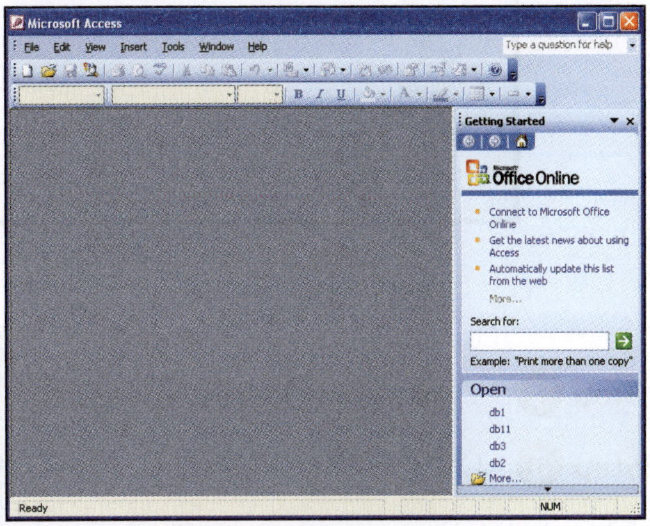

Fig 2.2 *MS Access window*

➤ Creating a Database

Follow the given steps to create a database in MS Access.

Step 1 Click **File ▶ New** (Fig. 2.3). The **New File** task pane appears on the right side of the window (Fig. 2.4).

Step 2 Click the **Blank Database** link from the New File task pane. The **File New Database** dialog box appears (Fig. 2.5).

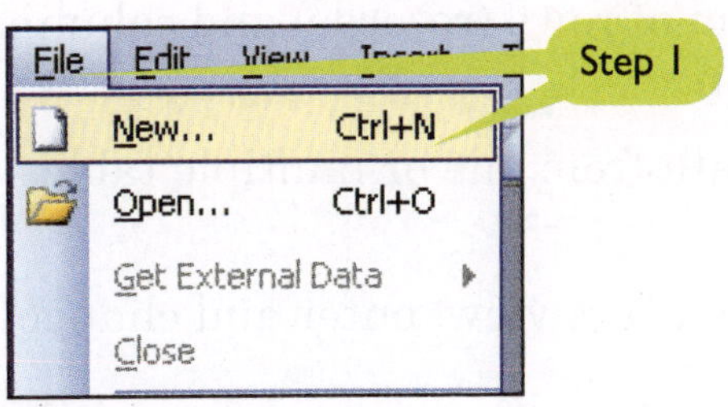

Fig 2.3 *Choosing File▶New*

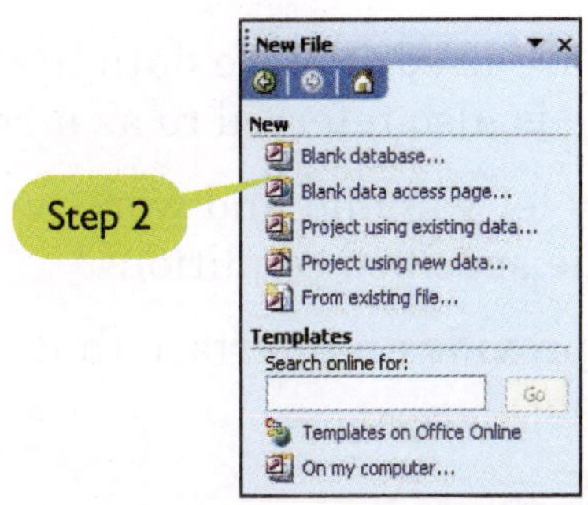

Fig 2.4 *New File task pane*

Step 3 Choose the appropriate drive or the folder where you want to save your database file.

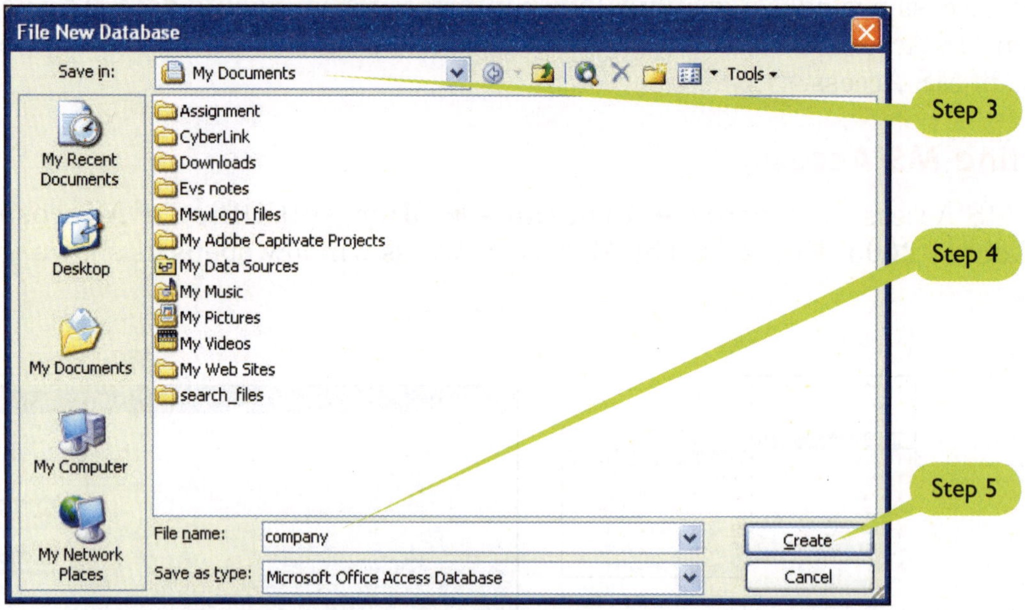

Fig 2.5 *File New Database dialog box*

Step 4 Type a name for the database.

Step 5 Click the **Create** button.

A blank database gets created. The new database window appears on the screen. Using this window, you can create various database objects (Fig. 2.6). Let us learn about various objects that can be created in MS Access database.

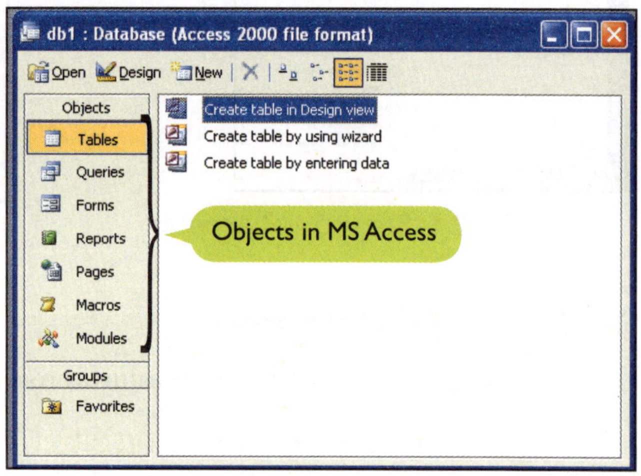

Fig 2.6 *Database window*

➤ Objects in MS Access

The various objects that can be created in MS Access are as follows:

- **Tables.** They are used to store data in the form of rows (records) and columns (fields). A table is also referred to as a **relation**.
- **Queries.** They let you find and work on the data from one or multiple tables according to the specified conditions.
- **Forms.** They provide an interface that lets the users view, enter and change data in the tables.

- **Reports.** If forms are for input, then reports are for output. Reports are used to display the information stored in a database in a professional format for printing purposes.
- **Pages.** They are used for entering or displaying data on the Internet.
- **Macros.** They are programming codes for performing various tasks. They can be easily created from the list of available macro actions.
- **Modules.** They are used for storing programming codes in MS Access.

In this chapter, you will learn to work with tables in MS Access.

TABLES IN MS ACCESS

The **tables** are the building blocks of a database and are used for storing data. A table is made up of rows and columns. A database can have one or more tables.

Consider Table 2.1 that stores data about the employees in an organisation.

Primary key

Record

Field

Table 2.1 *Information about the employees in an organisation*

Table: Employee

Eno	Ename	Esalary (in ₹)	Eaddress
E001	Harish	10000	12-Park Street, New Delhi
E002	Ramesh	25000	Flat No. 5, Vikas Apartment, Rohini, New Delhi
E003	Kiran	7500	23/78, Hari Ganj, New Delhi
E004	Harshita	12000	C-1/2 Rising Sun Apartments, Paschim Vihar, New Delhi

➤ Components of a Table

The important components of a table are:

1. **Field or Attribute.** The columns in a table are known as fields or attributes. A field is a named unit of information. A field stores one type of information about all the objects or items. Every field has a data type that determines the type of values that can be stored under it. For example, the above table has four fields or attributes. The field **Ename** stores text values and the field **Esalary** stores numeric values.
2. **Record.** The rows in a table are known as records. A record stores complete information about an object or an item. For example, **Table Employee** (Table 2.1) has five records. Each record contains the complete information about an employee.
3. **Primary Key.** A primary key is a field or combination of fields that uniquely identifies the records in a table. A primary key field cannot have repetitive values and cannot be left blank. In Table 2.1, **Eno** field can be made the primary key as every employee has a unique employee number.

QUICK QUESTION

1. **Fill in the blanks.**

a) A ____________ is an organised collection of related data.

b) DBMS stands for ________________________.

c) A ____________ uses tables to store data.

d) The databases created in MS Access are saved with the extension ____________.

e) The rows in a table are called ____________, whereas the columns are known as ____________.

➤ Creating a Table

There are various ways to create tables in MS Access. They are:

- Creating tables in Design view
- Creating tables by using Wizard
- Create table by entering data

In this chapter, you will be learning to create tables in the Design view. This view lets you design the structure of a table by specifying the field names, their data types and properties.

The steps to create a table in the Design view are:

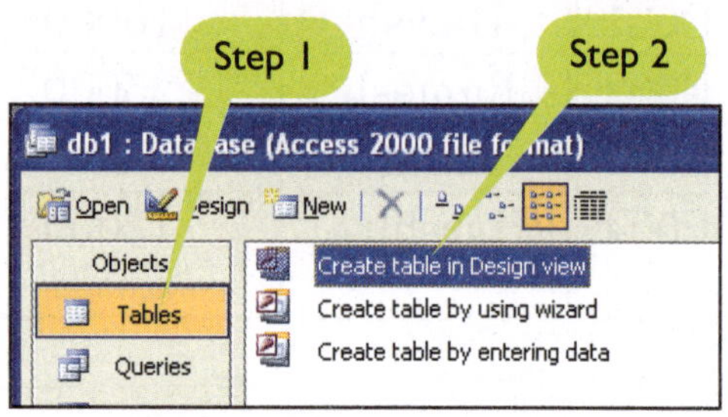

Fig 2.7 *Steps 1 and 2 to create a table*

Step 1 Click the **Tables** tab in the Database window (Fig. 2.7).

Step 2 Double-click the **Create table in Design view** option. The **Table Design** window appears as shown in Fig. 2.8. The Table Design window is divided into two areas:

- **Field Grid pane.** You use this pane to specify the structure of the table by providing the names of the fields and their data types.
- **Field Properties pane.** You use this pane to specify the field properties.

You will learn more about data types and field properties later in this chapter.

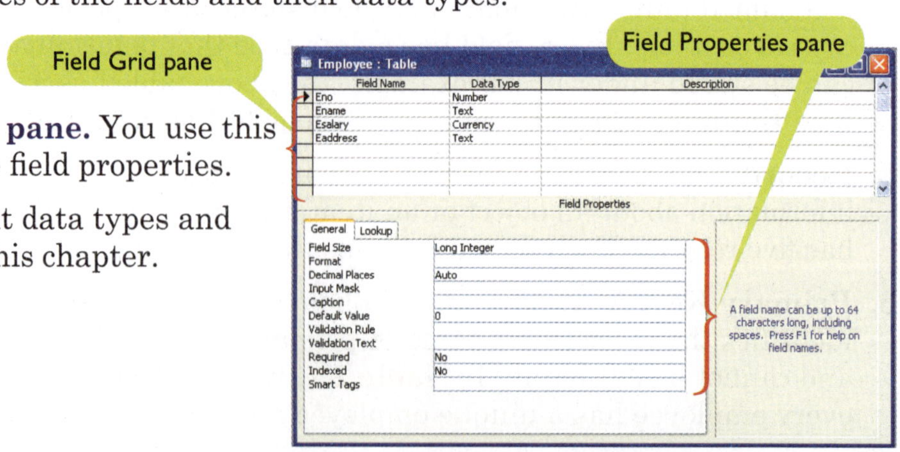

Fig 2.8 *Table Design window*

Step 3 Click **File ▶ Close** (**Fig. 2.9**) or click the **Close** button of the Table Design window.

Step 4 A message box appears (**Fig. 2.10**); click **Yes** to save the table.

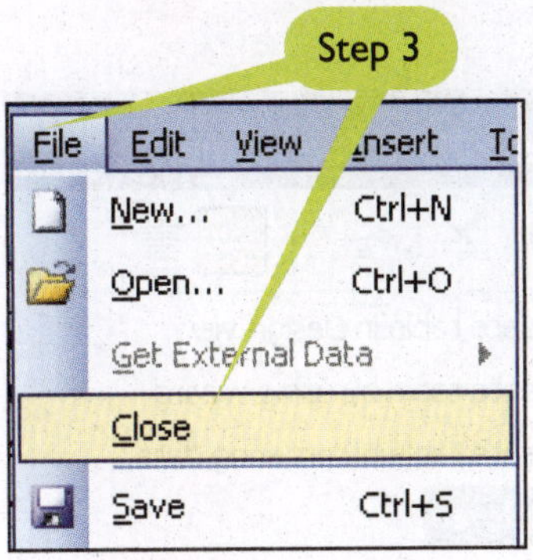

Fig 2.9 *Choosing File▶ Close*

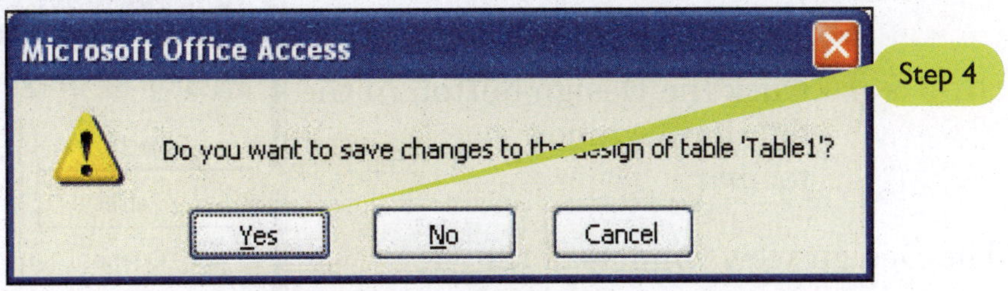

Fig 2.10 *Message box*

Step 5 The **Save As** dialog box appears. Type the table name and click **OK** (**Fig. 2.11**).

Step 6 A **message box** appears that asks whether you want to create a primary key or not (**Fig. 2.12**). Click **No**.

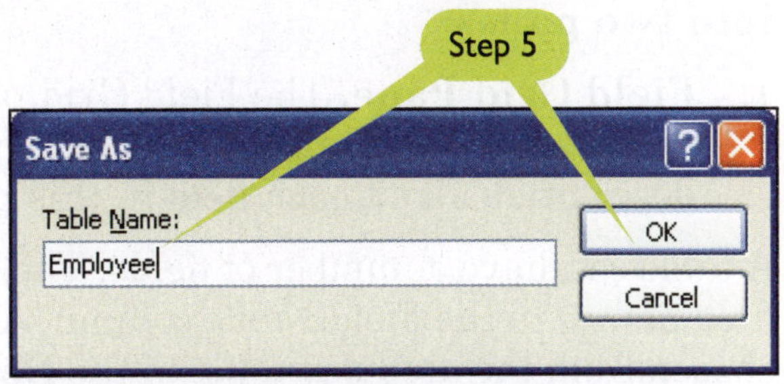

Fig 2.11 *Save As dialog box*

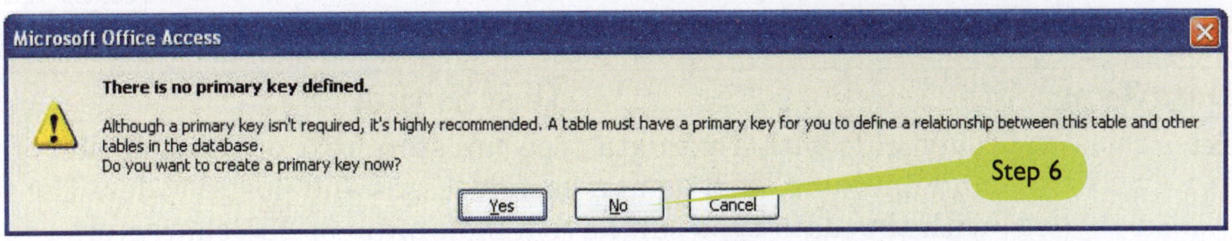

Fig 2.12 *Message box*

The table gets created and appears in the Database window (**Fig. 2.13**).

Fig 2.13 *Database window displaying the new table*

➤ Views of a Table

You can work on a table in two views—Design view and Datasheet view. Let us learn more about them.

- **Design View**

In the Design view of the table, you can enter the field names, their data types and description. You can also set the field properties. Earlier, in this chapter, you learnt how to create a table using the Design View. To open an already existing table in the Design view, follow the given steps.

Step 1 Click the table name in the Database window.

Step 2 Click the Design button in the database window toolbar.

The Design view window of the selected table appears (**Fig. 2.8**).

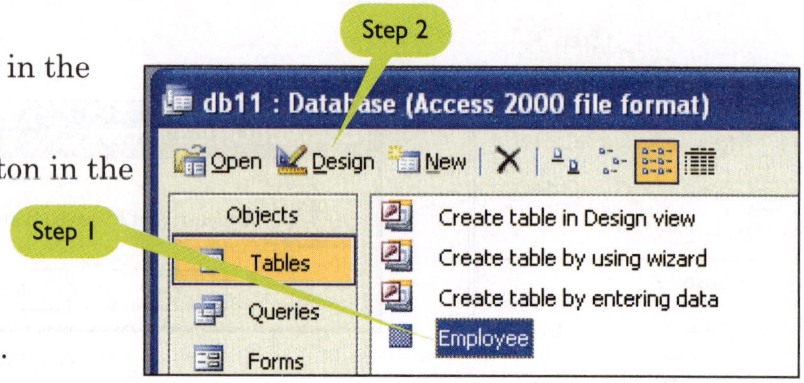

Fig 2.14 *Opening a table in the Design view*

The Design view window is divided into two panes:

1. **Field Grid Pane.** The Field Grid pane is used for entering field names and their data types. You can also give an optional description about each field in this pane.

A table can have a number of fields. The fields are created by writing field names in the Field Name column. A data type for the field is chosen from the drop-down list in the **Data Type** column (**Fig. 2.15**). Some of the data types in MS Access are listed in **Table 2.2.**

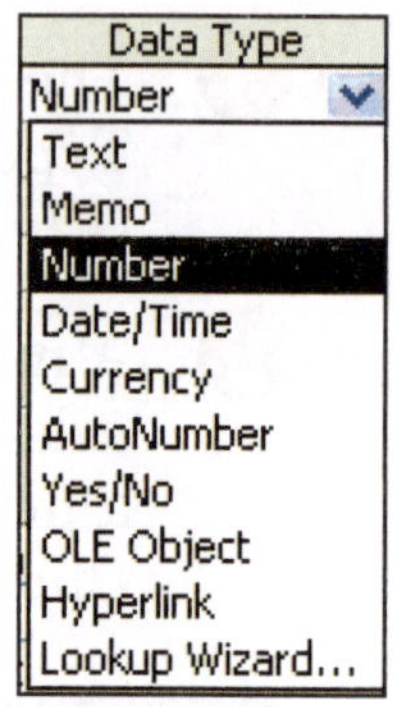

Fig 2.15 *Data types*

Table 2.2 *Data types in MS Access*

Data Type	Description
Text	The fields with Text data type can store text or combination of text and numbers such as names, addresses and postal codes. The fields with this data type can have a maximum of 255 characters.
Memo	The fields with Memo data type can store lengthy text, that is, up to 65,536 characters. It can be used for storing detailed information such as synopsis of a book or a patient's medical history.
Number	The fields with this data type can store numbers.
Date/Time	The fields with this data type can store date and time values.
Currency	The fields with this data type can store currency values and then display them in different formats.
AutoNumber	The fields with this data type store integers that are incremented automatically when a new row or record is added to a table.
Yes/No	The fields with this data type can store only one of the two possible values such as Yes/No, True/False or ON/OFF.

2. **Field Properties Pane.** The Field Properties pane is used to set properties for the fields in a table. Some of the field properties are:

- **Field Size.** This property can be set for fields with Text or Number data types.

  For Text data types, you can use this property to set the maximum number of characters for a text field. For example, if the value of this property is 20 then the user cannot enter more than 20 characters in the field. The default value for Field Size property is 50 for the Text data type.

  For Number data types, the user can choose from one of the following options—Byte, Integer, Long Integer, Single, Double. These options determine the range of values and size of the field (**Fig. 2.16**).

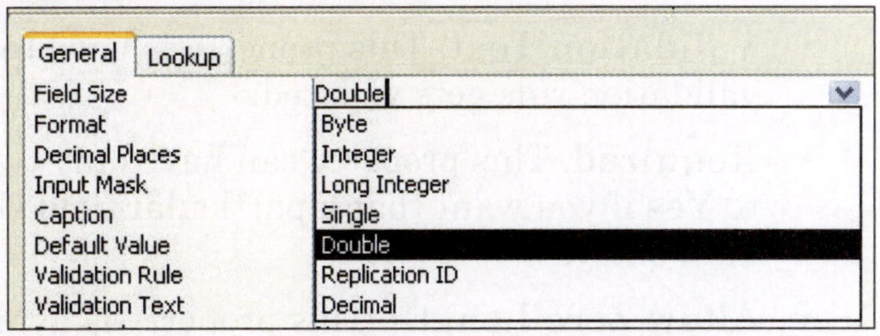

Fig 2.16 *Field Size options for the Number data type*

- **Format.** This property controls the manner in which data gets displayed. For example, for Number and Currency data types, you can choose the format from the given list of options (**Fig. 2.17**).

  For Date and Time data types, you can choose the different styles of displaying date and time (**Fig. 2.18**).

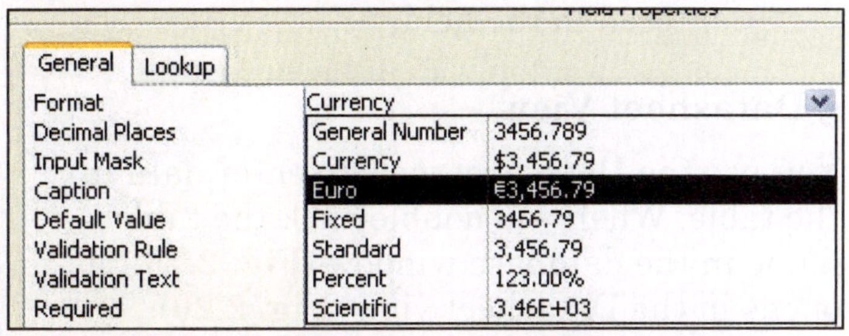

Fig 2.17 *Format options for the Number and the Currency data types*

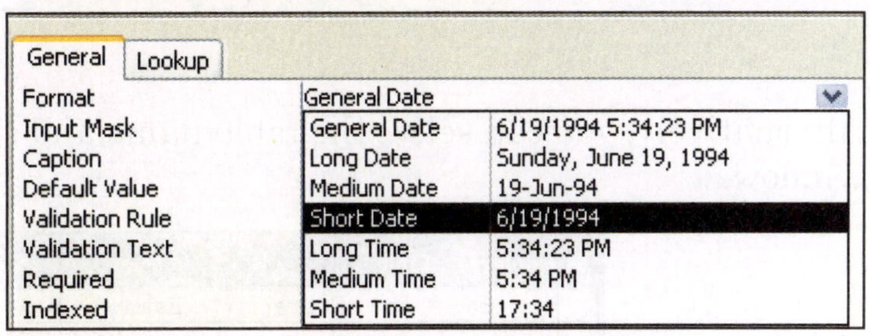

Fig 2.18 *Format options for the Date/Time data type*

- **Decimal Places.** This property is valid for Number and Currency data types. It is used to specify the number of digits to be displayed to the right of the decimal point. Its value may vary from 1 to 15.

- **Caption.** This property is used to give an alternate, more descriptive name to a field.

- **Default Value.** This property is used to specify a value that gets displayed automatically when the records are created.

- **Validation Rule.** This property is used to put conditions on the data that can be entered in a field. You cannot enter a value if it is not according to the validation rule.

Table 2.3 shows some examples of validation rule.

Table 2.3 *Examples of validation rule*

>=0	value in the field must be greater than or equal to zero
Between 10 and 20	value in the field must be between 10 and 20
="Delhi"	value in the field can only be 'Delhi'
In ("Delhi", "Mumbai")	value in the field can only be 'Delhi' or 'Mumbai'

- **Validation Text.** This property is used to display an error message when the validation rule gets violated.
- **Required.** This property can have only two values—Yes or No. It should be set to **Yes** if you want that a particular field should always get a value during the data entry.
- **Allow Zero Length.** This property is available for fields with Text and Memo data types. It can have two values—Yes or No. If the Required property is set to 'Yes' and the Allow Zero Length property is set to 'No', then a value must be entered in the field.

• Datasheet View

You use the Datasheet view to enter data in the table. When you double-click the table name in the database window (**Fig. 2.19**), it opens in the Datasheet view (**Fig. 2.20**).

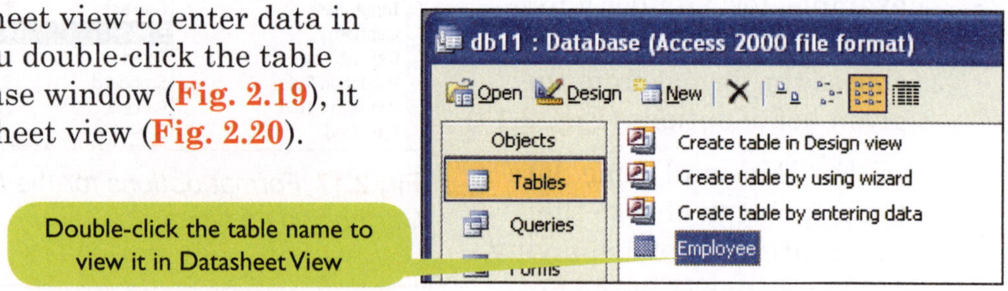

Fig 2.19 *Database window*

Alternatively, you can select the table name and click the **Open** button in the database window.

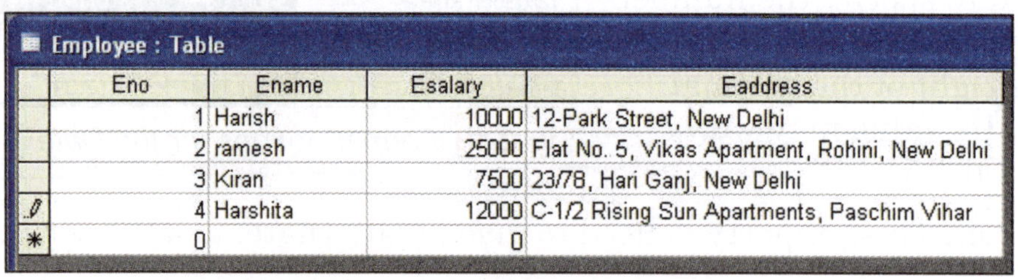

Employee : Table

Eno	Ename	Esalary	Eaddress
1	Harish	10000	12-Park Street, New Delhi
2	ramesh	25000	Flat No. 5, Vikas Apartment, Rohini, New Delhi
3	Kiran	7500	23/78, Hari Ganj, New Delhi
4	Harshita	12000	C-1/2 Rising Sun Apartments, Paschim Vihar
0		0	

Fig 2.20 *Datasheet view of the table*

• Switching between Design View and Datasheet View

You can quickly switch from one view to another by following either of the two options:

Click the drop-down arrow on the **View** button on the toolbar and choose the desired option (**Fig. 2.21**).

Fig 2.21 *Table Datasheet toolbar*

OR

Click **View ▶ Design View** or **View ▶Datasheet View** (Fig. 2.22).

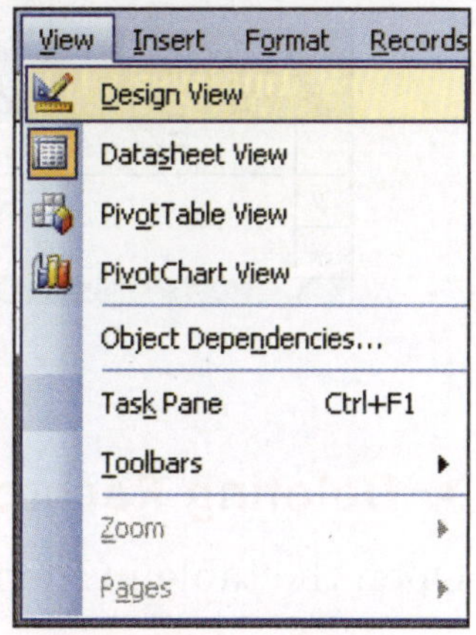

Fig 2.22 *View Menu*

QUICK QUESTION

2. Consider the table 'Patient' and answer the questions that follow.

Table: Patient

P_no	P_name	P_dob	P_ailment	P_history
P1	Mitali	12 Aug 1960	joint pain	thyroid, diabetes, high blood pressure, anaemic, has undergone bypass surgery, problem of water retention in lungs
P2	Shivika	11 Jan 1955	leg fracture	low blood pressure
P3	Raman	23 Apr 1965	blocked arteries	high cholesterol, overweight, cataract operation both eyes, has undergone angioplasty

a) Suggest suitable data types for various fields in the table 'Patient'.

b) Which view would you use to enter more records in the table?

c) You want to set the Field Size of the field P_name to 40. Which view of the table would you use?

d) What is the default field size for the Text data type?

➤ Adding Records or Data in a Table

The steps to enter records in a table are as follows:

Step 1 Open the table in the Datasheet view (**Fig. 2.23**).

Step 2 Type the values for various fields.

When you start entering data, a new record gets inserted automatically at the end of a table.

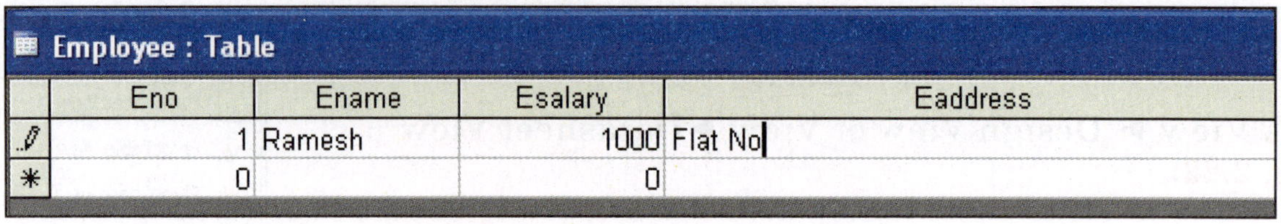

Fig 2.23 *Adding records in a table*

➤ Deleting Records in a Table

Open the table in the Datasheet view and follow these steps to delete a record.

Step 1 Click the record that needs to be deleted (**Fig. 2.24**).

Step 2 Click **Edit ▶ Delete Record** (**Fig. 2.25**).

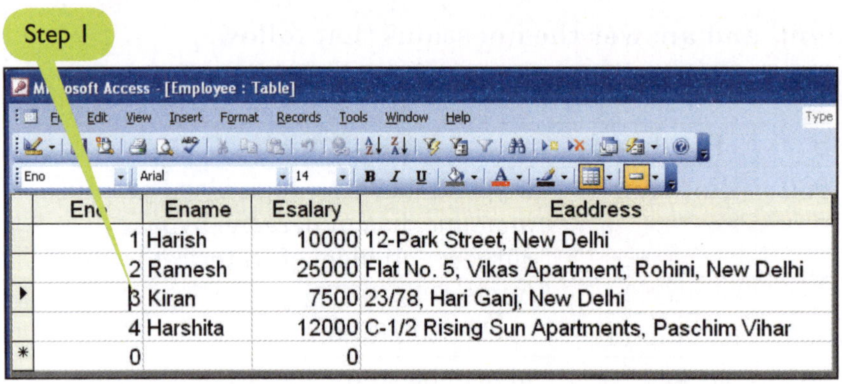

Fig 2.24 *Clicking the record to be deleted*

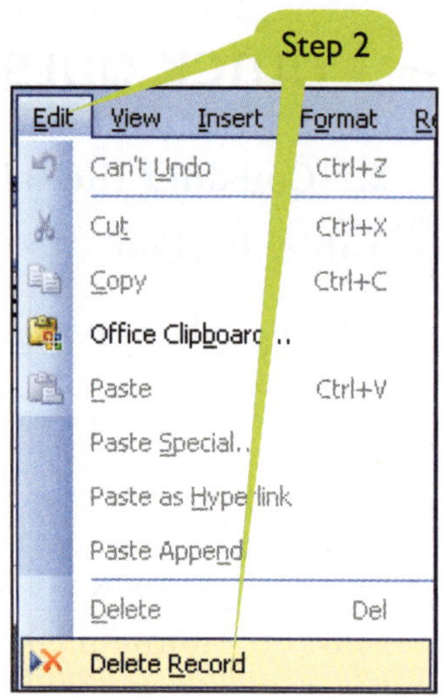

Fig 2.25 *Choosing Edit▶Delete Record*

✓ QUICK TIP

To delete a record, click the record and then click the Delete Record button on the Toolbar.

CHECK YOUR PROGRESS

1. **Create the table 'Book' with the following structure and enter six records in the table.**

Field Name	Data Type	Properties
No	Auto Number	
Name	Text	Field Size=40
Price	Number	Field Size=Single
Publisher	Text	Default Value="Pearson"
Category	Text	Validation Rule: Value can only be fiction or autobiography Validation Text: "Enter appropriate value"
Synopsis	Memo	Required="Yes", Allow Zero Length="No"

➤ Setting a Primary Key

A **primary key** is a field which has a unique value for every record in a table. Open a table in Design view and follow the given steps to set the primary key.

Step 1 Click the field to be set as the primary key (**Fig. 2.26**).

Step 2 Click **Edit ▶ Primary Key** (**Fig. 2.27**) or click the **Primary Key** button on the Toolbar.

The chosen field is set as the primary key and a symbol of key appears against it (**Fig. 2.28**).

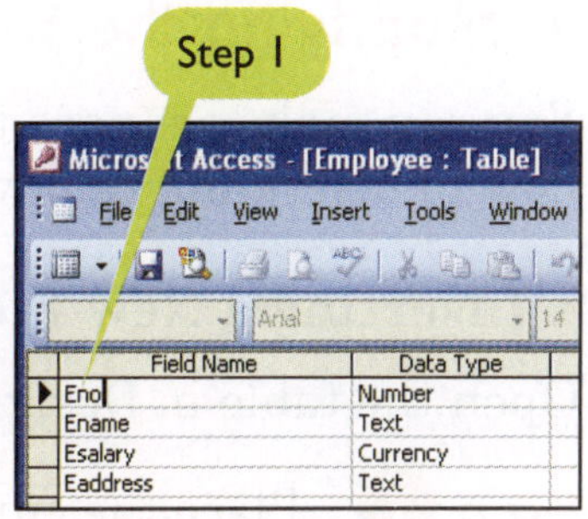

Fig 2.26 *Clicking the desired field*

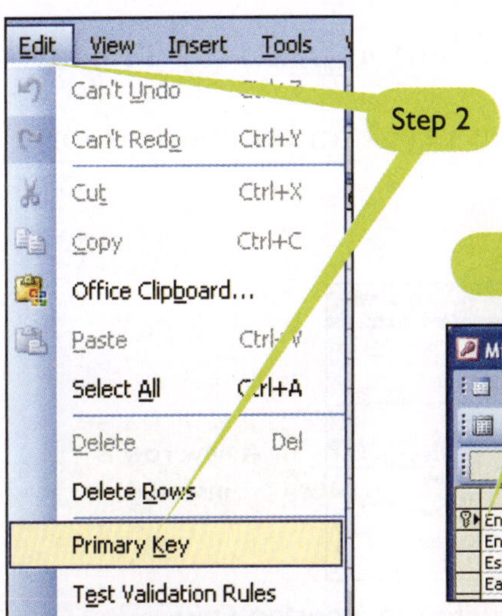

Fig 2.27 *Choosing Edit▶Primary Key*

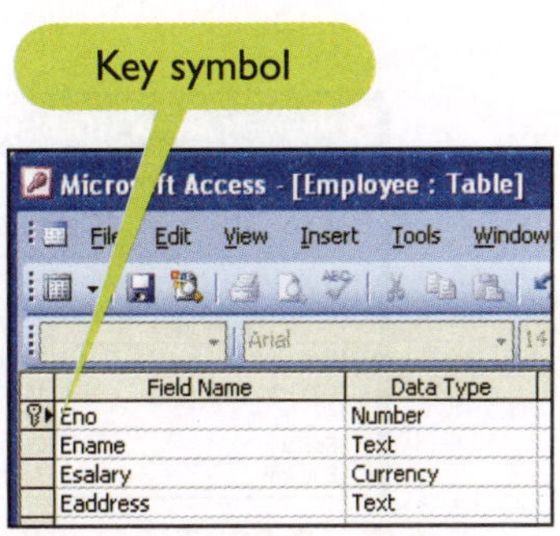

Fig 2.28 *Field with the key symbol*

QUICK TIP

You can also set a primary key by right-clicking a field in the Design view and choosing the Primary Key option from the shortcut menu.

➤ Removing a Primary Key

Open the table in Design view and follow the given steps to remove a primary key.

Step 1 Click the field that has been set as the primary key (**Fig. 2.29**).

Step 2 Click the **Primary key** button on the Toolbar or **Edit ▶ Primary Key** option (**Fig. 2.30**). The field is no longer a primary key (**Fig. 2.31**).

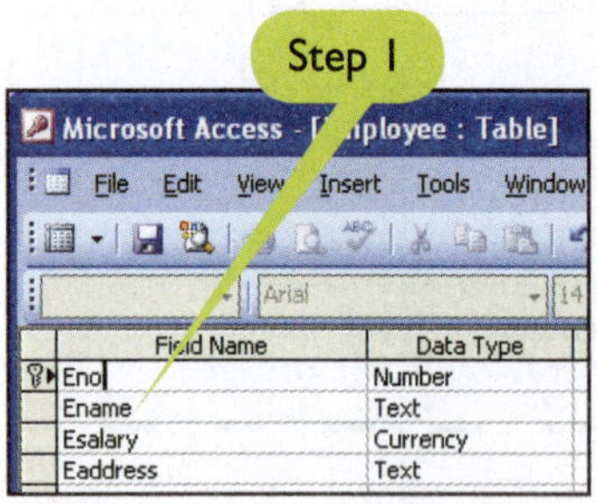

Fig 2.29 *Clicking the desired field*

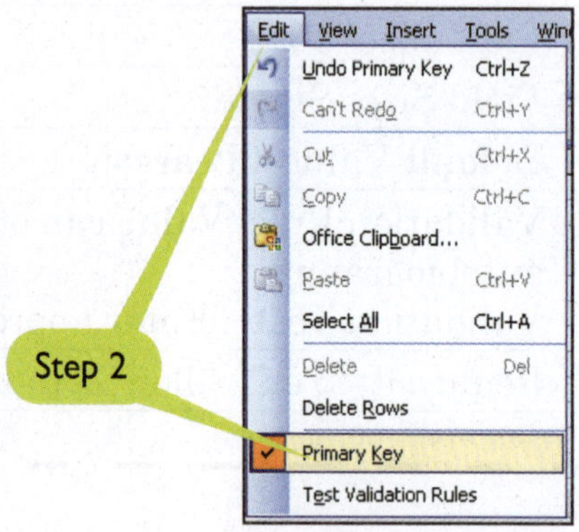

Fig 2.30 *Choosing Edit ▶ Primary Key*

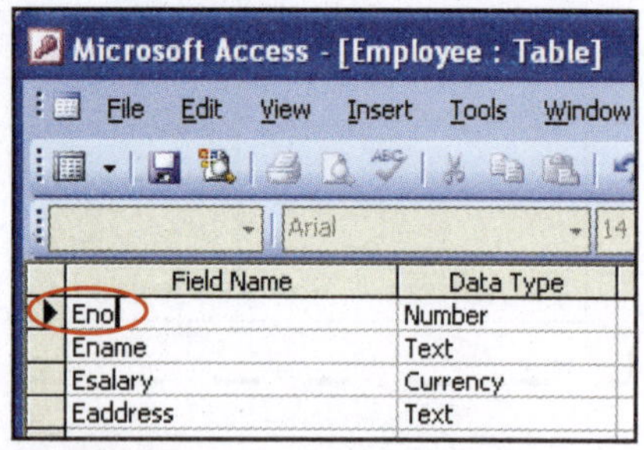

Fig 2.31 *The primary key is removed from the table*

➤ Modifying the Table Design

You can make changes to the design of a table after it has been created. Let us learn how to insert and remove a field from a table.

• Inserting a New Field

Open the table in Design view and follow the given steps to insert a field in the table:

Step 1 Place the cursor on the field before which you want to insert a new field (**Fig. 2.32**).

Step 2 Click **Insert ▶ Rows** or click the **Insert Rows** button on the Toolbar.

A new row is inserted (**Fig. 2.33**). Enter the field name, data type and properties for the new field.

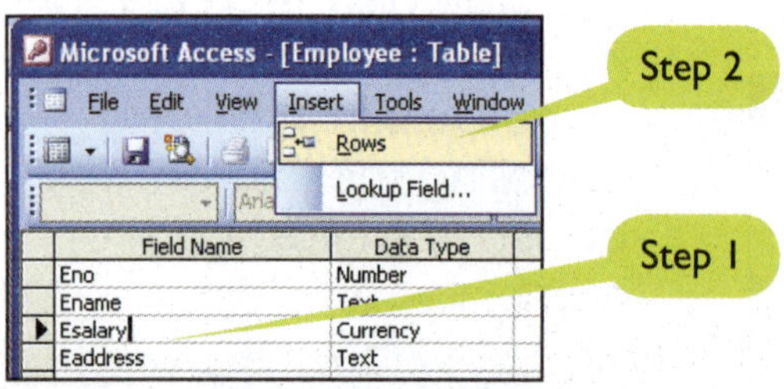

Fig 2.32 *Steps 1 and 2 for inserting a new field*

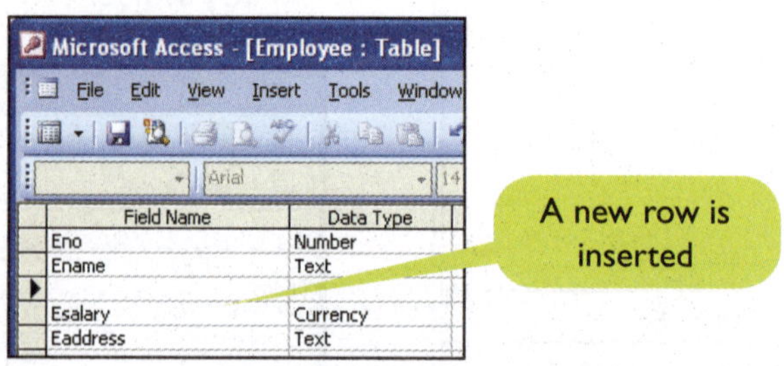

Fig 2.33 *Table with the inserted field*

- **Deleting a Field**

Open the table in Design view and follow the given steps to delete a field in the table.

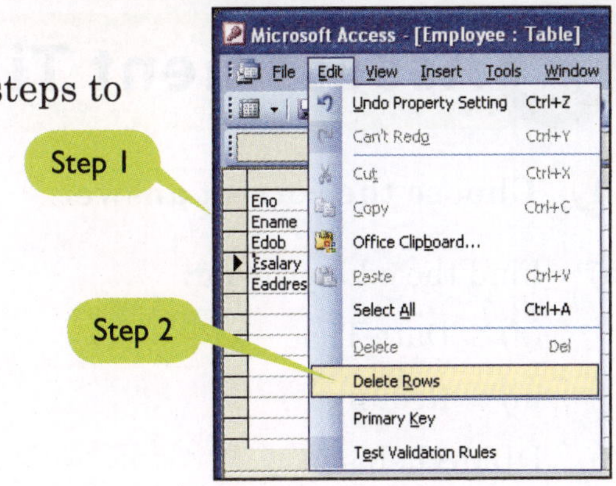

Fig 2.34 *Deleting a field*

Step 1 Click the field that has to be removed.

Step 2 Click **Edit ▶ Delete Rows** or click the **Delete Rows** button on the Toolbar.

The field is deleted from the table.

Recap Time

- A database is an organised collection of related data.
- A Database Management System (DBMS) is a software program that enables you to create, modify and extract data from a database.
- A Relational Database Management System (RDBMS) is a DBMS that is based on the relational model and stores data in the form of tables.
- MS Access is an example of RDBMS. It is a part of the Microsoft Office suite.
- Various objects that can be created in MS Access are—Tables, Queries, Forms, Reports, Pages, Macros and Modules.
- A field or an attribute is a column in a table that contains data of the same type.
- A record is a row in a table that stores complete information about an object or an item.
- A primary key is a field or a combination of fields that uniquely identifies the records in a table.
- The Design view of a table is used to enter field names, their data types, properties and description.
- The Datasheet view of a table is used to enter data in a table.

Answers to Quick Questions

1. a) Database b) Database Management System c) RDBMS d) *.mdb
   e) Records, Fields
2. a)

Field_Name	Data Type
P_no	Text
P_name	Text
P_dob	Date/Time
P_ailment	Text
P_history	Memo

   b) Datasheet view c) Design view d) 50

Assessment Time

1 **Choose the correct answer.**

a) Find the odd term out.

i) Date/Time ii) Field Size

iii) Required iv) Allow Zero Length

2) DBMS helps in

i) reducing data redundancy. ii) ensuring data security.

iii) enforcing standards. iv) All of these

3) A field that has a unique value for every record and cannot be left blank is called the

i) primary key. ii) unique key. iii) special key. iv) none of these

4) Which of the following field properties lets you specify the conditions on the data that can be entered in a table?

i) Field Size ii) Format iii) Validation Rule iv) Required

5) The 🔑 button is used to

i) open a table. ii) save a table.

iii) insert a field. iv) set a primary key.

2 **Fill in the blanks using the words given below.**

Default value	RDBMS	Design	Tables	Primary key	Datasheet

a) MS Access is an example of ______________.

b) In a relational database, data is stored in the form of ______________.

c) The ______________ view lets you enter data in a table.

d) You can set the field data types and their properties in the ______________ view.

e) The ______________ property is used to specify a value that is displayed automatically when the records are created.

f) The ______________ field cannot contain duplicate values.

3 **Answer the following questions.**

a) Define the following: i) Table ii) Database iii) DBMS

b) What are the advantages of using a DBMS?

c) Distinguish between the following pairs.

i) Record and Field
ii) Number and AutoNumber data type
iii) Text and Memo data type
iv) Validation rule and Validation text

d) What is a primary key? How do we set primary key in MS Access?

e) What are the two areas of the Design view of a table?

Activity Time

1 A sports complex wants to store the details of all the coaches in a database. Design the following table in MS Access and enter five records.

Table: Coach

Field Name	Data Type	Properties
CNo	Text	Primary Key
CName	Text	Field Size=60
CSalary	Number	Field Size=Double Validation Rule: Salary should be more than 1000 Validation Text: "Enter Appropriate Salary"
CSports	Text	Default Value="Badminton"
Address	Text	Required="Yes", Allow Zero Length="No"

2 A school wants to keep a record of details of all its students. Design the following table in MS Access and enter five records.

Table: Student

Field Name	Data Type	Properties
Sno	Auto Number	Primary Key
Name	Text	Field Size=40
Dob	Date/Time	Caption="Date of Birth"
Class	Text	Default Value="Nursery"
Address	Text	Required="Yes", Allow Zero Length="No"

Notes for the Teacher

- The teacher should discuss the various application areas of the databases.
- A class discussion on 'the database administration as an important field with good job opportunities' would be useful for the students.

INSERTING IMAGES AND CREATING LISTS IN HTML

Chapter 3

OBJECTIVES

After having studied this lesson, you will be able to:

- insert images in HTML.
- create lists in HTML.

In the previous class, you learnt about the basic formatting tags used for designing a webpage in HTML. Some of these tags include <BODY>, <P>, <FONT>, <HR> and heading tags. The description and attributes related to these tags are outlined in **Table 3.1**.

Table 3.1 *Basic formatting tags*

Tag Name	Description	Attribute(s)
<BODY>	It encloses all the tags that describe the content and layout of a webpage.	bgcolor, background, text, leftmargin and topmargin
<P>	It marks the beginning of a paragraph by inserting a blank line before and after the text.	align
<FONT>	It is used to change the appearance of the text to be displayed on a webpage.	face, color and size
<HR>	It is used to insert a straight horizontal line across a webpage.	color, align, noshade, size and width
Heading tags (<H1> to <H6>)	It displays the text in a larger and bolder font than the normal body text.	align

In this chapter, we will learn how to incorporate images and lists in a webpage.

INSERTING IMAGES (<IMG> TAG)

Images enhance the overall appearance of a webpage. Images make the websites look interesting. While designing the webpages, you should maintain a balance between the use of text and images. However, excessive use of images may slow down the download of a webpage. The various image file formats that are supported by most of the web browsers include GIF, JPEG and PNG.

QUICK FACT

GIF stands for Graphic Interchange Format, JPEG (JPG) stands for Joint Photographic Experts Group, and PNG stands for Portable Network Graphics. These three formats are currently the primary file types for formatting the graphics on the Internet.

In HTML, the images are inserted using the `<IMG>` tag. It is an empty tag. **Table 3.2** lists the attributes of the <IMG> tag.

Table 3.2 *Attributes of `<IMG>` tag*

Attribute	Description	Example
src	This attribute is used to specify the URL or path of the image to be displayed.	`<IMG src="flowers.jpg">`
height, width	This attribute is used to specify the height and width of the image in pixels.	`<IMG height=200 width=200>`
align	This attribute is used to align the image with respect to the margins or the inline text. • use **left** or **right** value to align the image with respect to margins • use **top**, **middle**, **bottom** to align the image with respect to inline text	`<IMG align=right>`
alt	This attribute is used to specify an alternative text that a browser will display if the image cannot be displayed.	`<IMG alt="flowers image">`
border	This attribute is used to specify the width of the border around an image.	`<IMG border=6>`

The following HTML code uses different attributes of the `<IMG>` tag to display the output as shown in **Fig. 3.1**.

```
<HTML>
<HEAD>
<TITLE> Flowers </TITLE>
<BODY bgcolor=pink>
<HR size=4 color=blue width=50%>
<H1 align=center> Beauty of Flowers</H1>
<HR size=4 color=blue width=50%>
```

```
<IMG src="tulips.jpg"
height=100 width=100
border=6>
<FONT color=purple> A
thing of beauty is a
joy forever. Flowers
are a symbol of
nature's divine beauty.
</FONT>
<IMG src="sunflower.jpg"
height=100 width=100
border=6 alt="Flowers
image">
</BODY>
</HTML>
```

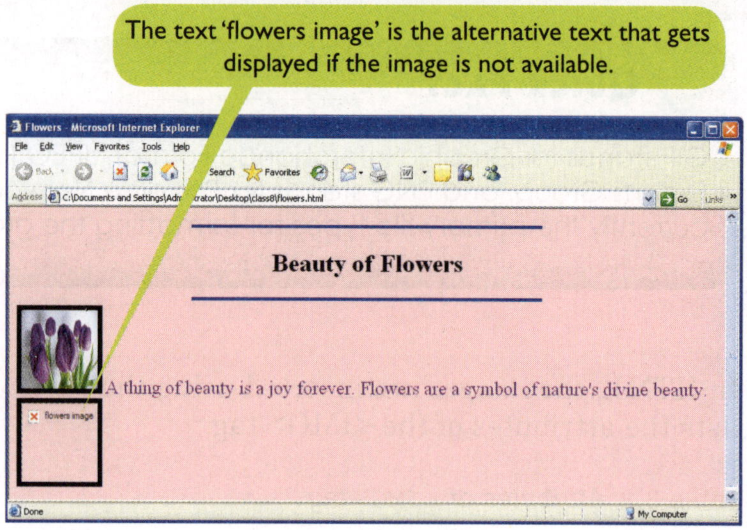

Fig 3.1 *Output*

➤ Using the Align Attribute of <IMG> Tag

The **align** attribute of the <IMG> tag lets you specify the placement of image on a webpage. To align an image with respect to margins, you use **left** or **right** as the attribute value as shown in the following HTML code:

```
<HTML>
<HEAD>
<TITLE> Flowers </TITLE>
<BODY bgcolor=pink>
<HR size=4 color=blue
width=50%>
<H1 align=center> Beauty
of Flowers</H1>
<HR size=4 color=blue
width=50%>
<IMG src="tulips.jpg"
height=100 width=100
border=6 align=left>
<FONT color=purple> A
thing of beauty is a joy
forever. Flowers are a symbol of nature's divine beauty.
<IMG src="sunflower.jpg" height=100 width=100 align=right border=6>
<BR><BR><BR><BR>
<P align=right> Looking at flowers makes us feel happy and pleasant.
Flowers are the greatest gift of God. </p></FONT>
</BODY>
</HTML>
```

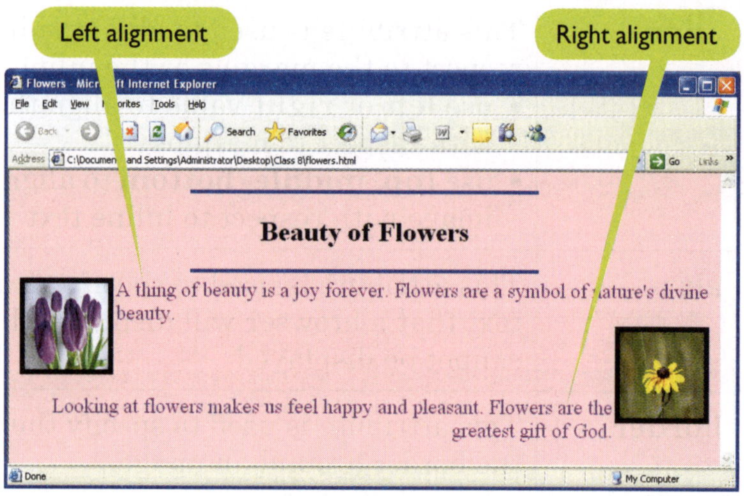

Fig 3.2 *Output*

The other three values that can be assigned to the align attribute are—**top**, **middle**, and **bottom**. These values align an image with respect to the text on a webpage. The following HTML code uses these attribute values and displays the output as shown in **Fig. 3.3**.

```
<HTML>
<HEAD>
<TITLE> Flowers </TITLE>
<BODY bgcolor=pink>
<HR size=4 color=blue width=50%>
<H1 align=center> Beauty of Flowers</H1>
<HR size=4 color=blue width=50%>
<IMG src="tulips.jpg" height=100 width=100 border=6 align=top>
<FONT color=purple> A thing of beauty is a joy forever. Flowers are
a symbol of nature's divine beauty. <BR><BR>
<IMG src="sunflower.jpg" height=100 width=100 border=6 align=middle>
Looking at flowers makes us feel happy and pleasant. Flowers are the
greatest gift of God.
<BR><BR>
<IMG src="bouquet.jpg" height=100 width=100 border=6 align=bottom>
So, present a bouquet of flowers to somebody you love today!!</FONT>
</BODY>
</HTML>
```

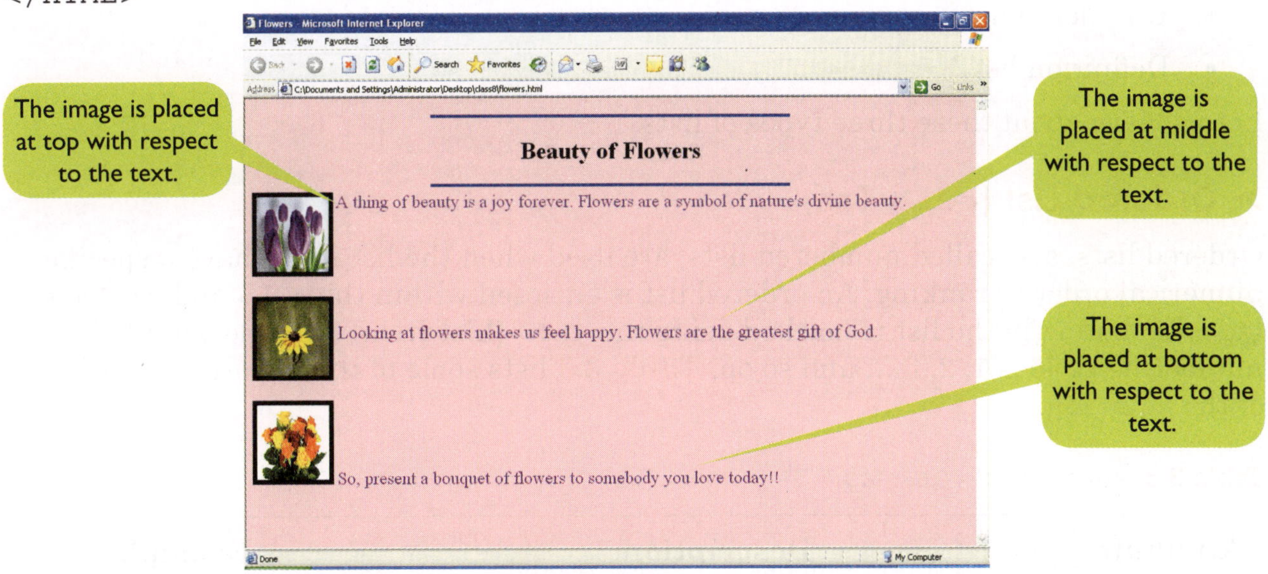

Fig 3.3 *Output*

QUICK TIP

To align an image in the center with respect to the margins, enclose the `<IMG>` tag inside the `<CENTER>` tag as: `<CENTER> <IMG src="tulips.jpg"></CENTER>`

CHECK YOUR PROGRESS

1. **Design a webpage as shown alongside using various formatting and <IMG> tags.**

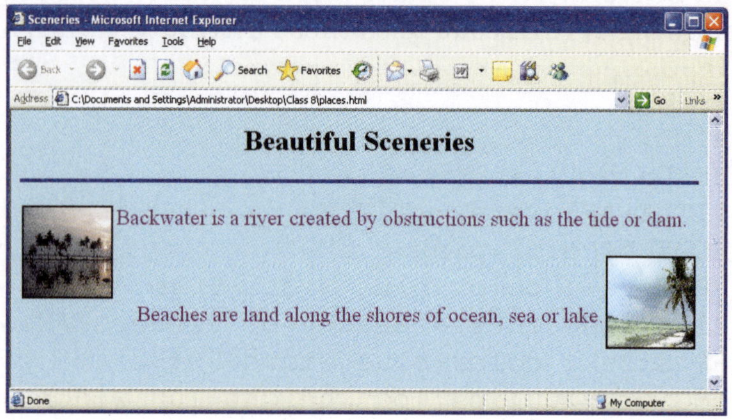

CREATING LISTS

Lists are a great way of organising a lot of information in webpages. Lists are indispensable tool for cataloging and indexing various objects and events. HTML supports three types of lists:

- Ordered list
- Unordered list
- Definition list

Let us learn about these three types of lists.

➤ Ordered List (<OL> Tag)

Ordered lists, also called numbered lists, are used when the list items have a specific numerical order or ranking. An ordered list is enclosed within the `<OL>` and `</OL>` tags. Each item in the list is marked using the `<LI>` (List Item) tag. The default numbering style is 1, 2, 3 ... and so on. **Table 3.3** lists some of the important attributes of the `<OL>` tag.

Table 3.3 *Attributes of <OL> tag*

Attribute	Description	Example
type	This attribute specifies the type of numbering to be used for each list item. The values that can be given are—A, a, I, i, and 1(default).	<OL type=A / a / I / i / 1>
start	This attribute lets you start the list numbering from a different letter or a number, that is, other than the default numbers.	<OL start=n> where 'n' denotes a number

The following HTML code uses different attributes of the <OL> tag and displays the output as shown in **Fig. 3.4**.

```
<HTML>
<BODY bgcolor=pink>
<H1 align=center> Online Books Library</H1>
Books are our best friends. We
can obtain many thoughts from
books.
<BR>
The various categories of books
featured in our library are:
<OL type=A>
<LI> Fiction
<LI> Motivational Books
<LI> Autobiographies
<LI> Mystery
<LI> Adventure
</OL>
</BODY>
<HTML>
```

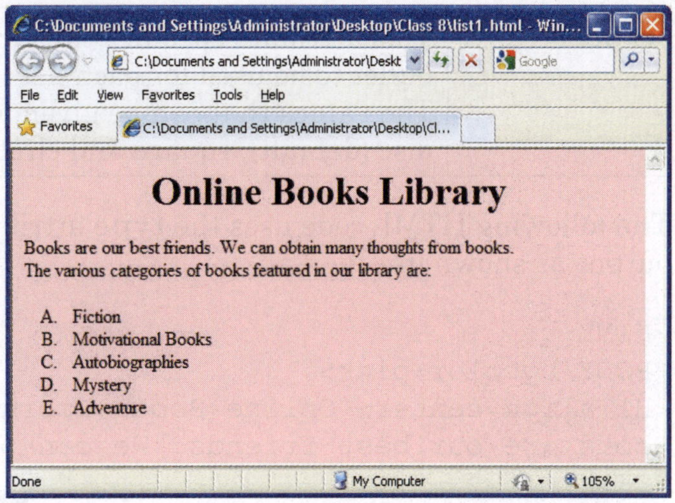

Fig 3.4 *Output (displaying an ordered list)*

Table 3.4 shows some examples of **type** and **start** attributes of the <OL> tag.

Table 3.4 *Examples of type and start attributes for ordered lists*

Type and Start Values	Output
<OL type=A start=1>	A. Fiction B. Motivational Books C. Autobiographies
<OL type=a start=1>	a. Fiction b. Motivational Books c. Autobiographies
<OL type=I start=2>	II. Fiction III. Motivational Books IV. Autobiographies
<OL type=i start=3>	iii. Fiction iv. Motivational Books v. Autobiographies
<OL type=1> or <OL> (default)	1. Fiction 2. Motivational Books 3. Autobiographies

➤ Unordered Lists (<OL> Tag)

Unordered lists are also known as bulleted lists. In unordered lists the list items do not have a specific order. An unordered list is enclosed within the <UL> and </UL> tags. Each item in the list is marked using the <LI> (List Item) tag. **Table 3.5** lists some of important attributes of the <UL> tag.

Table 3.5 *Attributes of <UL> tag*

Attribute	Description	Example
type	This attribute specifies the type of bullet to be used for each list item. The values that can be given are disc (default), square and circle.	<UL type=disc/circle/ square>

The following HTML code uses the **type** attribute of the <UL> tag and displays the output as shown in **Fig. 3.5**.

```
<HTML>
<BODY bgcolor=pink>
<H1 align=center> Online Books Library</H1>
Books are our best friends. We can obtain many thoughts from books.
<BR>
The various categories of books
featured in our library are:
<UL type=square>
<LI> Fiction
<LI> Motivational Books
<LI> Autobiographies
<LI> Mystery
<LI> Adventure
</UL>
</BODY>
<HTML>
```

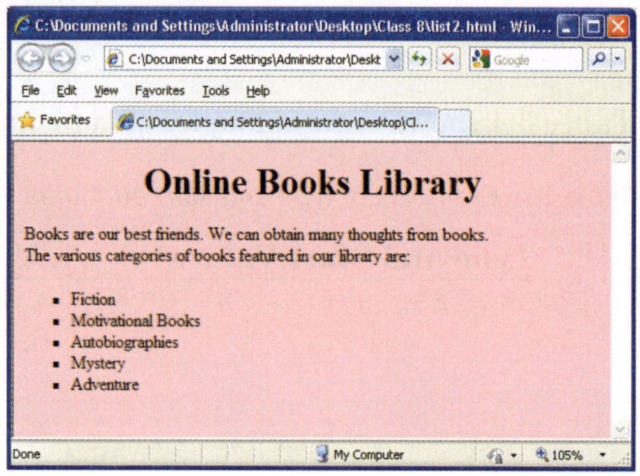

Fig 3.5 *Output (displaying an unordered list)*

Table 3.6 outlines the output displayed when you use different values for the **type** attribute of the <UL> tag.

Table 3.6 *Examples of type attribute for unordered lists*

Type Value	Output
<UL type=disc> OR <UL>	• Fiction • Autobiographies • Motivational Books
<UL type=circle>	○ Fiction ○ Autobiographies ○ Motivational Books
<UL type=square>	■ Fiction ■ Autobiographies ■ Motivational Books

QUICK QUESTION

1. **Find out the errors in the following code segment and write the corrected code:**

(a)
```
<OL type=a start=c>
<LI> Carbohydrates
<LI> Minerals
<LI> Proteins>
</OL>
```

(b)
```
<UL type=i>
<LI> Delhi
<LI> Mumbai
<LI> Kolkata
</UL>
```

(c)
```
<LI type=disc>
<UL> Keyboard
<UL> Mouse
</UL>
```

➤ Definition Lists

Definition lists vary slightly from the other lists. Definition lists comprise two parts—a term and its description. A definition list consists of three tags—<DL>, <DT> and <DD>. The <DL> and </DL> tags mark the beginning and end of a definition list.
The <DT> tag marks the definition terms in a definition list. It is an empty tag.
The <DD> tag marks the definition description in a definition list. It is also an empty tag.

The following HTML code uses the <DL>, <DT> and <DD> tags to display the output as shown in **Fig. 3.6**.

```
<HTML>
<BODY bgcolor="pink">
<H1 align=center>Glossary</H1>
<DL>
<DT>Internet
<DD>Internet is a network of interconnected computers.
<DT>HTML
<DD>HyperText Markup Language, it is a language to design webpages.
</DL>
</BODY>
```

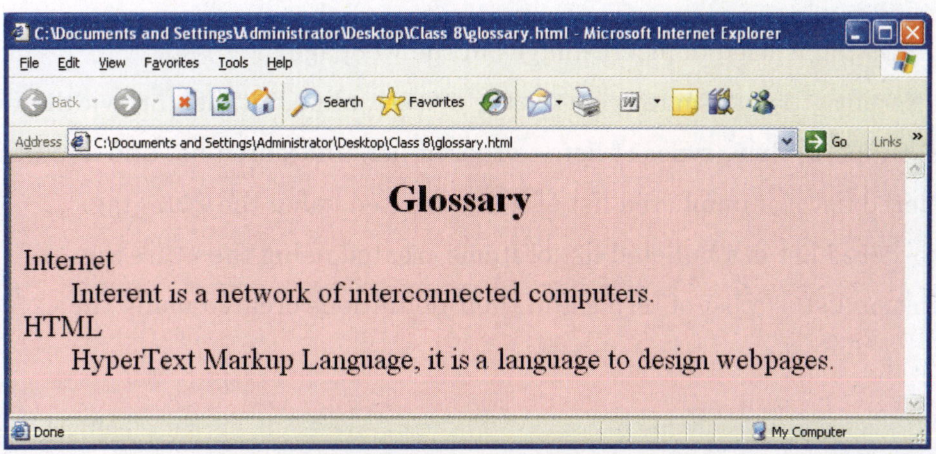

Fig 3.6 *Output (displaying a definition list)*

➤ Nested Lists

Ordered and unordered lists can be nested within each other to form multilevel lists. The following HTML code displays the output as shown in **Fig. 3.7**.

```
<HTML>
<BODY bgcolor=pink>
<H1 align=center> Online Books Library</H1>
Books are our best friends. We can obtain many thoughts from books.
<BR>
The various categories of books featured in our library are:
<OL type=A>
<LI> Autobiography
     <OL type=a>
     <LI> My Experiments with Truth
     <LI> Wings of Fire
     </OL>
<LI> Fiction
     <UL type=circle>
     <LI> Bacon Death
     <LI> Pride and Prejudice
     </UL>
<LI> Adventure
     <UL type=square>
     <LI> Gulliver's Travels
     <LI> The Phantom Tollbooth
     </UL>
</OL>
</BODY>
<HTML>
```

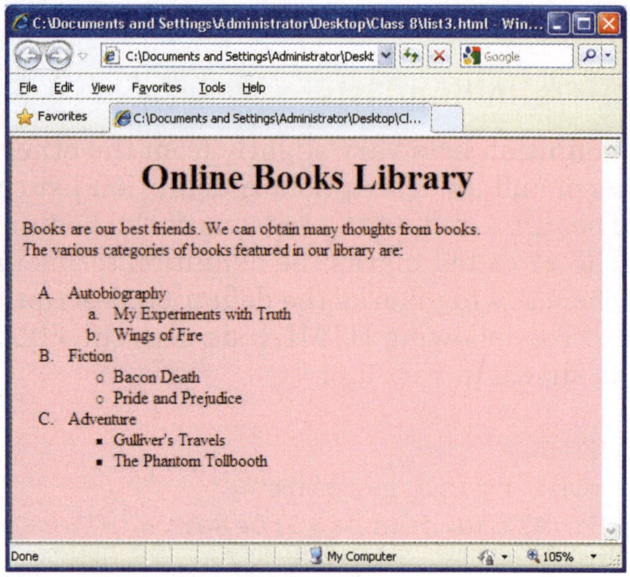

Fig 3.7 *Output (displaying a nested list)*

Recap Time

- The <IMG> tag is used to insert images in the webpage.
- The different attributes of the <IMG> tag are src, align, alt, height, width and border.
- HTML supports three types of lists—ordered list, unordered list and definition list.
- An ordered list is a numbered list of items created using the <OL> tag.
- An unordered list is a bulleted list of items created using the <UL> tag.
- A definition list is a list of terms and their definitions created using the <DL>, <DT> and <DD> tags.

Answers to Quick Questions

1. (a)
```
<OL type=a start=3>
<LI> Carbohydrates
<LI> Minerals
<LI> Proteins>
</OL>
```
(b)
```
<UL type=square/
disc/circle>
<LI> Delhi
<LI> Mumbai
<LI> Kolkata
</UL>
```
(c)
```
<UL type=disc>
<LI> Keyboard
<LI> Mouse
</UL>
```

Assessment Time

1 Choose the correct answer.

a) Which of the following is the correct way of using the start attribute of the <OL> tag?

i) `<OL start=3>` ii) `<OL start=iii>` iii) `<OL start=C>` iv) `<OL start=disc>`

b) Which one of the following is an attribute of the <IMG> tag?

i) alternate ii) alt iii) source iv) size

c) Which one of the following values cannot be assigned to the align attribute of the <IMG> tag?

i) top ii) right iii) center iv) bottom

d) Which of the following holds true for a definition list?

i) It is a numbered list of items.
ii) It is a bulleted list of items.
iii) It is a list of terms and definitions of terms.
iv) It is a combination of bulleted list and numbered list.

2 Fill in the blanks using the words given below.

Type	Src	<DL>	Alt	Align

a) A list of terms and their definitions can be created using the _______________ tag.

b) You use the _______________ attribute of the <OL> tag to specify the type of numbering to be used in front of each list item.

c) The _______________ attribute of <IMG> tag lets you specify the name of the image file to be displayed on a webpage.

d) The text to be displayed when an image cannot be shown can be specified using the _______________ attribute of the <IMG> tag.

e) Using the _______________ attribute of the <IMG> tag, you can specify the placement of an image with respect to inline text.

3 **Answer the following questions.**

a) What is the use of <IMG> tag?

b) What is the purpose of src and alt attributes of the <IMG> tag?

c) Differentiate between <OL> and <UL> tags.

d) Which three tags are used to create definition lists?

e) What is the use of type attribute of the list tags?

f) Write the HTML code for the following:

   i) To display square bullets in an unordered list.

   ii) To start an ordered list with the number 3.

   iii) To insert an image 'picture.gif' on a webpage and center align it in the browser's window.

   iv) To display the text 'building image' if the image 'building.jpg' cannot be displayed.

Activity Time

1 Write the HTML codes to generate the following webpages.

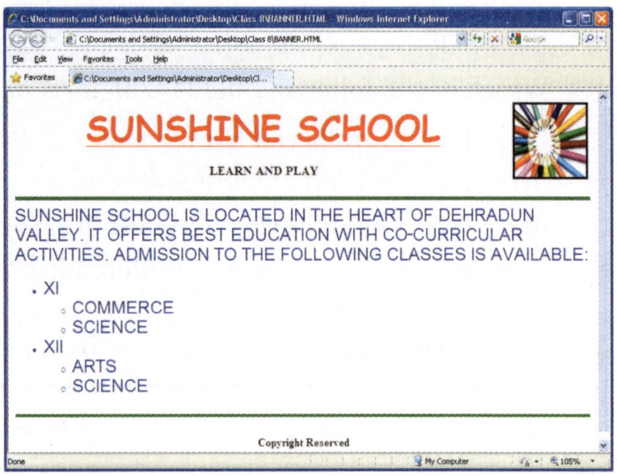

Notes for the Teacher

Teachers can briefly discuss the different types of image file formats that can be inserted in a webpage.

CREATING TABLES AND HYPERLINKS IN HTML

Chapter 4

OBJECTIVES

After having studied this lesson, you will be able to:

- create tables in HTML.
- create hyperlinks in HTML.

In the previous chapter, you learnt about inserting lists and images in a webpage. Your knowledge of HTML is incomplete without learning about tables and hyperlinks. Tables help you organise data in a structured manner in a webpage whereas hyperlinks enable you to connect different webpages. Look at the webpage shown in Fig. 4.1. It contains tables and hyperlinks.

In this chapter, you will learn about creating tables and hyperlinks in HTML.

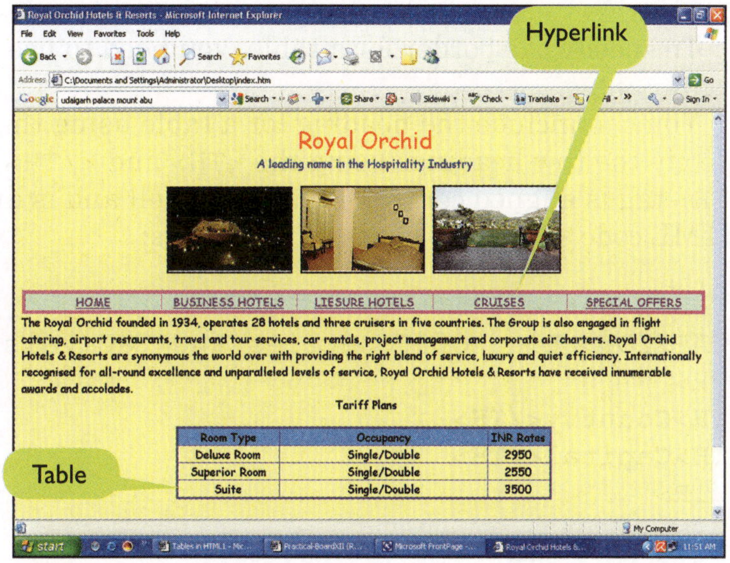

Fig 4.1 *A webpage showing a table and hyperlinks*

CREATING TABLES IN HTML

Tables let you present data in a row and column format. You can use tables to format and organise information systematically in a webpage.

The basic structure of a table consists of the following tags:

1. <TABLE>...</TABLE> tags
2. <TR> and </TR> tags
3. <TD> and </TD> tags

The <TABLE> and </TABLE> tags mark the beginning and end of a table in an HTML document. A table is divided into rows using the <TR> tag. Each row is divided into data cells using the <TD> tag.

You can include text, images, lists, form elements or a hyperlink in a data cell. The number of pairs of <TR> and </TR> determines the number of rows in a table. The given HTML code uses the basic table tags to display a table without borders.

```
<TABLE>
<TR>
<TD>Country</TD>
<TD>Capital</TD>
</TR>
<TR>
<TD>India</TD>
<TD>Delhi</TD>
</TR>
<TR>
<TD>Germany</TD>
<TD>Berlin</TD>
</TR>
</TABLE>
```

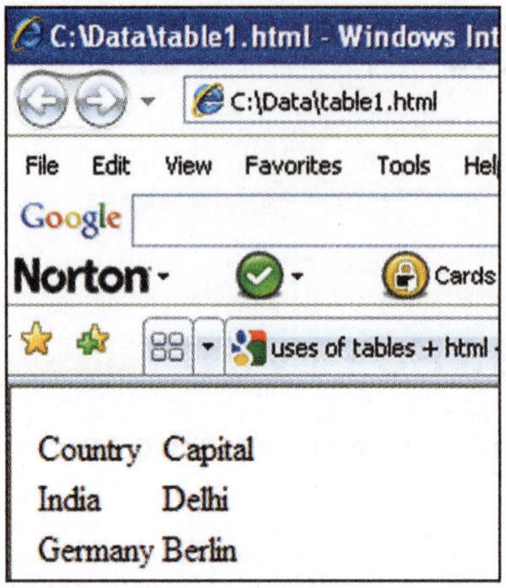

Fig 4.2 *Output (table without borders)*

QUICK FACT

Some of the well known document markup languages similar to HTML are—Extensible HyperText Markup Language (XHTML), Mathematical Markup Language (MathML), and Rich Text Format (RTF).

To specify the border for a table, you need to use the border attribute of the <TABLE> tag.

You can include the heading for a table using the <CAPTION> tag. You can also specify the row headings using the <TH> and </TH> tags. The text enclosed within the <TH> tag is aligned centrally inside the cell and is displayed in a bolder font. The given HTML code shows the usage of these tags:

```
<TABLE border="5">
<CAPTION> List of Countries and Capitals </CAPTION>
<TR>
<TH>Country</TH>
<TH>Capital</TH>
</TR>
<TR>
<TD>India</TD>
<TD>Delhi</TD>
</TR>
<TR>
<TD>Germany</TD>
<TD>Berlin</TD>
</TR>
</TABLE>
```

Let us now learn about some more attributes of the <TABLE> tag to enhance the appearance a table.

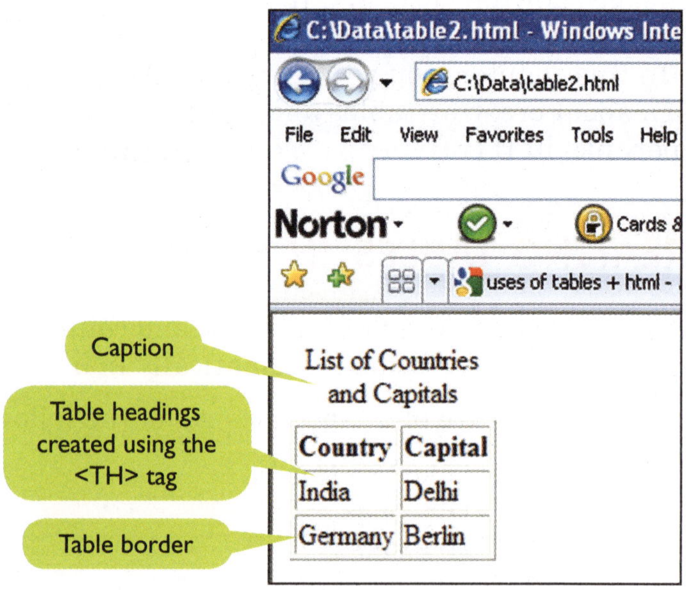

Fig 4.3 *Output (table with border, caption and row heading)*

➤ Attributes of <TABLE> Tag

Some of the other attributes of <TABLE> tag include bordercolor, bgcolor, background, width, height, cellspacing and cellpadding. **Table 4.1** provides a brief description about these attributes.

Table 4.1 *Attributes of <TABLE> tag*

Attributes	Description	Example
border	This attribute specifies the thickness of the border around the table. The value is specified in pixels.	`<TABLE border="3">`
bordercolor	This attribute specifies the colour of the border of a table.	`<TABLE bordercolor="blue">`
bgcolor	This attribute specifies the background colour of a table.	`<TABLE bgcolor="pink">`
background	This attribute specifies the URL of an image file to be displayed as background of a table.	`<TABLE background="C:\roses.jpg">`
width, height	This attribute specifies the width or height of a table. The value is specified in pixels or in percentage.	`<TABLE width=100% height=200>`
cellspacing	This attribute specifies the space between two adjacent cells. The value is specified in pixels.	`<TABLE cellspacing=3>`
cellpadding	This attribute specifies the space between the edge of a cell (cell wall) and the contents of the cell. The value is specified in pixels.	`<TABLE cellpadding=3>`

The following HTML code uses different attributes of the <TABLE> tag to display the output as shown in **Fig. 4.4**.

```
<TABLE border="3"
bordercolor="blue"
bgcolor="yellow" width=50%
cellspacing=3 cellpadding=3>
<TR>
<TH>Country</TH>
<TH>Capital</TH>
</TR>
<TR>
<TH>India</TH>
<TH>Delhi</TH>
</TR>
<TR>
<TD>Germany</TD>
<TD>Berlin</TD>
</TR>
</TABLE>
```

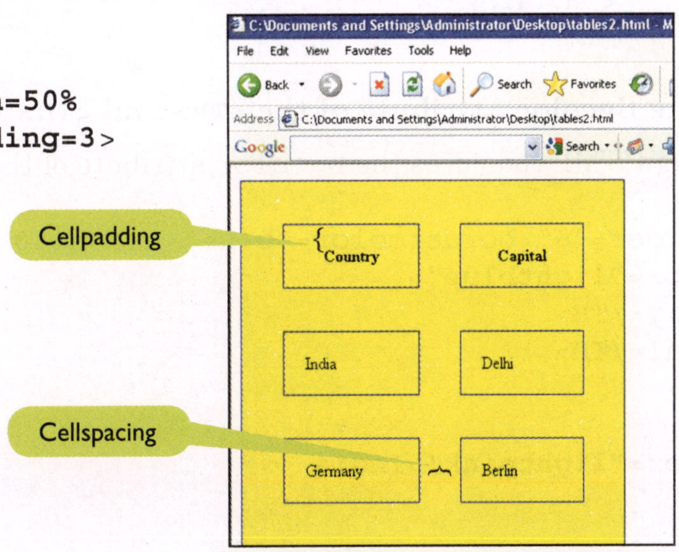

Fig 4.4 *Output of a table using cellspacing and cellpadding attributes*

CHECK YOUR PROGRESS

1. **Global International Company wants to display books-related information in a tabular format on their website. Design a webpage that displays a table listing the books name, authors and price list of five books.**

➤ Attributes of <TR>/<TD>/<TH> Tags

You can use attributes of <TR>, <TD> or <TH> tag to control aspects like alignment and background colour at the row or cell level. Table 4.2 lists some of the important attributes of the <TR>, <TD> and <TH> tags.

Table 4.2 *Attributes of <TR>, <TD> and <TH> tags*

Attributes	Description	Example
align	This attribute specifies the horizontal alignment of the text within a cell. The values can be left, right, or center.	`<TR align="right">`
bgcolor	This attribute specifies the background colour of a row or a data cell.	`<TR bgcolor="red">`
rowspan	This attribute specifies the number of rows a data cell should span. This attribute is used with the <TD> tag or the <TH> tag.	`<TD rowspan="2">`
colspan	This attribute specifies the number of columns a data cell should span. This attribute is used with the <TD> tag or the <TH>tag.	`<TD colspan="2">`

• Using the Bgcolor Attribute of the <TR> and <TD> Tags

The following HTML code uses the bgcolor attribute of the <TR> and <TD> tags.

```
<TABLE border="6" bordercolor="blue" width=50%>
<TR bgcolor="lightblue">
<TH>Country</TH>
<TH>Capital</TH>
</TR>
<TR>
<TD bgcolor="lightpink">India
</TD>
```

```
<TD bgcolor="mistyrose">Delhi
</TD>
</TR>
<TR>
<TD bgcolor="yellow">Germany</TD>
<TD bgcolor="yellowgreen">Berlin
</TD>
</TR>
</TABLE>
```

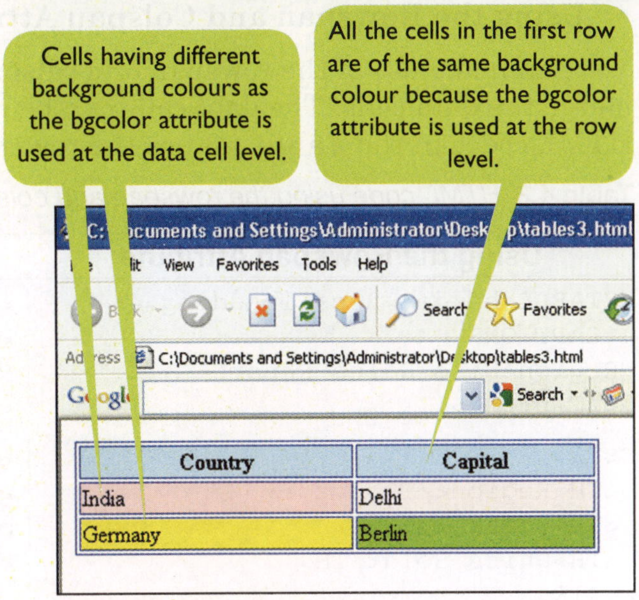

Fig 4.5 *Output of a table using bgcolor attribute at the row and cell level*

- ### Using the Align Attribute of the <TR> and <TD> tags

In **Fig. 4.6**, the contents of the header row are centrally aligned by default. To change the horizontal alignment of the text in the other rows, you can make use of the align attribute.

```
<TABLE border="6" bordercolor="blue" width=50%>
<TR bgcolor="lightblue">
<TH>Country</TH>
<TH>Capital</TH>
</TR>
<TR align="center">
<TD bgcolor="lightpink">India
</TD>
<TD bgcolor="mistyrose">Delhi
</TD>
</TR>
<TR>
<TD bgcolor="yellow">Germany
</TD>
<TD bgcolor="yellowgreen"
align="right">Berlin</TD>
</TR>
</TABLE>
```

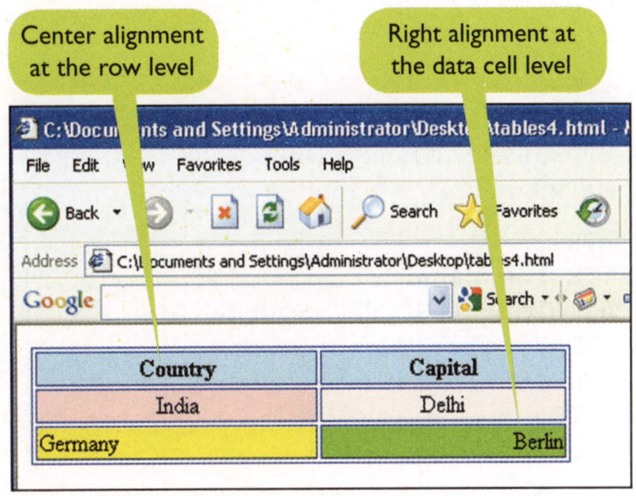

Fig 4.6 *Output of a table using row/cell level align attribute*

QUICK TIP

To include an image or a list item inside a data cell, you can enclose the <IMG> tag or the <UL> tag inside the <TD> or the <TH> tag.

- **Using the Rowspan and Colspan Attributes of the <TD> Tag**

You can make use of the rowspan and colspan attributes when there is a need to merge the data cells. The data cells can be merged column-wise or row-wise. The HTML codes in the **Table 4.3** use the rowspan and colspan attributes of the <TD> tag.

Table 4.3 *HTML code using the rowspan and colspan attributes*

Using the Rowspan Attribute

```
<TABLE border=2 cellpadding=4>
<CAPTION>
Region Wise Sales Report
</CAPTION>

<TR>
<TH>Region</TH>
<TH>States</TH>
<TH>Units Sold</TH>
</TR>

<TR>
<TH rowspan=2
bgcolor="#99CCFF">North</TH>
<TD>Jammu and Kashmir</TD>
<TD>1493</TD>
</TR>

<TR>
<TD>Haryana</TD>
<TD>3829</TD>
</TR>

<TR>
<TH rowspan=2
bgcolor="#99CCFF">South</TH>
<TD>Kerala</TD>
<TD>4827</TD>
</TR>

<TR>
<TD>Tamil Nadu</TD>
<TD>7246</TD>
</TR>

</TABLE>
```

Using the Colspan Attribute

```
<TABLE border=2 cellpadding=4>
<CAPTION>
Region Wise Sales Report
</CAPTION>

<TR>
<TH colspan=2
bgcolor="#99CCFF">North</TH>
</TR>

<TR>
<TD>Jammu and Kashmir</TD>
<TD>1493</TD>
</TR>

<TR>
<TD>Haryana</TD>
<TD>3829</TD>
</TR>

<TR>
<TD>Uttar Pradesh</TD>
<TD>0283</TD>
</TR>

<TR>
<TH colspan=2
bgcolor="#99CCFF">South</TH> </TR>

<TR>
<TD>Kerala</TD>
<TD>4827</TD>
</TR>

<TR>
<TD>Tamil Nadu</TD>
<TD>7246</TD>
</TR>

<TR>
<TD>Karnataka</TD>
<TD>5689</TD>
</TR>
</TABLE>
```

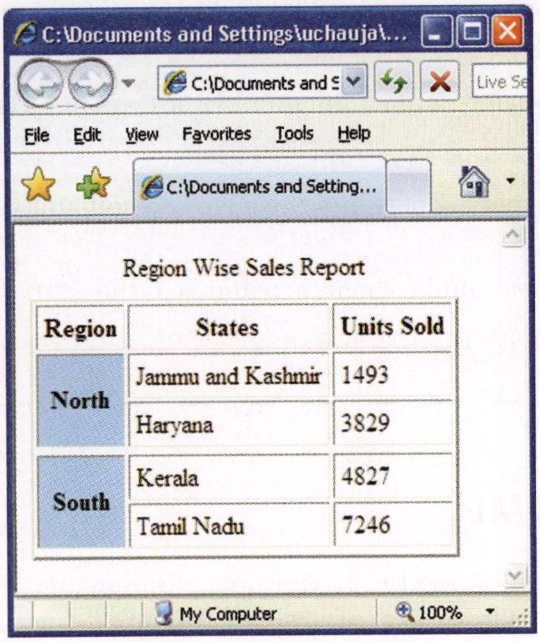

Fig 4.7 *Output (using the rowspan attribute)*

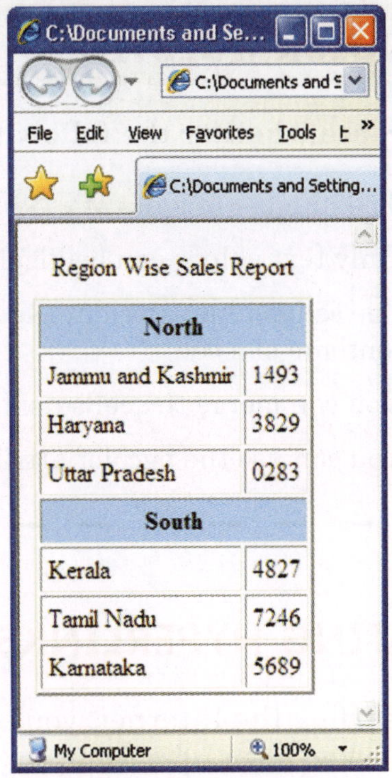

Fig 4.8 *Output (using the colspan attribute)*

CHECK YOUR PROGRESS

2. **Design a webpage that displays a list of some of the best tourist places in India in a tabular format. You may consider the following layout for the page.**

List of Best Tourist Places in India

Tourist Places	Hotels
Manali	Hotel Apple Country
	Mapple River Crescent Resort
Shimla	Eastbourne Resort & Spa
	Shingar Hotel
Mount Abu	Hotel Hillock
	Palanpur Palace

QUICK QUESTION

1. **State whether the following statements are true or false.**

a) The number of pairs of <TR> and </TR> determines the number of rows in a table.

b) Only text values can be displayed as a part of <TD> and <TH> tags.

c) The cellpadding attribute specifies the spacing between the edge of a cell and the contents of a cell.

d) You can merge the cells using the rowspan and colspan attributes of the <TD> tag.

e) You can use the bgcolor attribute only with the <TABLE> tag.

CREATING HYPERLINKS IN HTML

While surfing the Internet, you come across several text strings or images which when clicked open up a different webpage. These text strings or images are called **hyperlinks**. Hyperlinks interconnect the webpages over the World Wide Web.

➤ Anchor (<A>) Tag

The Anchor (<A>) tag is used to create hyperlinks in a webpage. It is a container tag. Any text or image enclosed within the <A> and </A> tags is displayed as a hyperlink. Table 4.4 illustrates some of the important attributes of the <A> tag.

Table 4.4 *Attributes of <A> tag*

Attribute	Description
href	This attribute indicates the destination of the link.
name	This attribute is used for linking sections on the same webpage. It indicates the name of the section within a webpage.

➤ Types of Linking in HTML

There are three types of linking in HTML. They are:

1. External linking
2. Internal linking
3. E-mail linking

QUICK TIP

You can use the target attribute of the <A> tag to specify the name of a window where the linked page should be displayed. For example, setting the target attribute to _blank opens the linked information in a new window.

- **External Linking**

The external linking involves connecting two different webpages. When you click a hyperlink, a new webpage to which the hyperlink is linked gets displayed in the browser window. You can link pages within the same directory or to any other page over the Internet. **Table 4.5** illustrates some of the examples of external linking.

Table 4.5 *Examples of external linking*

Linking pages within the same directory	Linking pages to pages over the Internet
first.html---link to---> second.html HTML source code in first.html `<A href="second.html"> Click to open Second file</A>`	first.html---link to---> Google Web Page HTML source code in first.html `<A href="http://www.google.com"> Click here to visit Google Web Page</A>`

The following HTML code illustrates the use of <A> tag in the file **first.html** to link to different webpages.

```
<HTML>
<A href="second.html"> Click to open Second file </A><BR><BR>
<A href="http:\\www.google.com"> Click here to visit Google Web
Page </A>
</HTML>
```

The output of the aforementioned HTML code is shown in **Fig. 4.9**.

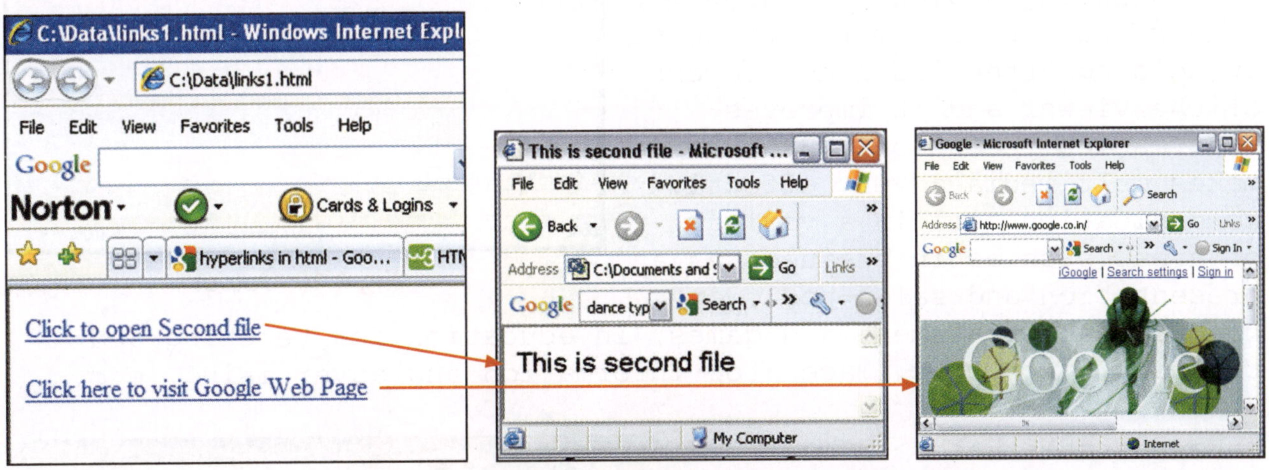

Fig 4.9 *Output of clicking different links*

When you click the first link, the contents of the webpage 'second.html' are displayed in the browser window. When you click the second link, the home page of Google gets displayed in the browser window.

- **Internal Linking**

Internal linking involves linking various sections of the same webpage, This type of linking is useful when a webpage is very long. It lets the user view the desired section of a page quickly. Internal linking serves as a bookmark to go to a particular segment of the webpage. This helps the user to quickly jump to the information he/she is looking for. For example, **Go to top of the page** link in webpages is an example of internal linking.

Internal linking is a two step process.

Step 1 Use the **name** attribute of the `<A>` tag to give a name to the section that has to be linked to.

Example, `<a name="xyz"> You will be linked here</A>`

Step 2 Use the **href** attribute of the `<A>` tag to refer to the named section preceded by the # symbol.

Example, `<a href="#xyz"> You will be taken to the linked section</A>`

The following HTML code demonstrates the use of **name** and **href** attributes of `<A>` tag to link the text 'Go to top of the page' to the top of the page.

```
<A name="top"><H1>Introduction</H1></A>
<FONT face="comic sans ms" size="5">
Multimedia is any combination
of text, graphic art, sound,
animation and video delivered to
the user by means of a computer
or other electronic media. An
effective multimedia presentation
not only presents information
in a dazzling and entertaining
manner, but is also more effective
in holding attention and interest
of the viewer and it improves
information retention. <BR>This
makes multimedia a very effective
communication tool in a variety
of areas such as in business as a
presentation and sales tool, in
home for entertainment and games, in education for teaching and
training, in public places for information and advertising, etc.
</font>
<BR><BR><BR><BR><BR>
<A href="#top"> Go to top of
the page </A>
```

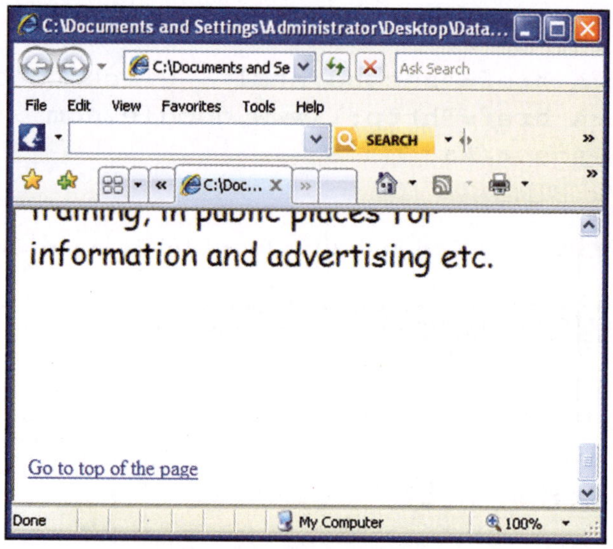

Fig 4.10 *Output*

> **QUICK TIP**
>
> The title attribute of the <A> tag can be used for displaying a tooltip that pops up when the mouse is moved over a hyperlink.

- **E-mail Linking (Linking to an E-mail Address)**

To link text to an e-mail address, you use the **mailto:** keyword before the e-mail address in the **href** attribute of the <A> tag. For example, to link the text 'Send an E-mail' to the e-mail address **maria_joseph@gmail.com**, you can write the following HTML code:

```
<a href="mailto:maria_joseph@gmail.com">Send an Email</a>
```

QUICK TIP

You may use the **link** attribute of <BODY> tag to specify a different colour for the links in a webpage. Also, you can use the **vlink** attribute of the <BODY> tag to specify a colour for the visited links.

CHECK YOUR PROGRESS

3. Design a webpage that provides information about our solar system. The list of planets should be displayed as hyperlinks. Clicking on the planet name should display the information about the planet stored in a separate html file. You may consider the layout given alongside for designing the webpage.

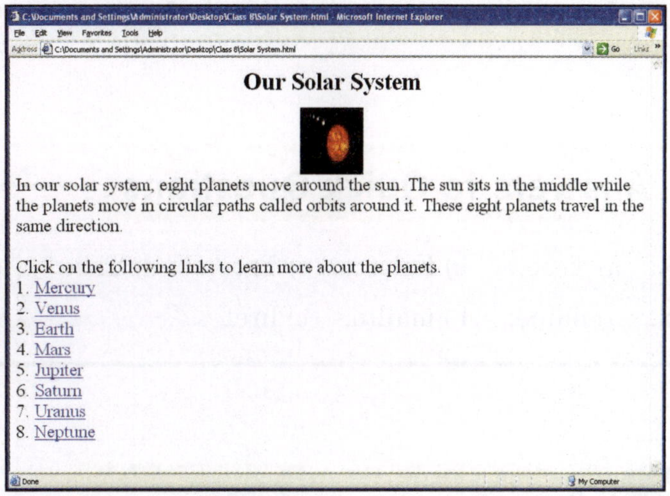

QUICK QUESTION

2. Give one word for the following:

a) Name the attribute of <A> tag that identifies a section in a webpage.

b) Name the keyword that should be used before the address in the href attribute of the <A> tag for linking text to an e-mail address.

c) Name the attribute of the <A> tag for specifying the location of the file to be displayed when you click a hyperlink.

Recap Time

- Tables are defined using the <TABLE> tag in an HTML document.
- A table is divided into rows using the <TR> tag and each row is divided into data cells using the <TD> tag.
- A table heading can be inserted using the <CAPTION> tag.
- The attributes of the <TABLE> tag include border, bordercolor, background, width, height, cellspacing, and cellpadding.
- The attributes of <TR>, <TD>, and <TH> tags include align, bgcolor, rowspan and colspan.
- Hyperlinks are the text strings or images in a webpage which when clicked, links to a different webpage or another section of the same webpage.
- The <A> tag can be used to create hyperlinks in a webpage.
- The three types of linking in HTML are—external, internal and e-mail linking.
- The two important attributes of <A> tag are href and name.

Answers to Quick Questions

1. a) True b) False c) True d) True e) False

2. a) name b) mailto: c) href

Assessment Time

1 Choose the correct answer.

a) Which of the following is not an attribute of the <TABLE> tag?

i) border ii) bgcolor

iii) background iv) rowspan

b) Which one of the following attributes of the <TABLE> tag specifies the space between two adjacent cells?

i) colspan ii) cellpadding

iii) cellspacing iv) border

c) Which of the following tags is used to add columns to a table?

i) <colspan> ii) <TD>

iii) <TR> iv) <A>

d) Which of the following is the correct code for creating a hyperlink?

i) `<A name=http://www.google.co.in> Google Home Page</A>`

ii) `<A url=http://www.google.co.in> Google Home Page</A>`

iii) `<A href=http://www.google.co.in> Google Home Page</A>`

iv) `<A> http://www.google.co.in</A>`

2 **Fill in the blanks using the words given below.**

<TR>	Hyperlink	Table	<CAPTION>	href	name

a) A grid of rows and columns is known as ___________.

b) The ___________ tag is used to add rows to the table.

c) The tag used for inserting a table heading is ___________.

d) A ___________ connects one webpage to another.

e) ___________ and ___________ are the two attributes of the <A> tag.

3 **Write the HTML commands for the following:**

a) To create a table with four pixels thick border of blue colour.

b) To create a table with background colour as yellow.

c) To set the background colour of a row as yellow.

d) To center align the contents of a cell.

e) To set the image 'flower.jpg' as a hyperlink to the file 'Garden.html'.

4 **Answer the following questions.**

a) Which tags are used to define the basic structure of a table in HTML?

b) Differentiate between cellspacing and cellpadding attributes of <TABLE> tag.

c) Give the use of Anchor (<A>) tag.

d) Differentiate between internal and external linking.

e) How is internal linking done in a webpage?

f) Explain with the help of an example how to link any text to an e-mail address.

Activity Time

1. You are the activity incharge of your school. You have been assigned the responsibility of putting up the schedule for various activities to be conducted during the summer vacations in your school on the school portal. Design a webpage for this task. You may consider the given layout for the page.

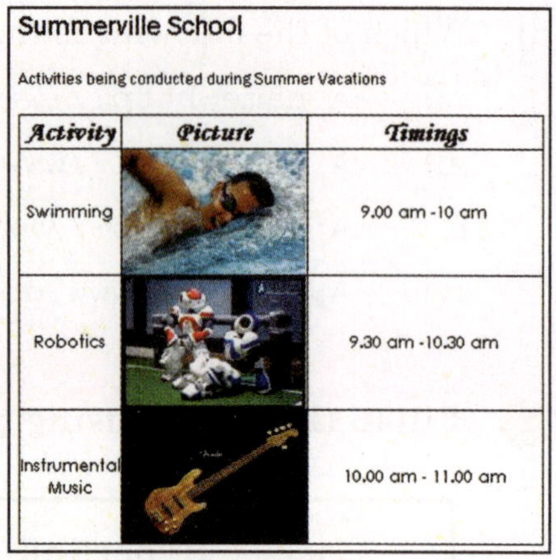
Summerville School

Activities being conducted during Summer Vacations

Activity	Picture	Timings
Swimming		9.00 am -10 am
Robotics		9.30 am -10.30 am
Instrumental Music		10.00 am - 11.00 am

2. Kala Natya Samiti wants to put up information about various dance forms like Ballet, Jazz, Hip Hop and Classical. Design a website for the organisation. You can consider having different pages for various dance forms.

3. Your class teacher has observed that a lot of students in the class eat junk food regularly. She wants to highlight the importance of a balanced diet. She wants you to design a webpage that brings out the importance of various nutrients in our diet and their functions. You may consider the given layout.

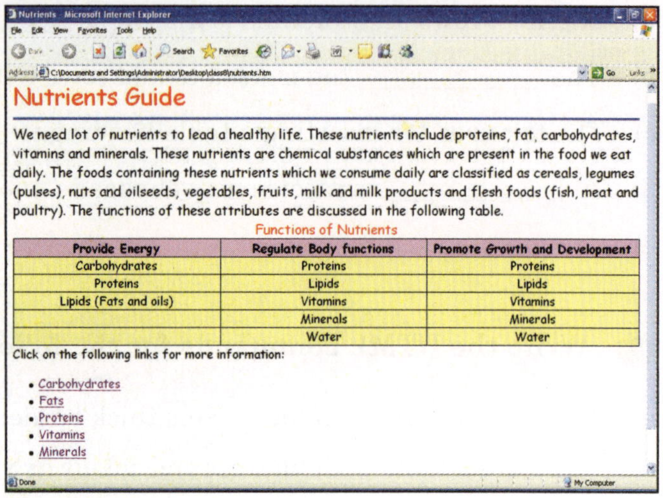
Nutrients Guide

We need lot of nutrients to lead a healthy life. These nutrients include proteins, fat, carbohydrates, vitamins and minerals. These nutrients are chemical substances which are present in the food we eat daily. The foods containing these nutrients which we consume daily are classified as cereals, legumes (pulses), nuts and oilseeds, vegetables, fruits, milk and milk products and flesh foods (fish, meat and poultry). The functions of these attributes are discussed in the following table.

Functions of Nutrients

Provide Energy	Regulate Body functions	Promote Growth and Development
Carbohydrates	Proteins	Proteins
Proteins	Lipids	Lipids
Lipids (Fats and oils)	Vitamins	Vitamins
	Minerals	Minerals
	Water	Water

Click on the following links for more information:

- Carbohydrates
- Fats
- Proteins
- Vitamins
- Minerals

Link the list items to the following pages.

- Carbohydrates to **carbo.html**
- Fats to **fats.html**
- Proteins to **pro.html**
- Vitamins to **vit.html**
- Minerals to **min.html**

Notes for the Teacher

- The teacher can explain the students how tables can be effectively used for organising information in a webpage.
- While surfing the Internet, students should be encouraged to observe the layout of various webpages. This way they will be able to design their webpages in a better way.

MICROSOFT FRONTPAGE 2003

Chapter 5

OBJECTIVES

After having studied this lesson, you will be able to:

- start Microsoft FrontPage.
- create a new webpage.
- use different page views.
- save a webpage.
- set page properties in Microsoft FrontPage.
- design a webpage.
- view a webpage in a web browser.

You already know how to create webpages by writing the HTML codes. For creating webpages in this manner, you need to learn about the various HTML tags and their attributes. These days, a number of software are available that let you create webpages or websites quickly, without writing any HTML code.

Microsoft FrontPage 2003 is one such application software used for website designing and management. It is a **WYSIWYG HTML editor** that provides the tools and templates necessary for quickly designing the HTML pages. You do not require prior knowledge of HTML or any other programming language in order to use MS FrontPage. Let us learn more about this software.

QUICK FACT

- FrontPage was initially created by the Cambridge, Massachusetts company Vermeer Technologies. Vermeer Technologies was acquired by Microsoft in January 1996 specifically so that Microsoft could add FrontPage to its product line-up.
- WYSIWYG stands for What You See Is What You Get.

STARTING MICROSOFT FRONTPAGE

To open MS FrontPage, click **Start** ▶ **Programs** ▶ **Microsoft Office** ▶ **Microsoft Office FrontPage 2003**.

MS FrontPage window appears (**Fig. 5.1**).

MS FrontPage is used for creation and management of websites. A website is a collection of interconnected webpages. In this chapter you will learn to design webpages using this software.

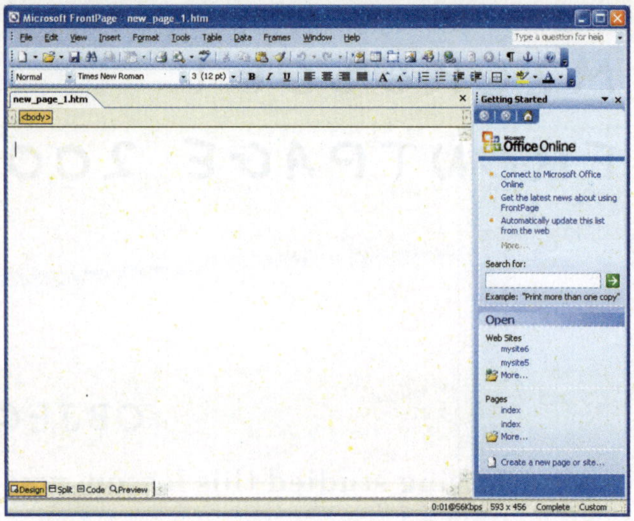

Fig 5.1 *MS FrontPage window*

CREATING A NEW WEBPAGE

To create a new webpage, follow the given steps.

Step 1 Click **File ▶ New** (**Fig. 5.2**). The **New** task pane appears on the right side of the screen.

Step 2 Click the **Blank page** option available under the **New page** section (**Fig. 5.3**). A new page appears as shown in **Fig. 5.1**.

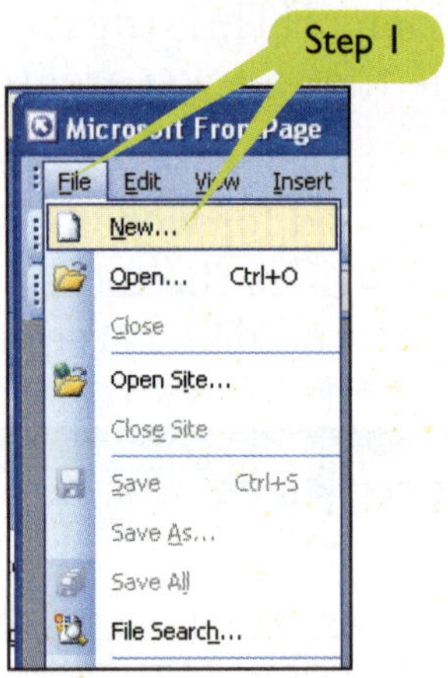

Fig 5.2 *Choosing File▶New*

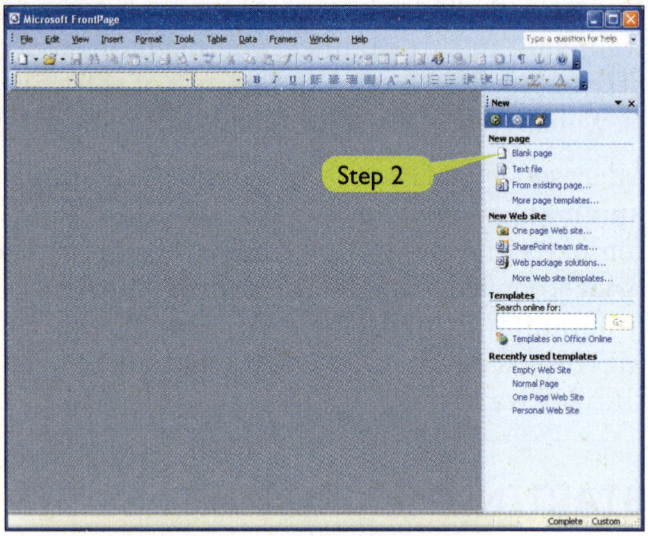

Fig 5.3 *New task pane*

PAGE VIEWS IN MS FRONTPAGE

MS FrontPage offers you a variety of ways to view and edit your webpages during the many stages of the design process. Each view has its own advantages. The View buttons at the bottom of the MS FrontPage window let you switch between the various Page views. Let us learn about the various Page views.

➤ Types of Page Views

1. **Design View.** This is the default view. You can design and edit pages in this view (**Fig. 5.4**).
2. **Code View.** This view shows the HTML code of the page that you are designing. You can use this view to add the HTML code or see the generated code (**Fig. 5.5**).

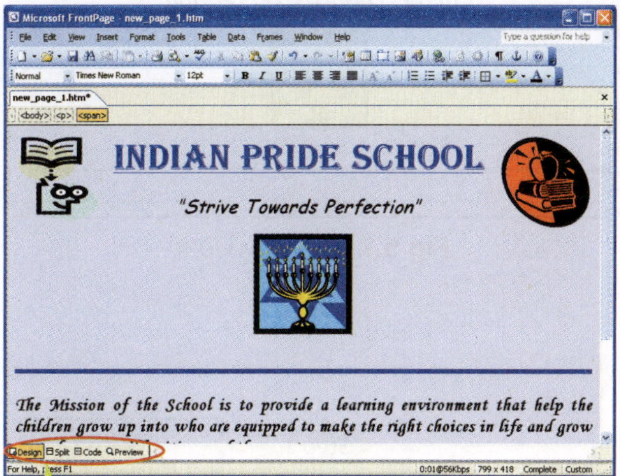

Page view buttons

Fig 5.4 *Design view*

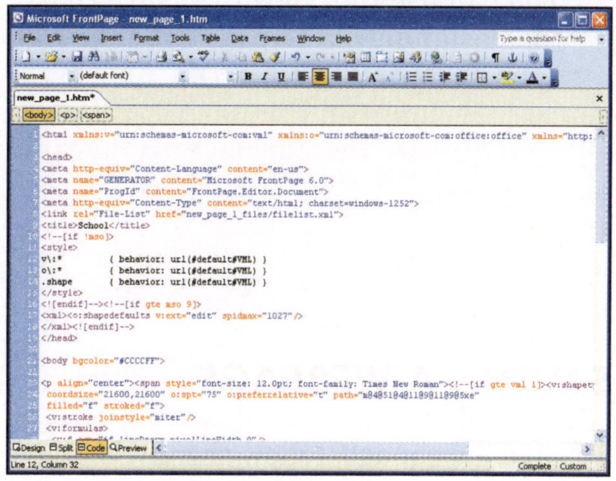

Fig 5.5 *Code view*

3. **Split View.** This view offers simultaneous access to both the **Code** and **Design** views. Here, the screen is divided into two halves. The upper half displays the Code view and the lower half displays the Design view (**Fig. 5.6**).

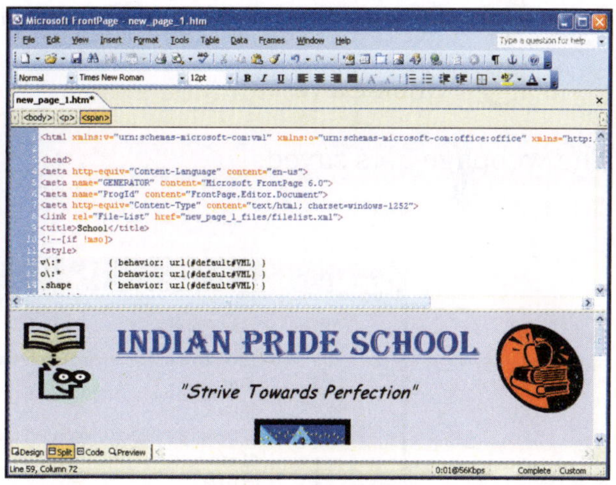

Fig 5.6 *Split view*

Quick Fact

'Intellisense' is a new feature in FrontPage 2003 that assists the user while typing in Code View. When working in Code View, Intellisense will suggest tags and/or properties for the code that the user is entering which significantly reduces the time to write a code.

4. **Preview View.** This view shows how the page will look in the web browser. You can use this view to ensure that the designing of the page is being done as desired (Fig. 5.7).

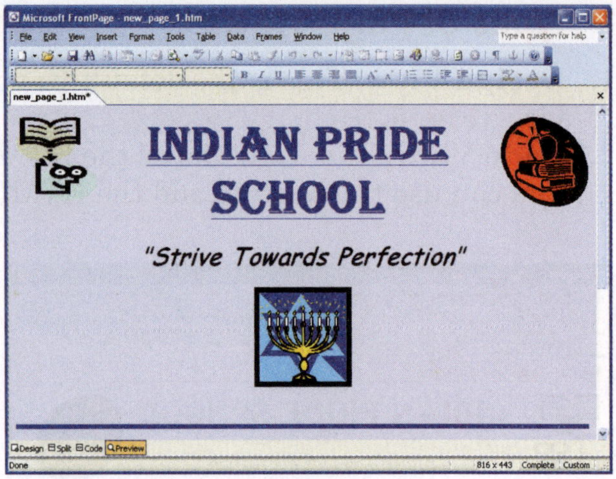

Fig 5.7 *Preview view*

SAVING A WEBPAGE

To save a webpage, follow the given steps.

Step 1 Click **File** ▶ **Save** (Fig. 5.8). The **Save As** dialog box appears (Fig. 5.9).

Step 2 Specify the location and name of the file.

Step 3 Click **Save**.

The webpage gets saved.

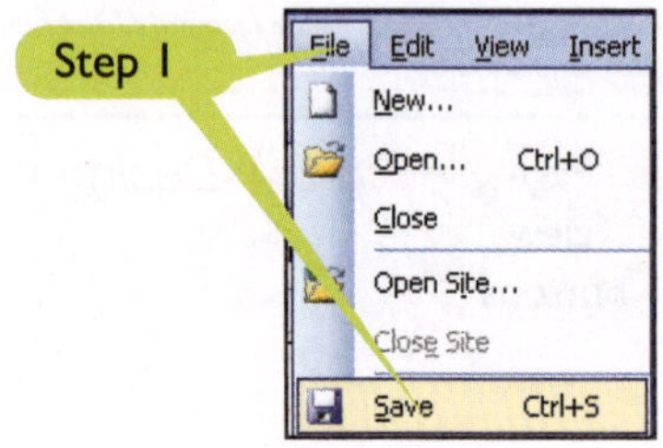

Fig 5.8 *Choosing File▶Save*

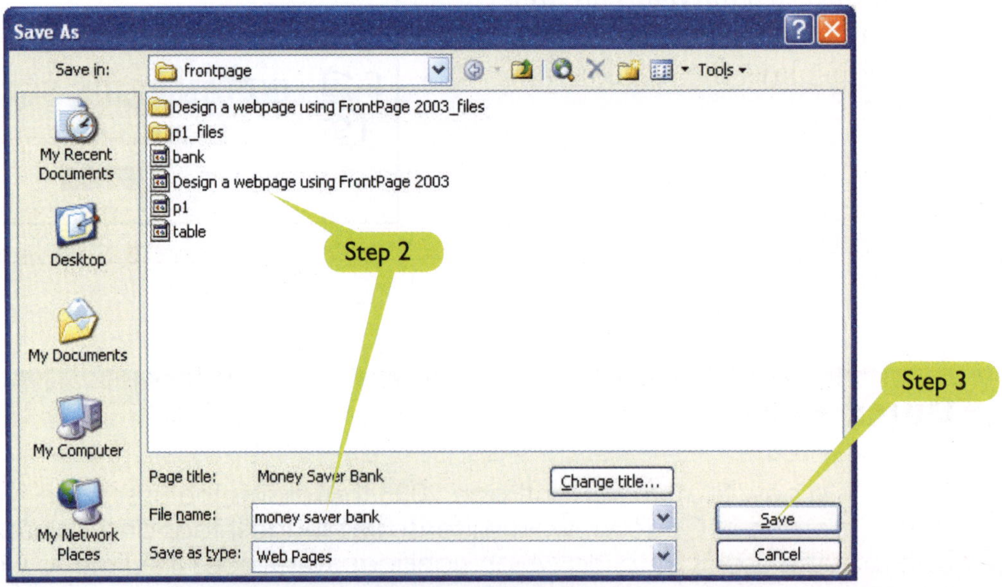

Fig 5.9 *Save As dialog box*

PAGE PROPERTIES

You can set the properties of a webpage such as background colour and page margins. To set the page properties, follow the given steps.

Step 1 Click **File ▶ Properties** (Fig. 5.10). The **Page Properties** dialog box appears (Fig. 5.11).

Step 2 Click the **General** tab and set the properties such as the Title (The title of the page appears in the Title bar of the browser window.)

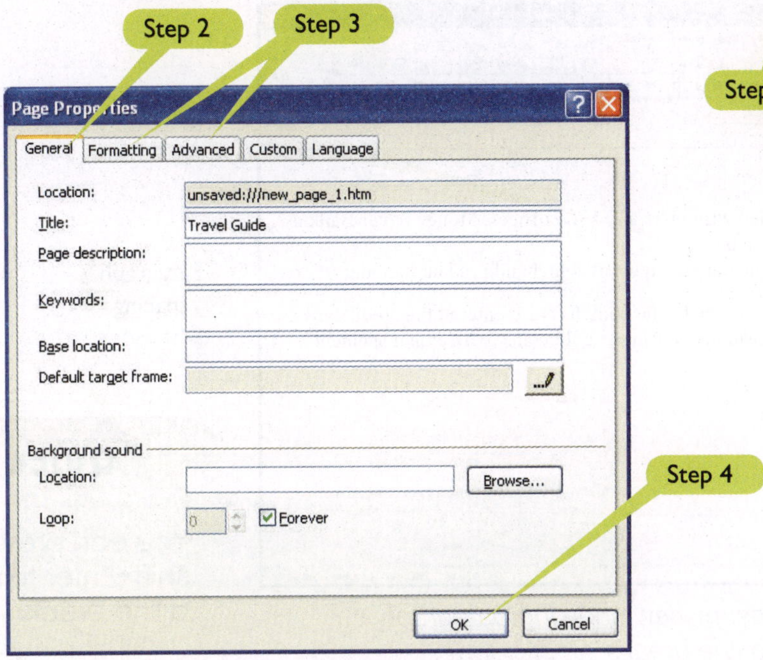

Fig 5.11 *Page Properties dialog box*

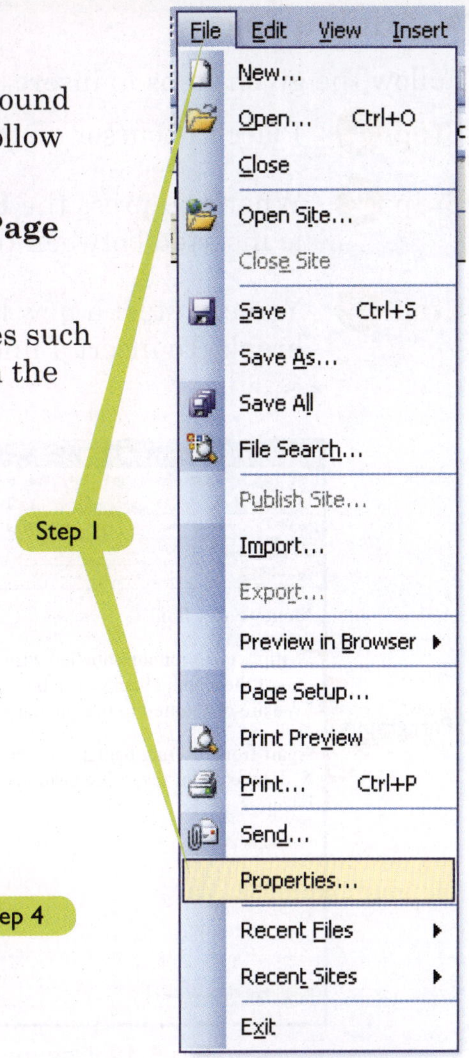

Fig 5.10 *Choosing File ▶ Properties*

Step 3 Similarly, you can click the **Formatting** and the **Advanced** tabs to set the properties such as background colour, background picture and margins for the webpage.

Step 4 Click **OK** to apply the settings.

> **QUICK TIP**
>
> You can also set the page properties by right-clicking on the page in Design view and choosing the **Page Properties** option from the shortcut menu.

DESIGNING A WEBPAGE

You can design a webpage by inserting text, pictures and various other components.

➤ Adding Text

Follow the given steps to insert text in a webpage.

Step 1 Place the cursor on the webpage (in Design view) and start typing.

Step 2 When you press the **Enter** key, a new paragraph begins and a double space is inserted between the two paragraphs.

Step 3 You can start a new line without changing the paragraph by inserting a line break. To insert a line break, click **Insert ▶ Break ▶ Line Break**.

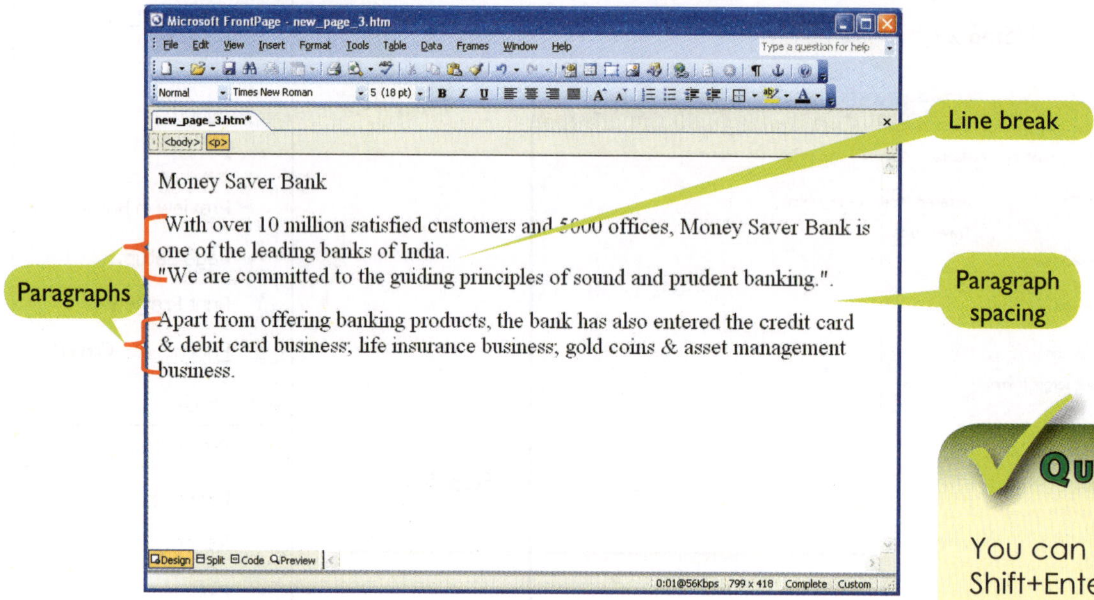

Fig 5.12 *Design view showing paragraph spacing and line breaks*

> **QUICK TIP**
> You can press Shift+Enter to insert a line break.

➤ Formatting Text

You can format the text to change the font style, size, colour, etc. To format text, select the text and follow the given steps.

Step 1 Click **Format ▶ Font** (Fig. 5.13). The **Format** dialog box appears (Fig. 5.14).

Step 2 Select the appropriate options such as font, font style and size.

Step 3 Click **OK**.

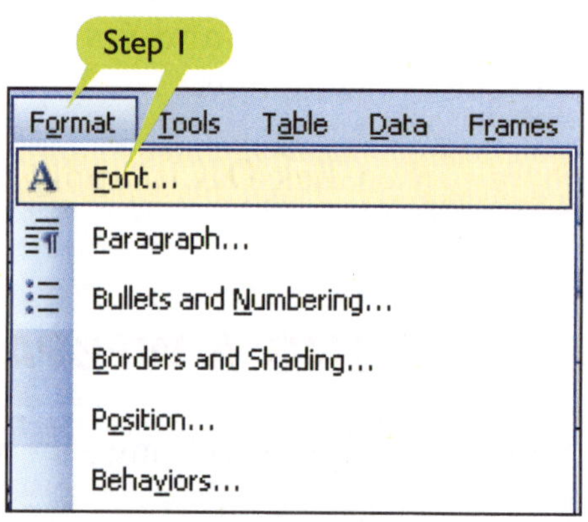

Fig 5.13 *Choosing Format▶Font*

The selected text gets formatted (**Fig. 5.15**).

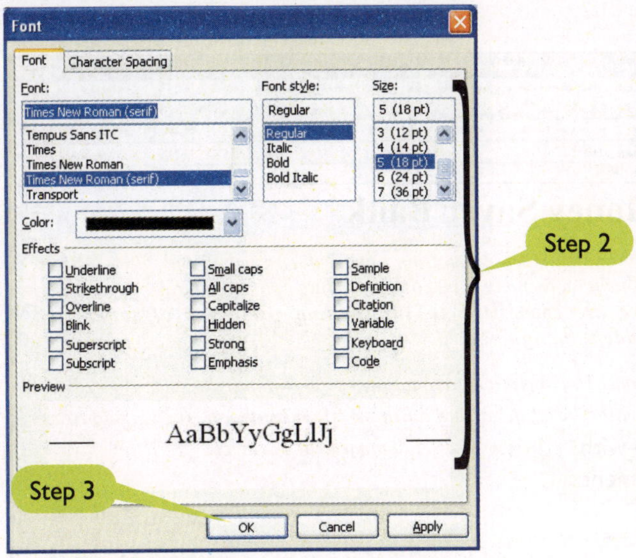

Fig 5.14 *Font dialog box*

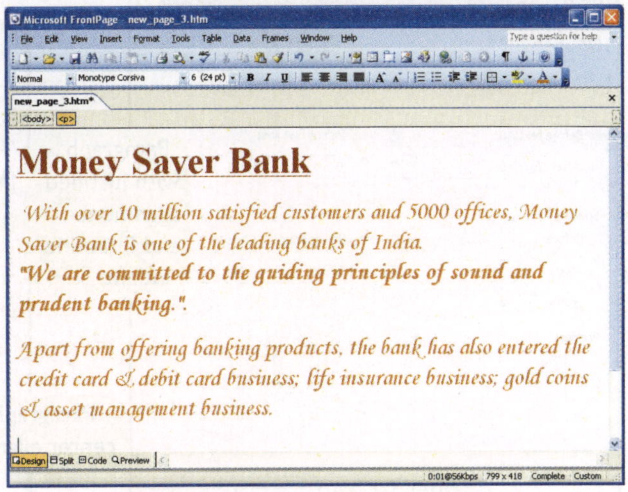

Fig 5.15 *Design view showing the formatted text*

QUICK TIP

You can also make use of the buttons on the Formatting toolbar to format the text.

➤ Formatting Paragraphs

MS FrontPage allows you to specify the paragraph alignment, indentation and spacing. To format a paragraph, select the paragraph and follow the given steps.

Step 1 Click **Format ▶ Paragraph** (**Fig. 5.16**). The **Paragraph** dialog box appears (**Fig. 5.17**).

Step 2 Select the appropriate options such as alignment, indentation and spacing.

Step 3 Click **OK**.

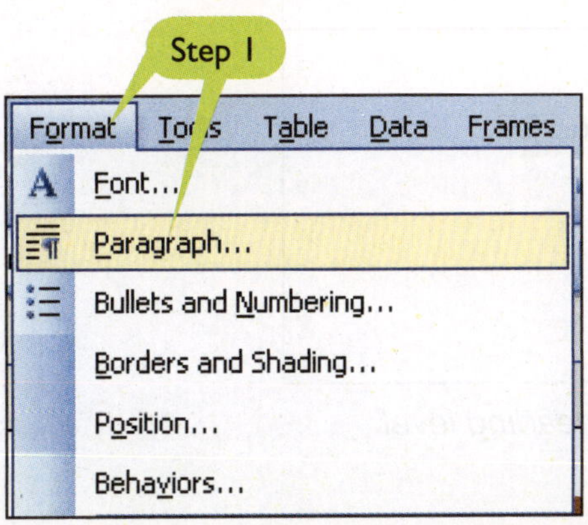

Fig 5.16 *Choosing Format ▶ Paragraph*

The selected paragraphs get formatted (**Fig. 5.18**).

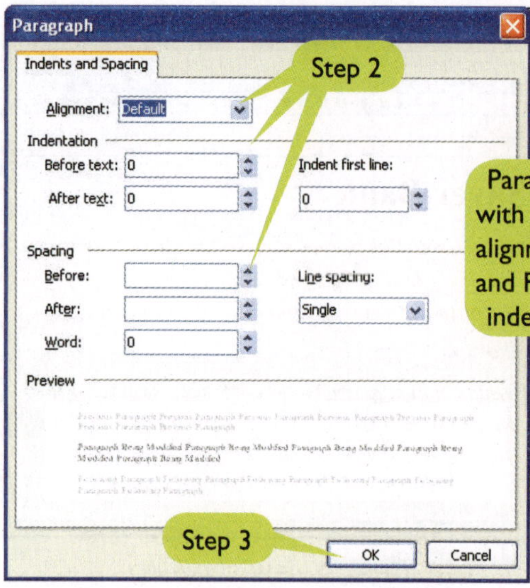

Fig 5.17 *Paragraph dialog box*

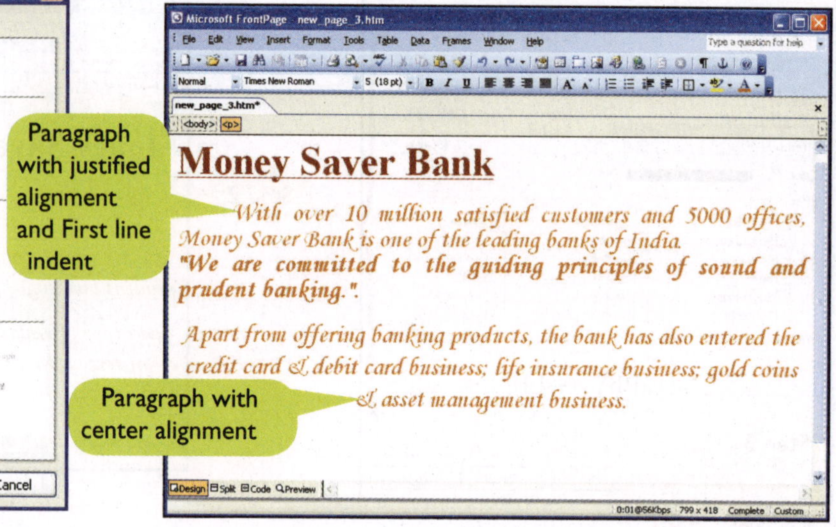

Fig 5.18 *Design view showing formatted paragraphs*

➤ Inserting Headings

You have learnt about the Heading tags (H1 to H6) in HTML. To create headings in FrontPage, click or select the text that should appear as the heading and follow the given steps.

Step 1 Click the **Style** drop-down list on the Formatting toolbar (**Fig. 5.19**).

Step 2 Choose the appropriate heading level.

The text appears as per the selected heading level (**Fig. 5.20**).

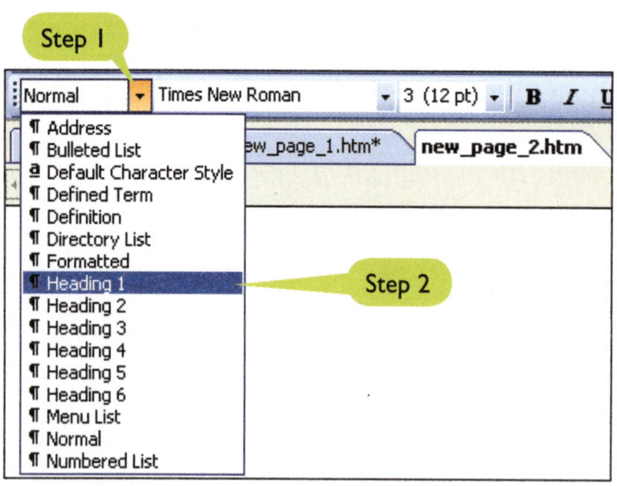

Fig 5.19 *Choosing the heading level*

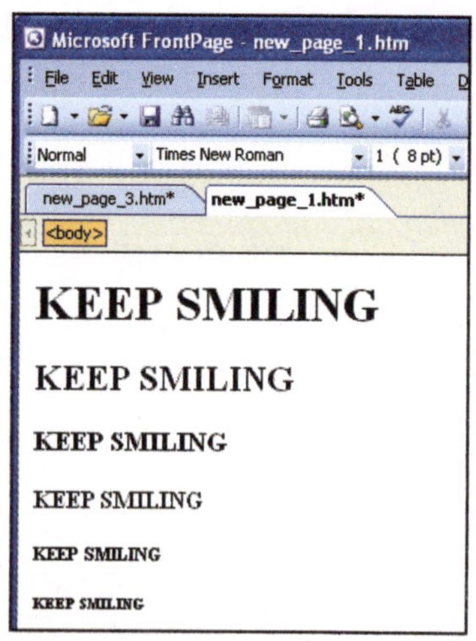

Fig 5.20 *Design view showing different heading levels*

CHECK YOUR PROGRESS

1. **Design the page shown here in MS FrontPage according to the given description.**

Title of the page: Save Environment

Background colour: Light Green

Level 1 heading: GO GREEN

Level 2 heading: REDUCE, REUSE, RECYCLE

Level 3 heading: THREE GREAT WAYS TO PROTECT ENVIRONMENT

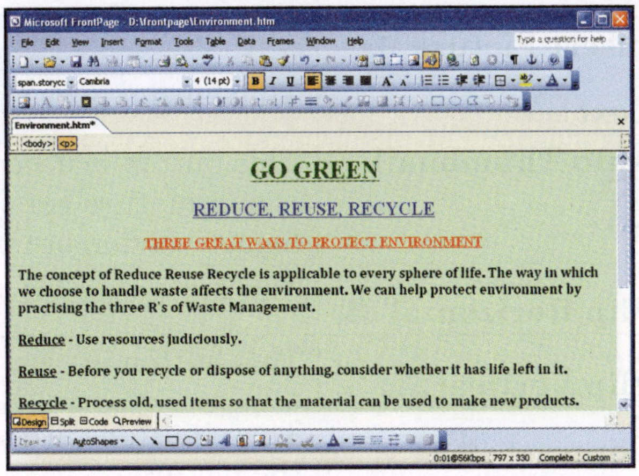

➤ Inserting Pictures and Clip Art

The way you add pictures or Clip Art in an MS Word document or an MS PowerPoint slide, the same way you can add pictures or Clip Art to a webpage. Click **Insert ▶ Picture ▶ Clip Art** or **Insert ▶ Picture ▶ From File** to insert pictures on a webpage (**Fig. 5.21**).

The inserted pictures can be dragged and placed at the desired position on a webpage.

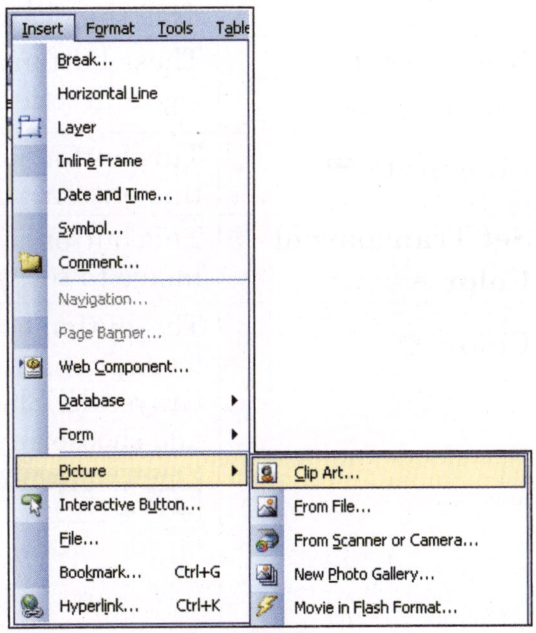

Fig 5.21 *Choosing Insert ▶ Picture ▶ Clip Art*

• Pictures Toolbar

You can format a picture by making use of the various buttons on the Pictures toolbar (**Fig. 5.22**). To display the Pictures toolbar, click **View ▶ Toolbars ▶ Pictures**.

Fig 5.22 *Pictures toolbar*

The use of some of the buttons on the Pictures toolbar is illustrated in **Table 5.1**.

Table 5.1 *Uses of some buttons on the Pictures toolbar*

Button	Description
Insert Picture	This button is used to insert pictures in a document.
Text	This button is used to place text over the pictures.
Auto Thumbnail	This button is used to create a thumbnail image. A thumbnail is a miniature version of an image that is often linked to the bigger version of the same image.
Flip Horizontal	This button is used to create a mirror image of the selected image.
Flip Vertical	This button is used to flip or turn a picture upside down.
Contrast	These buttons are used to increase or decrease the contrast of the picture.
Brightness	These buttons are used to increase or decrease the brightness of the picture.
Crop	This button lets you cut any part of the picture that is not required. To use this feature, click the Crop button and then drag the picture's sizing handles to crop the picture.
Rotate Left or **Right by 90°**	These buttons let you rotate a picture by 90° in the left or right direction.
Line Style	This button is used to put a border around a picture. Using this button, you can also choose different line styles.
Set Transparent Color	This button is used to change the background colour of an image to transparent.
Color	This button is used to adjust the colour of a picture. There are four options available when you click on this button—Automatic, Grayscale, Black & White and Washout. Click on the picture and choose any one of these four options for the desired result.   *Automatic* *Grayscale* *Black & White* *Washout*
Bevel	This button is used to add a three-dimensional edge effect to the border of a picture.
Reset Picture	This button lets you get back to the original picture on which you had started working.

- **Picture Properties**

You can change some properties of a picture such as its placement with the help of **Picture Properties** dialog box (**Fig. 5.23**). To display the **Picture Properties** dialog box, right-click on the picture and choose **Picture Properties** from the shortcut menu. The options that are available under the Appearance tab of the Picture Properties dialog box are:

- **Wrapping style.** It determines the placement of the text with respect to the picture.
- **Layout.** These options let you specify four properties—Alignment, Border thickness, Horizontal spacing and Vertical spacing. Horizontal and Vertical spacing determines the space between the picture and the surrounding text.
- **Size.** This option allows you to specify the size of a picture in pixels or in terms of percentage.

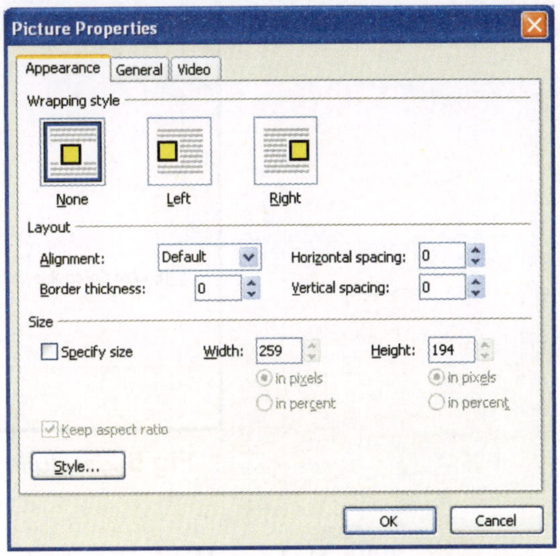

Fig 5.23 *Picture Properties dialog box*

➤ Creating Bulleted and Numbered Lists

You can easily create bulleted or numbered lists by using **Format ▶ Bullets and Numbering** option or by using the buttons on the Formatting toolbar.

MS FrontPage also lets you add pictures as bullets. Let us learn to use pictures as bullets.

Select the text on which bullets have to be applied and follow the given steps.

Step 1 Click **Format ▶ Bullets and Numbering** (**Fig. 5.24**). The **Bullets and Numbering** dialog box appears (**Fig. 5.25**).

Step 2 Click the **Picture Bullets** tab.

Step 3 Click the **Specify picture** checkbox.

Step 4 Click the **Browse** button.

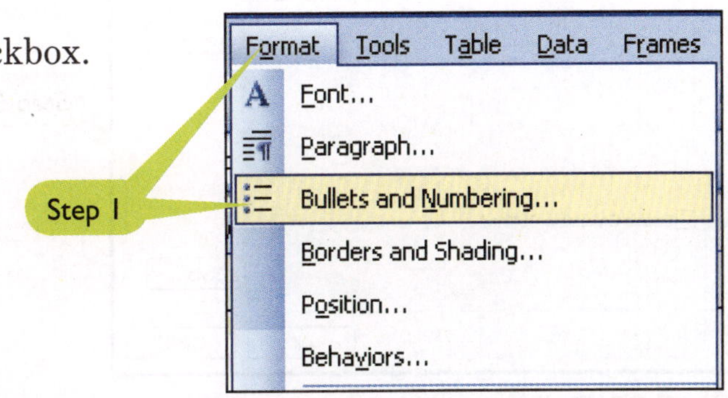

Fig 5.24 *Choosing Format ▶ Bullets and Numbering*

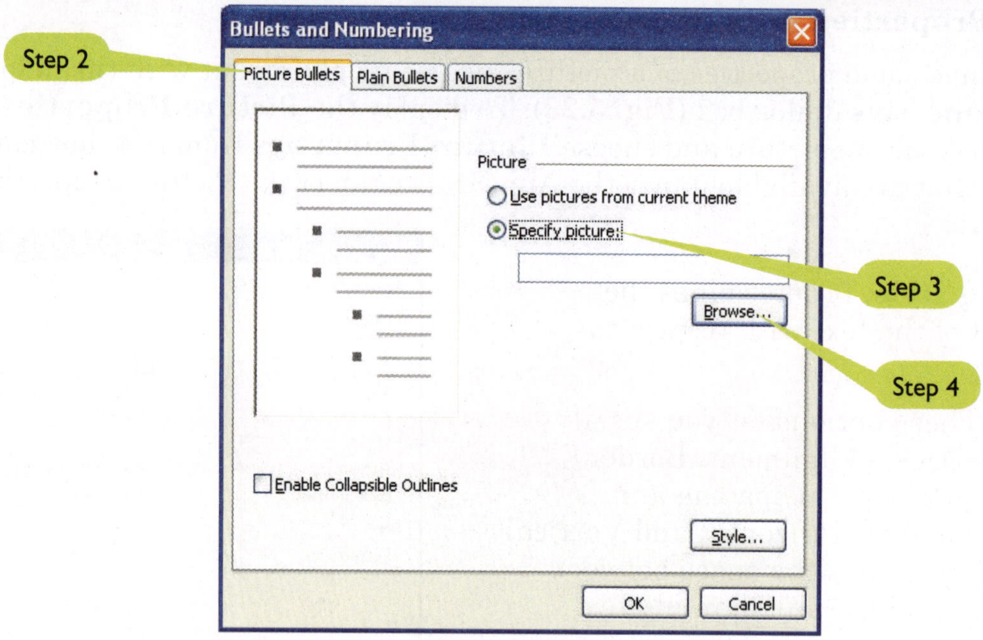

Fig 5.25 *Bullets and Numbering dialog box*

Step 5 The **Select Picture** dialog box appears (**Fig. 5.26**). Select the picture that is to be used as a bullet and click the **Open** button.

Step 6 Click **OK** in the **Bullets and Numbering** dialog box (**Fig. 5.27**).

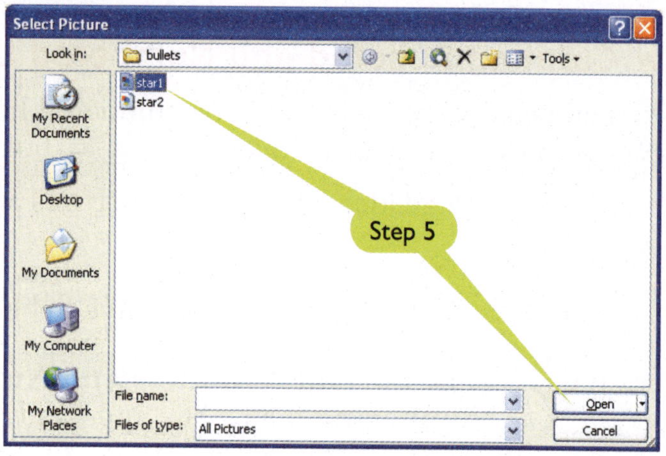

Fig 5.26 *Select Picture dialog box*

The selected picture is used as a bullet (**Fig. 5.28**).

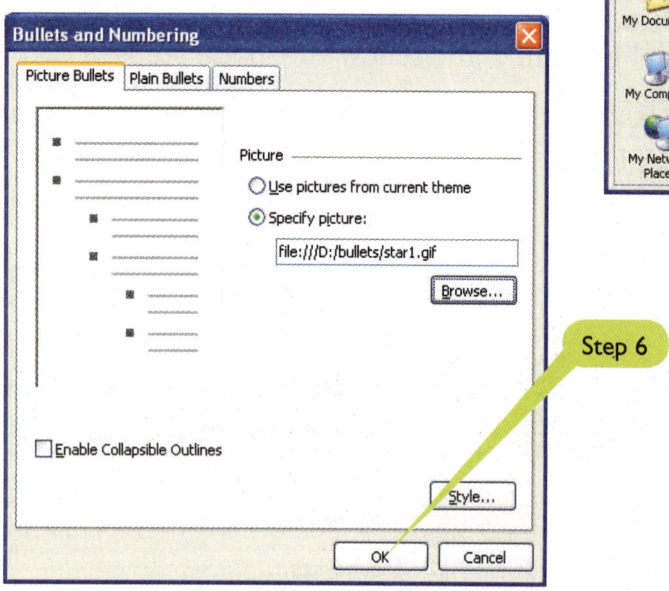

Fig 5.27 *Bullets and Numbering dialog box*

Fig 5.28 *List with picture bullets*

➤ Adding a Horizontal Line

You can add horizontal lines in a webpage to create sections of text. Open the page in Design view and follow the given steps to add a horizontal line.

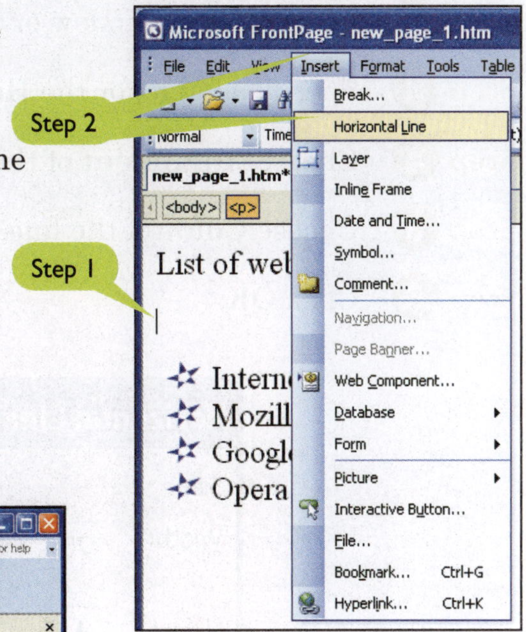

Fig 5.29 *Steps for inserting a horizontal line*

Step 1 Place the cursor at the position where the line needs to be inserted (**Fig. 5.29**).

Step 2 Click **Insert ▶ Horizontal Line**. A horizontal line gets inserted in the page (**Fig. 5.30**).

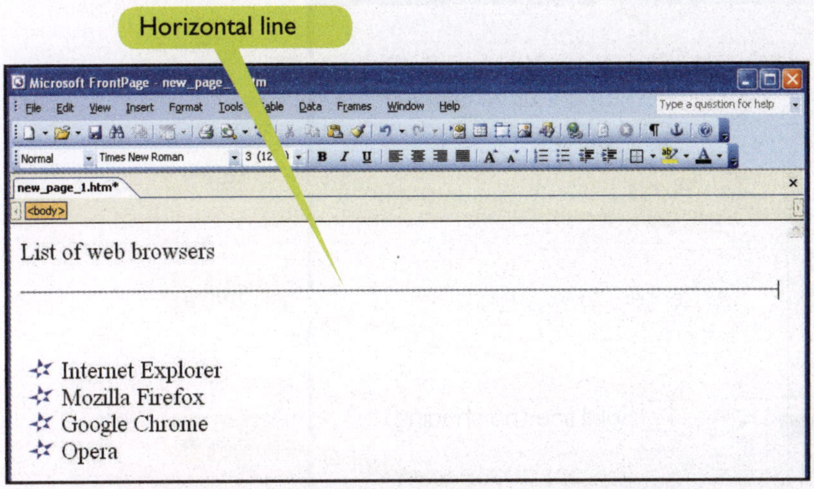

Fig 5.30 *Text with the inserted horizontal line*

You can also change the colour, thickness and width of a line by following the given steps.

Step 1 Double-click the line (**Fig. 5.31**). The **Horizontal Line Properties** dialog box appears (**Fig. 5.32**).

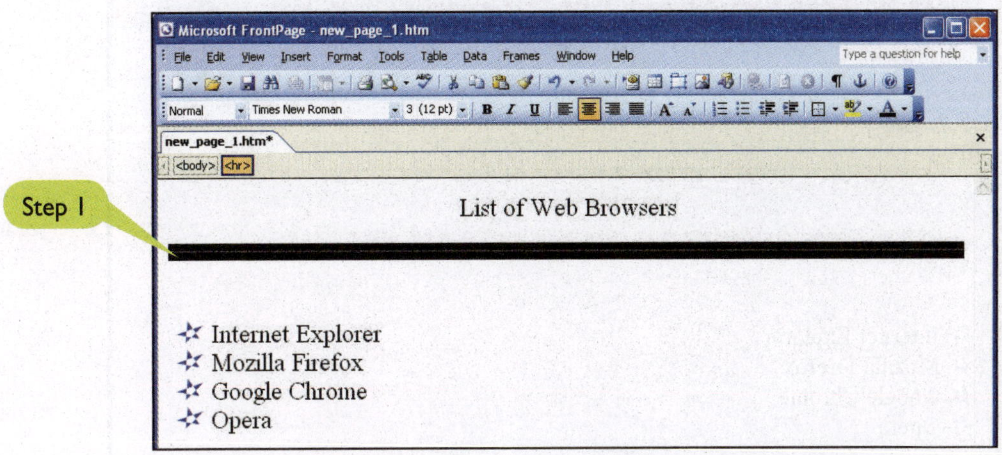

Fig 5.31 *Step 1 for setting horizontal line properties*

Step 2 Specify a value for **Width** of a line. The value can be in terms of percentage of window or pixels.

Step 3 Specify a value for the **Height** or the thickness of the line in pixels.

Step 4 Choose **Alignment** of the line.

Step 5 Choose **Color** of the line.

Step 6 Click **OK**.

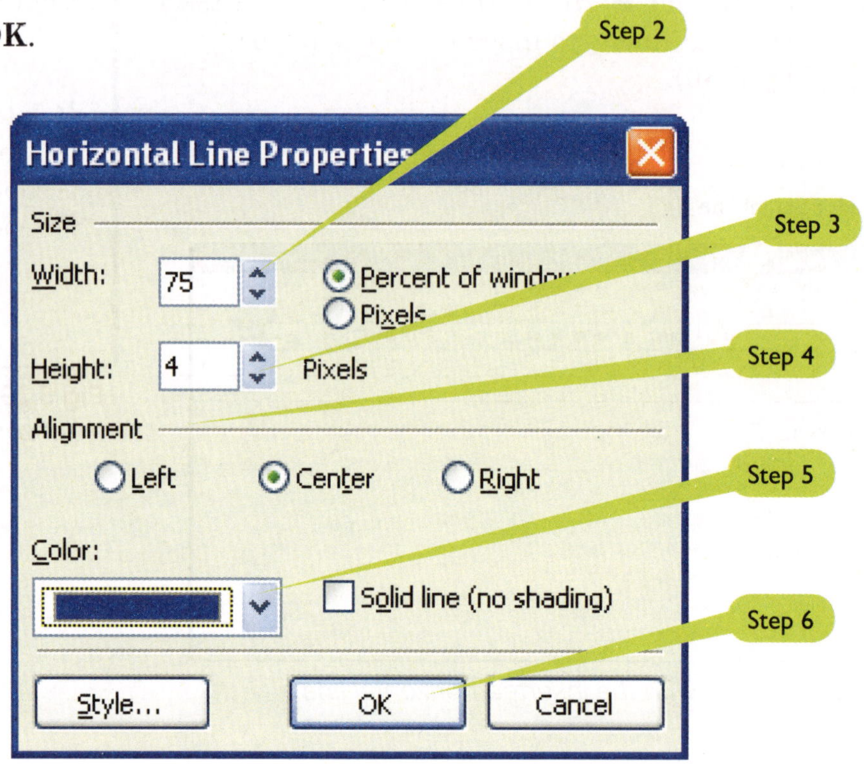

Fig 5.32 *Horizontal Line Properties dialog box*

The horizontal line is formatted according to the specified properties (**Fig. 5.33**).

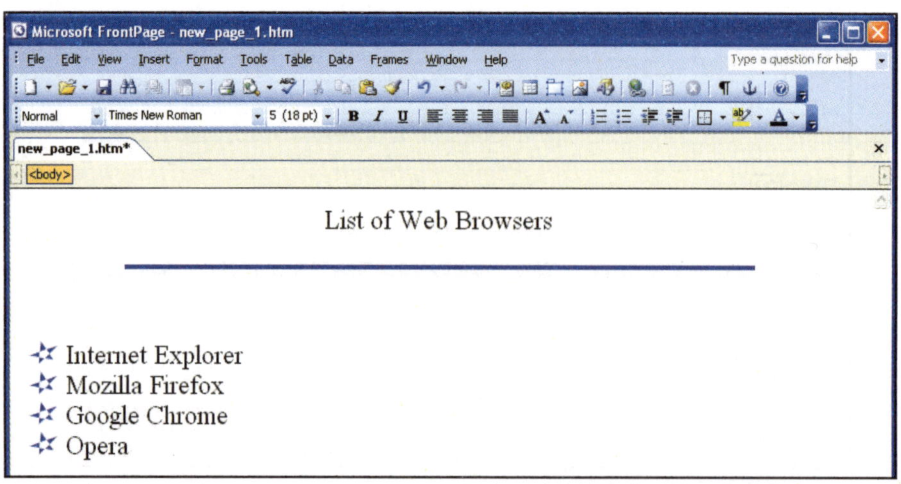

Fig 5.33 *Page showing the formatted horizontal line*

CHECK YOUR PROGRESS

2. **Design the webpage shown alongside in MS FrontPage by incorporating the specified features.**
   - Picture
   - Bullets and Numbering
   - Horizontal Line

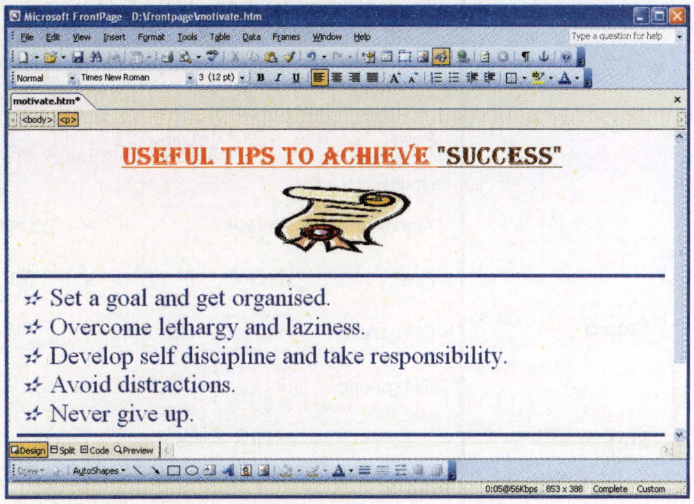

➤ Inserting Tables

Tables are very useful for organising information. MS FrontPage provides tools for designing the tables quickly. To insert tables, follow the given steps.

Step 1 Click **Table ▶ Insert ▶ Table** (**Fig. 5.34**). The **Insert Table** dialog box appears (**Fig. 5.35**).

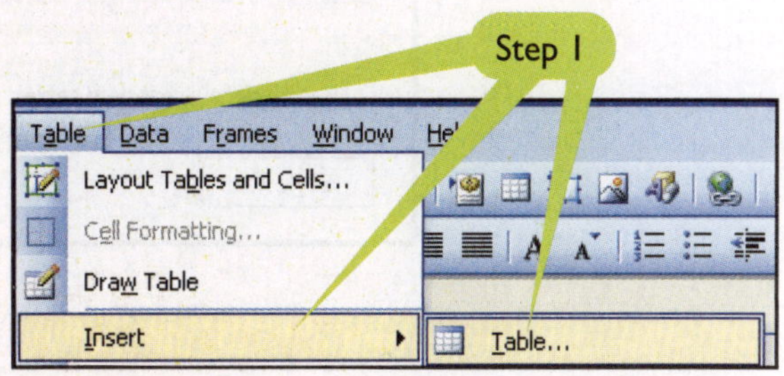

Fig 5.34 *Choosing Table ▶ Insert ▶ Table*

Step 2 Specify the number of **Rows** and **Columns** for the table.

Step 3 Choose the table alignment from the **Alignment** drop-down list.

Step 4 Set the **width** of the table. Setting the table width in a percentage is more desirable as tables with fixed pixels size do not adjust with the dimensions of the browser window and can result in a horizontal scroll bar if the table is wider than the browser window. It is desirable not to specify the **height** of the table. The table should have height according to its contents.

Step 5 Set the value of **Float** property. This property determines the table's position in relation to the other objects on the page.

Step 6 Specify a value for **Cell padding**. Cell padding is the amount of space between the text and the wall of the cell.

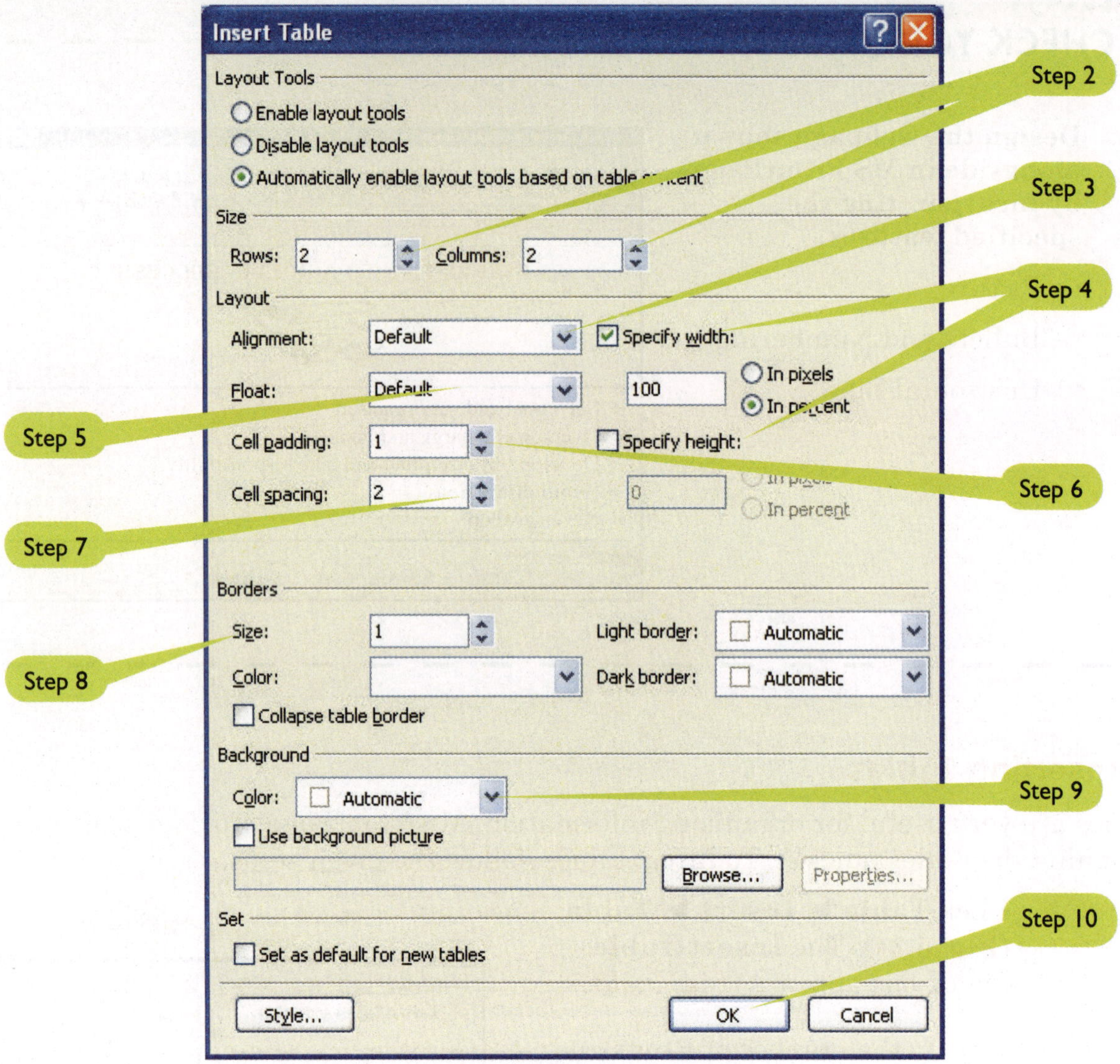

Fig 5.35 *Insert Table dialog box*

Step 7 Specify a value for **Cell spacing**. Cell spacing is the space between the cells of the table.

Step 8 Specify a value for table **Border Size** and **Color**.

Step 9 Specify a **Background Color** for the table.

Step 10 Click **OK**.

The table with the selected properties gets inserted in the page (**Fig. 5.36**).

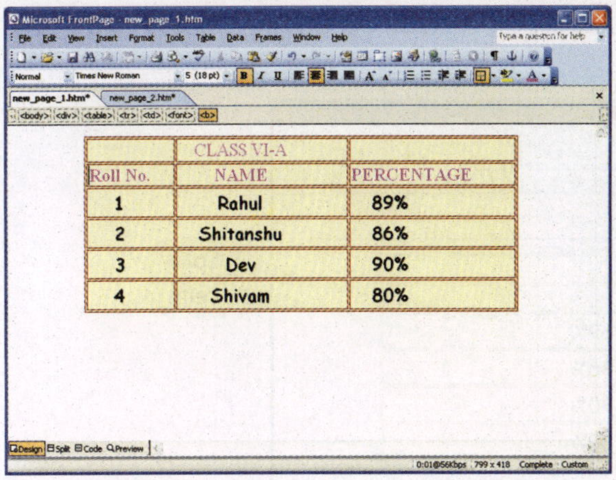

Fig 5.36 *Design view showing the formatted table*

> ✓ **QUICK TIP**
>
> You can change the table or cell properties by clicking anywhere in the table and choosing **Table ▶ Table Properties ▶ Table** or **Table ▶ Table Properties ▶ Cell**.

After inserting a table you can split and merge cells.

- **Splitting Cells**

Splitting cells refers to dividing a single cell into multiple cells. The steps for splitting cells are:

Step 1 Select the cell or cells that you want to split (**Fig. 5.37**).

Step 2 Click **Table ▶ Split Cells** (**Fig. 5.38**). The **Split Cells dialog box** appears (**Fig. 5.39**).

Step 3 Specify the number of rows or columns you wish to split the selected cells into.

Step 4 Click **OK**.

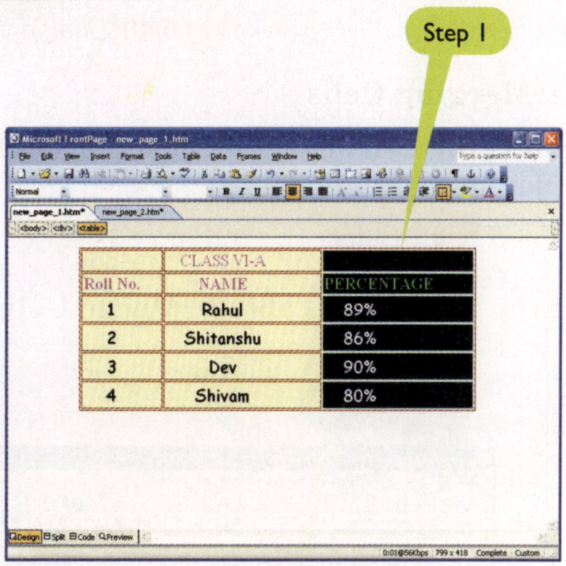

Fig 5.37 *Selecting the cells*

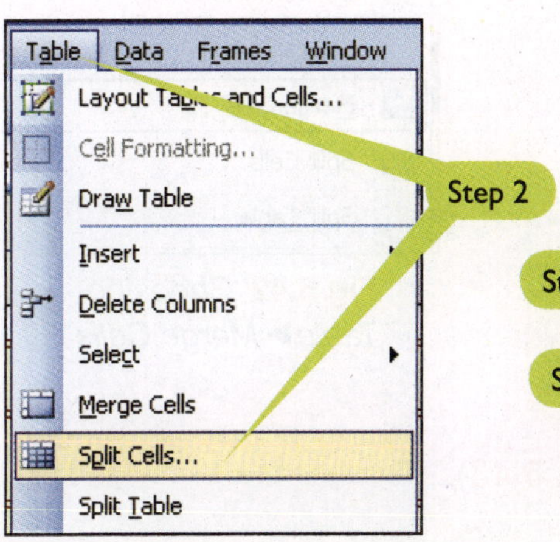

Fig 5.38 *Choosing Table▶Split Cells*

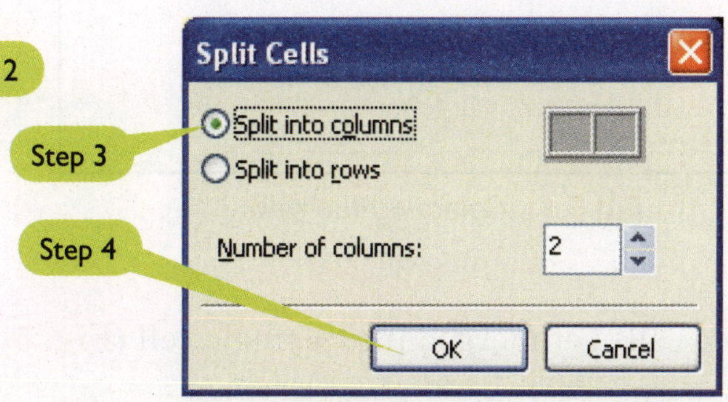

Fig 5.39 *Split Cells dialog box*

The selected cells are divided into a number of rows or columns as specified by you (**Fig. 5.40**).

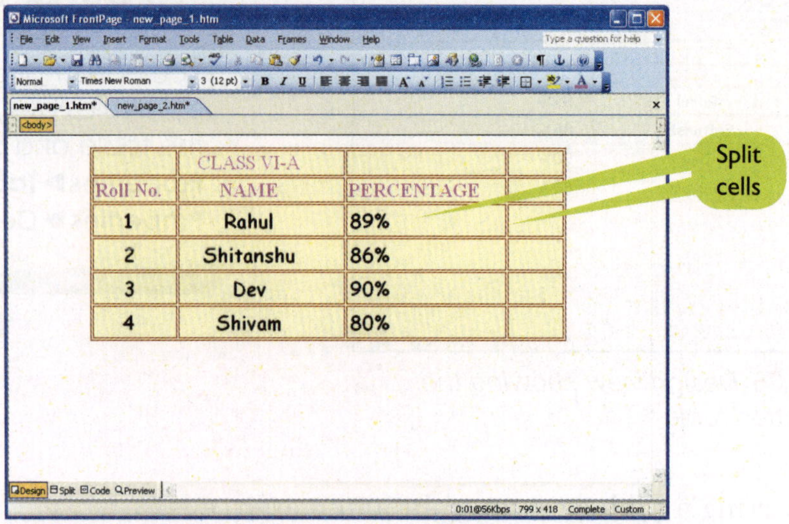

Fig 5.40 *Design view showing the table with split cells*

- ## Merging Cells

Merging cells refers to combining multiple cells into a single cell. The steps for merging cells are:

Step 1 Select the cell or cells that you want to merge (**Fig. 5.41**).

Step 2 Click **Table ▶ Merge Cells** (**Fig. 5.42**).

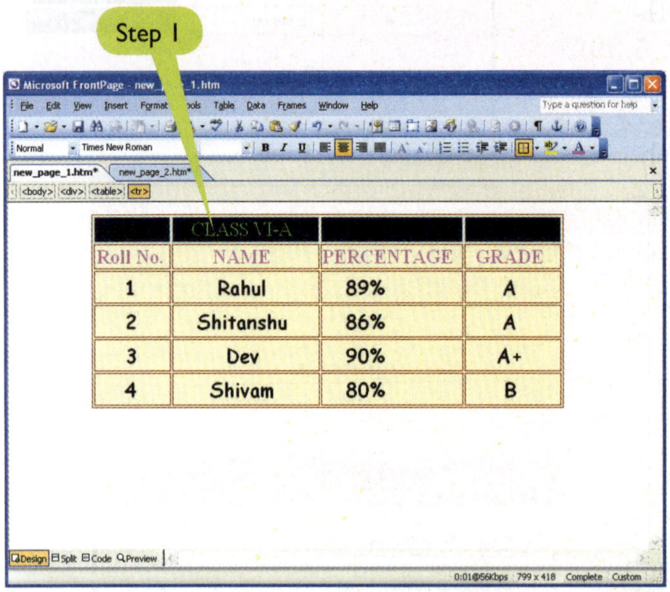

Fig 5.41 *Selecting the cells*

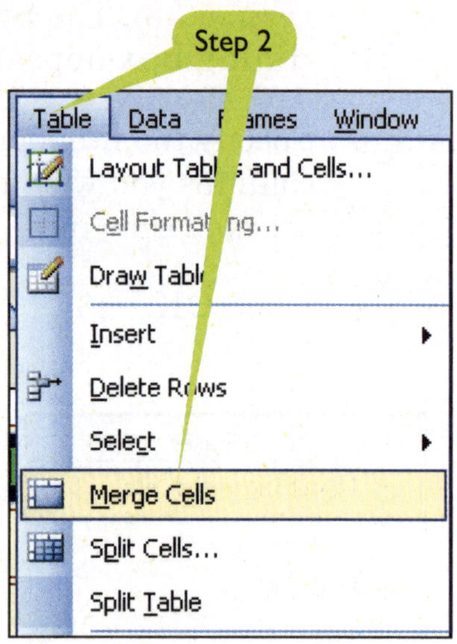

Fig 5.42 *Choosing Table ▶ Merge Cells*

The selected cells get merged into a single cell (**Fig. 5.43**).

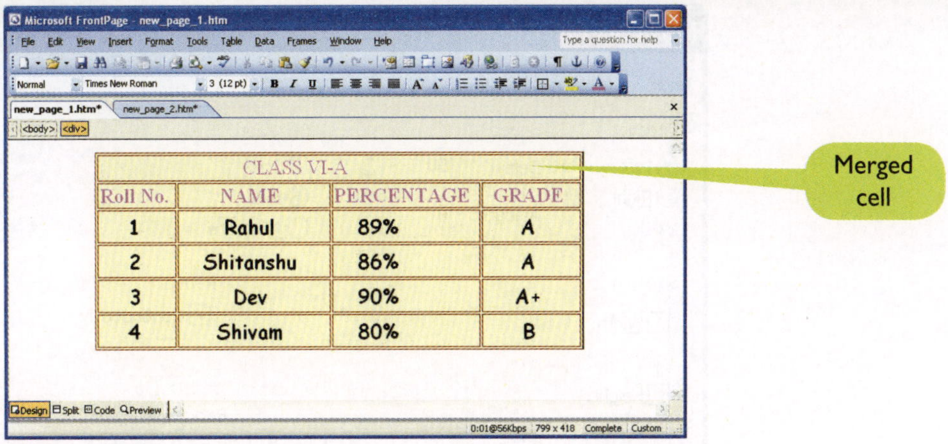

Fig 5.43 *Design view showing the table with merged cells*

➤ Adding Marquee Effect

You can add moving text with the help of **Marquee** effect. To add the effect, follow the given steps.

Step 1 Select the text that should have the Marquee effect (**Fig. 5.44**).

Step 2 Click **Insert ▶ Web Component**. The **Insert Web Component** dialog box opens (**Fig. 5.45**).

Step 3 Under the **Component type** section, choose the **Dynamic Effects** option.

Step 4 Under the **Choose an effect** section, double-click on **Marquee**. The **Marquee Properties** dialog box appears (**Fig. 5.46**).

Step 5 Set the desired properties in the dialog box.

Step 6 Click **OK**.

You can view the Marquee effect in the Preview view.

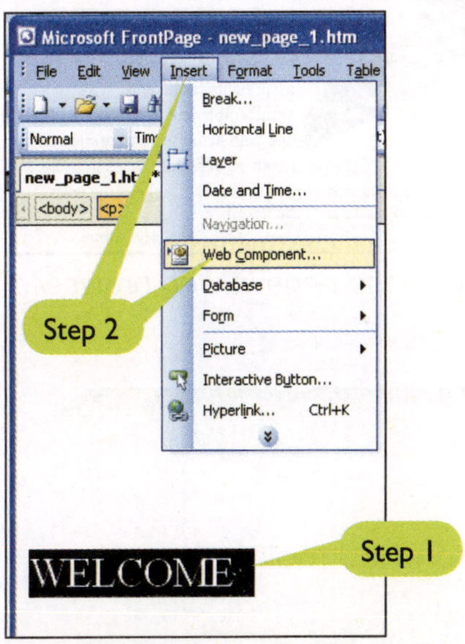

Fig 5.44 *Steps 1 and 2 for adding the marquee effect*

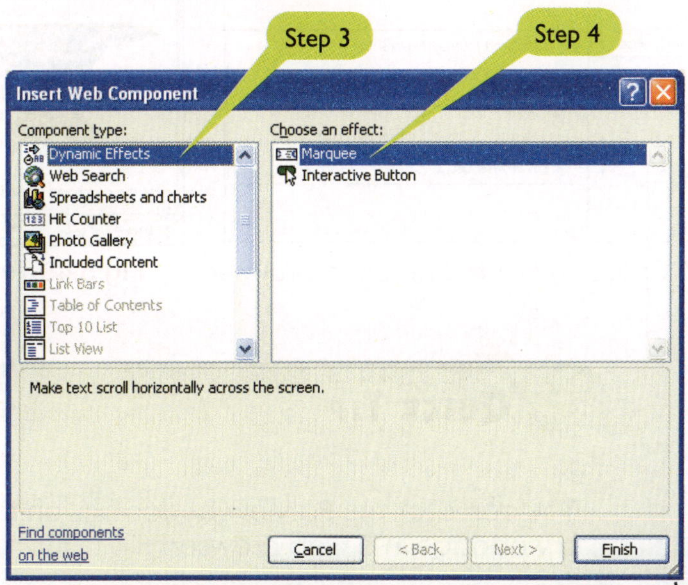

Fig 5.45 *Insert Web Component dialog box*

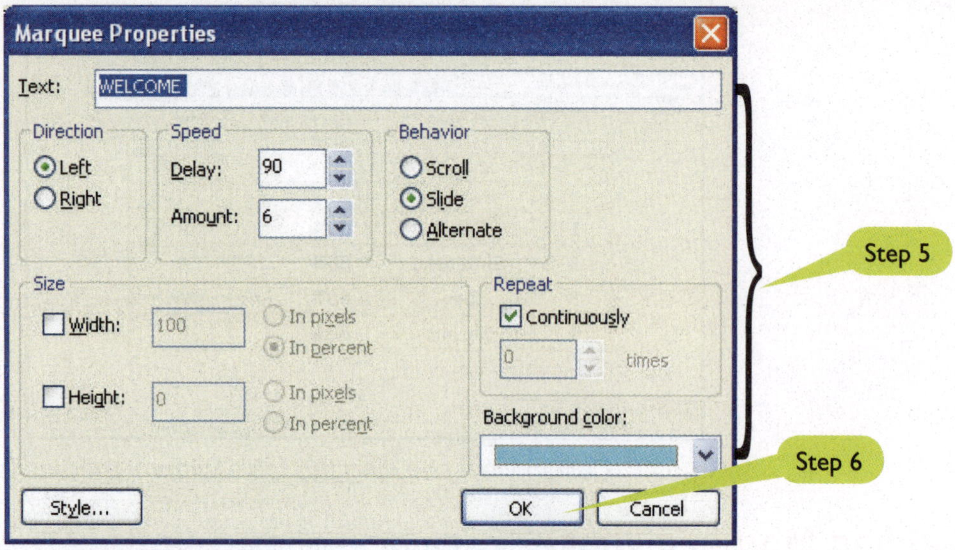

Fig 5.46 *Marquee Properties dialog box*

VIEWING A WEBPAGE IN A WEB BROWSER

After creating a webpage, you can view it in a browser window. To view a webpage in a browser, click **File ▶ Preview in Browser** (Fig. 5.47) and choose a browser from the submenu.

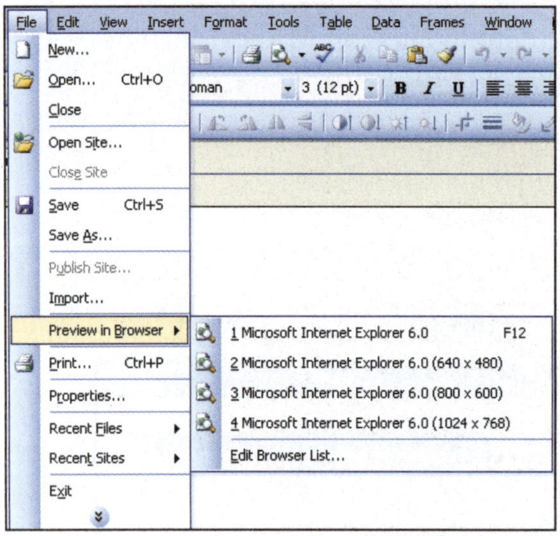

Fig 5.47 *Choosing File ▶ Preview in Browser*

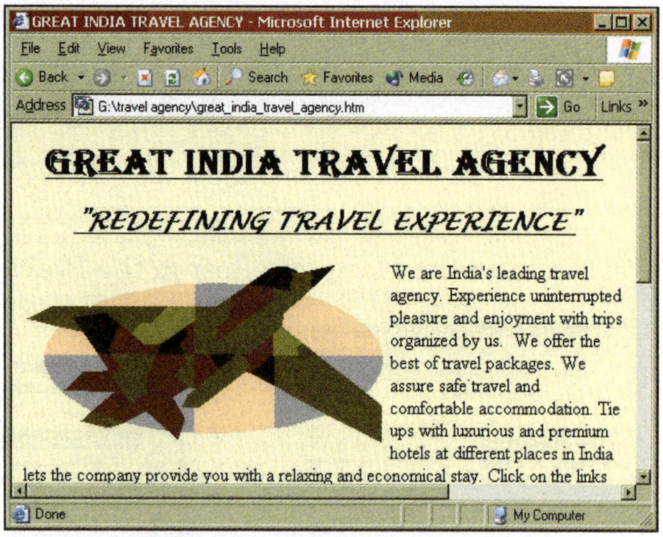

Fig 5.48 *Preview of the page in web browser*

QUICK TIP

You can click the Preview button on the Standard toolbar to view a webpage in a web browser.

Recap Time

- Microsoft FrontPage is a WYSIWYG HTML editor that provides the tools and templates necessary for designing and managing the websites quickly.
- There are four types of Page views—Design view, Code view, Split view and Preview view.
- Design view is the default page view. You can design and edit pages in this view.
- Code view shows the HTML code of a webpage.
- Split view offers simultaneous access to both the Code and Design views of a page.
- Preview view shows how the page will look in the web browser.
- The Page Properties dialog box is used to set page properties such as background colour, title and margins.
- You can design webpages by writing text, formatting paragraphs, adding horizontal lines, pictures, bullets and numbering, marquee effect, etc.

Assessment Time

1 Choose the correct answer.

a) Which of the following is an example of WYSIWYG HTML editor?

i) MS PowerPoint ii) MS Access iii) MS FrontPage iv) MS Excel

b) The view of a webpage that lets you design and see the code of the page is

i) Split view. ii) Code view. iii) Design view. iv) Preview view.

c) Which menu should be accessed in order to add bullets and numbering to a page?

i) Edit ii) Format iii) Insert iv) File

d) Miniature version of an image that is often linked to the bigger version of the same image is referred to as

i) Clip Art. ii) thumbnail. iii) marquee. iv) none of these

2 Fill in the blanks using the words given below.

Page Properties	Cell padding	Marquee	Format	Line Break	Code

a) The ______________ view can be used to view the various HTML tags that make up a webpage.

b) Moving or scrolling text can be added to an HTML page by using the ______________ effect.

c) The ______________ dialog box has options for setting the background colour or picture.

d) The paragraph option under the ______________ menu lets you set paragraph alignment, indentation and spacing.

e) In a table, ______________ is the amount of space between the text and the wall of the cell.

f) A ______________ is inserted in a webpage when you press SHIFT+ENTER in the Design view.

3 Answer the following questions.

a) What is the use of Microsoft FrontPage?

b) Discuss the various Page views briefly.

c) Write the steps for inserting the following elements on a webpage.

i) Horizontal line ii) Bullets and numbering iii) Marquee effect

d) Mention some table properties that can be set with the help of Table Properties dialog box.

e) What do you understand by the term 'theme' in MS FrontPage?

Activity Time

1 A shopping mall wants to advertise their products by setting up their website. Design a webpage for them. You may consider the layout shown here.

2 Design a webpage for your school website. The webpage should display the results of various inter-school competitions in a tabular format.

<table>
<tr><th colspan="5">INTER-SCHOOL COMPETITIONS</th></tr>
<tr><th>S.No.</th><th>School Name</th><th>Competition</th><th>Participants</th><th>Result</th></tr>
<tr><td rowspan="3">1</td><td rowspan="3">Royal High School</td><td rowspan="3">English Debate</td><td>Shreya Ghosh</td><td rowspan="3">I</td></tr>
<tr><td>Swapnil Pandey</td></tr>
<tr><td>Radha Menon</td></tr>
<tr><td rowspan="5">2</td><td rowspan="5">DAS Sr Sec School</td><td rowspan="5">Street Play</td><td>Rishita Tandon</td><td rowspan="5">II</td></tr>
<tr><td>Monica Sareen</td></tr>
<tr><td>Alka Gupta</td></tr>
<tr><td>Rahul Singh</td></tr>
<tr><td>Shreya Parmar</td></tr>
<tr><td rowspan="2">3</td><td rowspan="2">JM High School</td><td rowspan="2">PowerPoint</td><td>Ikshita Parihar</td><td rowspan="2">II</td></tr>
<tr><td>Devansh Mahajan</td></tr>
</table>

Notes for the Teacher

- The teacher should encourage the students to analyse the HTML codes generated by MS FrontPage.

MORE ON MS FRONTPAGE

Chapter 6

OBJECTIVES

After having studied this lesson, you will be able to:

- create hyperlinks in MS FrontPage.
- use interactive buttons as links.
- make use of hot spots and image maps in a website.
- learn about the various views for developing websites using MS FrontPage.
- create a website.

In the previous chapter, you learnt to design webpages using MS FrontPage. You can easily create websites by linking various webpages. Let us now learn about some more features of MS FrontPage that help us to design and create websites.

CREATING HYPERLINKS

In the earlier chapters, you learnt to create hyperlinks using HTML. Hyperlinks allow you link two different documents (**external linking**) or different sections of the same document (**internal linking**). A hyperlink can be a text string or an image. Let us now learn to create hyperlinks in MS FrontPage.

➤ Creating External Hyperlinks

To create an external hyperlink, open the webpage in the Design view and follow the given steps.

Step 1 Select the text or click the image to be linked to another webpage (**Fig. 6.1**).

Step 2 Click **Insert ▶ Hyperlink**. The **Insert Hyperlink** dialog box appears (**Fig. 6.2**).

Step 3 Under the **Link to** section, click the **Existing File** or **Web Page** option.

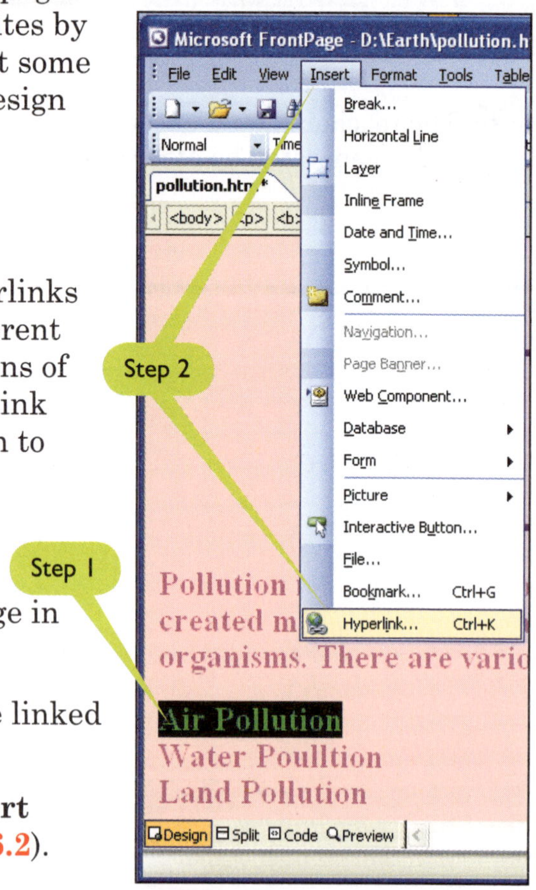

Fig 6.1 *Steps 1 and 2 for creating a hyperlink*

Step 4 Locate and select the file to be linked.

Step 5 Click **OK**.

The hyperlink gets created. View the page in the browser to test the hyperlink (**Fig. 6.3**).

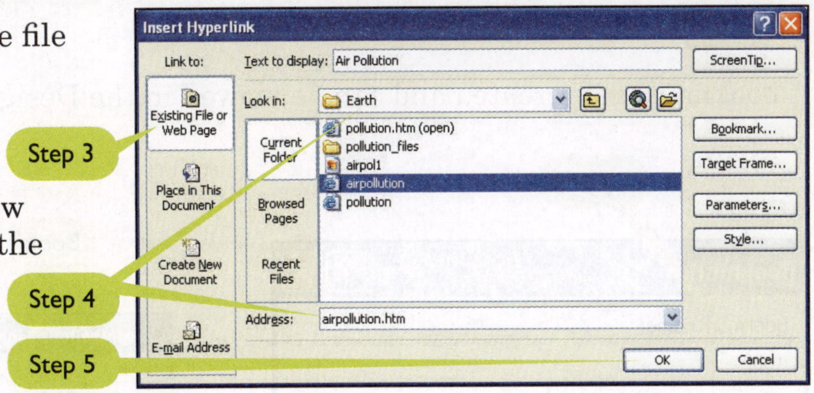

Fig 6.2 *Insert Hyperlink dialog box*

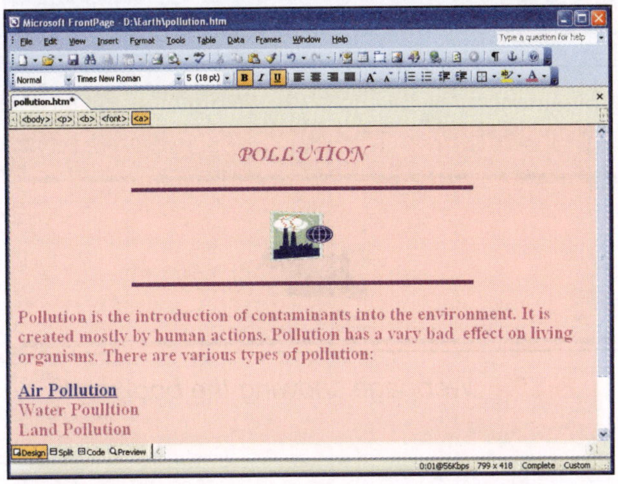

Fig 6.3 *HTML page with a hyperlink*

> **Quick Tip**
>
> You can click the **Insert Hyperlink** button on the Standard toolbar to create hyperlinks.

➤ Creating Internal Hyperlinks

Internal linking is useful when the page is very long. This type of linking lets the user view the desired part or section of the page quickly. To create internal links, follow the given steps.

I. Naming a Section of a Page

Step 1 Place the cursor on the part or the section of a webpage which needs to be linked (**Fig. 6.4**).

Step 2 Click **Insert ▶ Bookmark**. The **Bookmark** dialog box appears (**Fig. 6.5**).

Step 3 Type a name for the bookmark. (A **bookmark** link is used to identify different sections of a page by assigning them unique names so that they can be linked.)

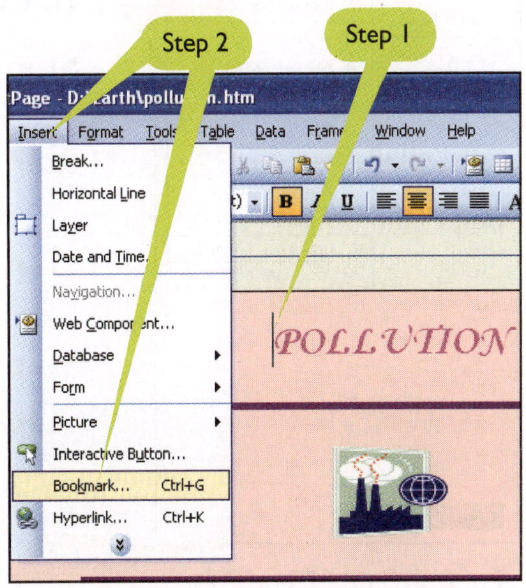

Fig 6.4 *Step 1 for naming the section of a page*

Step 4 Click **OK**.

A bookmark gets created and can be viewed in the Design view only (**Fig. 6.6**).

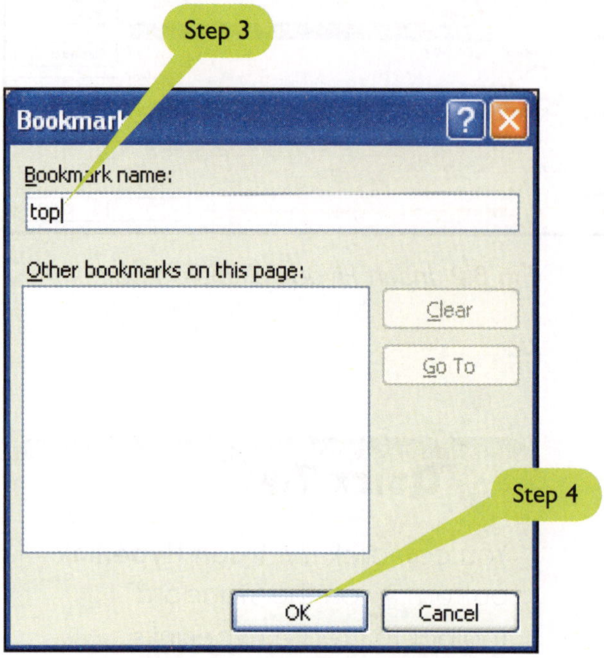

Fig 6.5 *Bookmark dialog box*

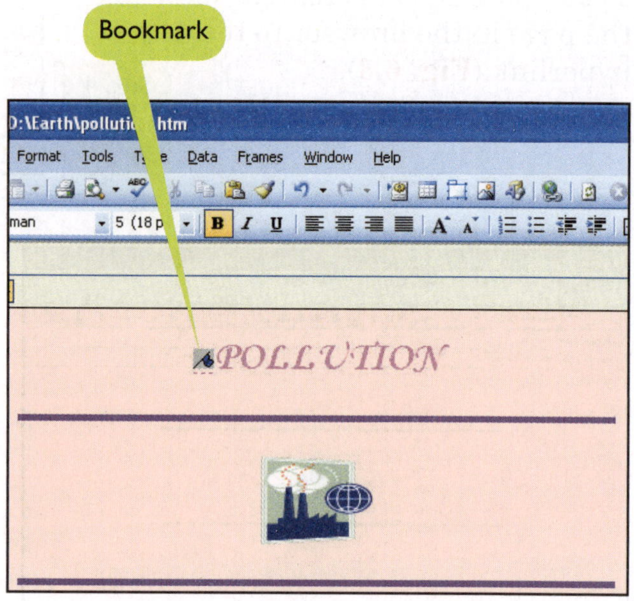

Fig 6.6 *Webpage showing the bookmark*

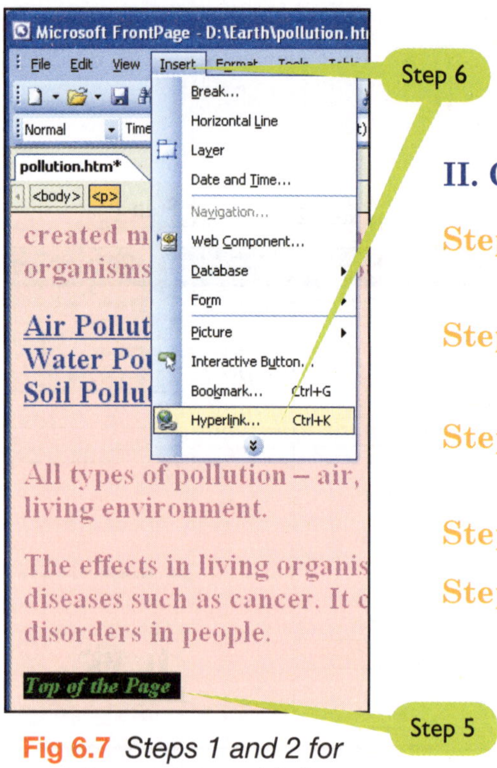

Fig 6.7 *Steps 1 and 2 for creating an internal link*

II. Creating Internal Link

Step 5 Select the text or click the image that should function as the hyperlink (**Fig. 6.7**).

Step 6 Click **Insert ▶ Hyperlink**. The **Insert Hyperlink** dialog box appears (**Fig. 6.8**).

Step 7 Under the **Link to** section, click **Place in This Document** option.

Step 8 Select the bookmark name.

Step 9 Click **OK**.

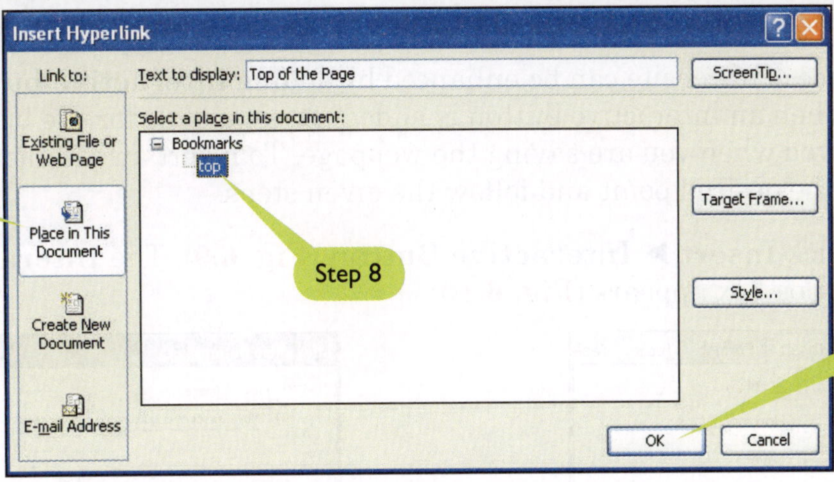

Fig 6.8 *Internal Hyperlink dialog box*

The internal link gets created.

CHECK YOUR PROGRESS

1. **Create a webpage that gives information about various types of operating system. Make use of internal linking to link the name of the operating system to its corresponding section on the same webpage. You may consider the following layout.**

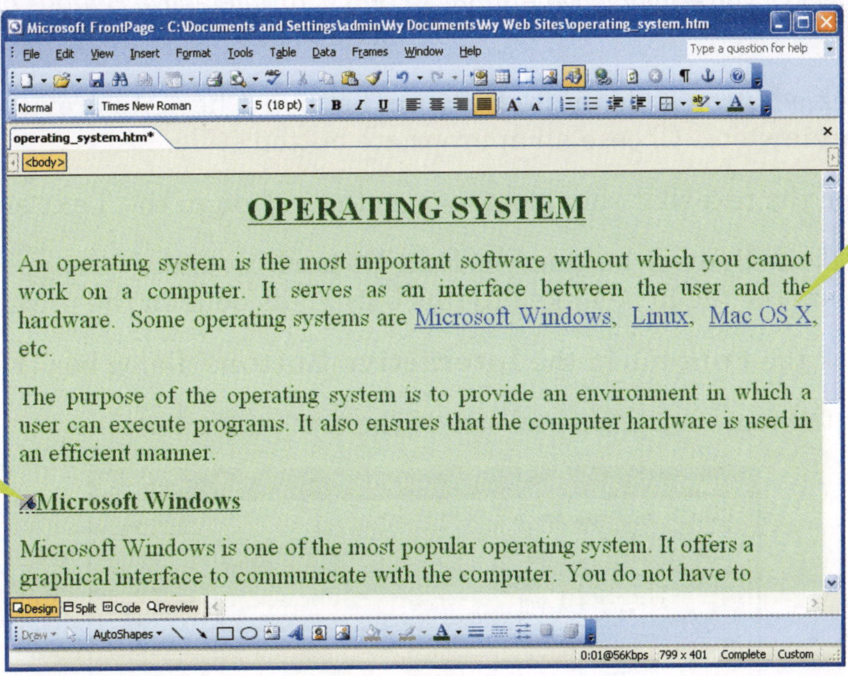

➤ Using Interactive Buttons as Links

The appearance of a website can be enhanced by adding **interactive buttons** as hyperlinks. When an interactive button is added, an image file for the button gets created and can be saved when you are saving the webpage. To insert an interactive button, place the cursor at the desired point and follow the given steps.

Step 1 Click **Insert ▶ Interactive Button** (**Fig. 6.9**). The **Interactive Buttons** dialog box appears (**Fig. 6.10**).

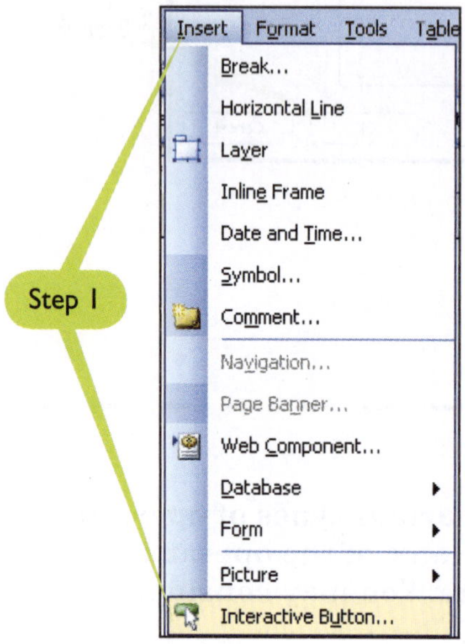

Fig 6.9 *Choosing Insert▶Interactive Button*

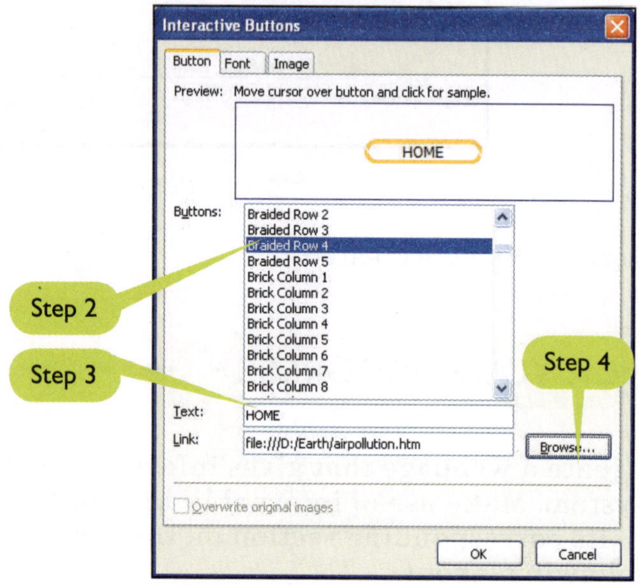

Fig 6.10 *Interactive Buttons dialog box (Button tab)*

Step 2 Click a button style in the **Buttons** list box. Check its preview in the **Preview** box. Choose an appropriate button style.

Step 3 Type the text that should appear on the button in the **Text** entry box.

Step 4 Click the **Browse** button. The **Edit Hyperlink** dialog box appears (**Fig. 6.11**). Locate the file to be linked to this button (as done in the previous section).

Step 5 Click the **Font** tab in the **Interactive Buttons** dialog box (**Fig. 6.12**).

Step 6 Set the font, font style and size of the text on the button.

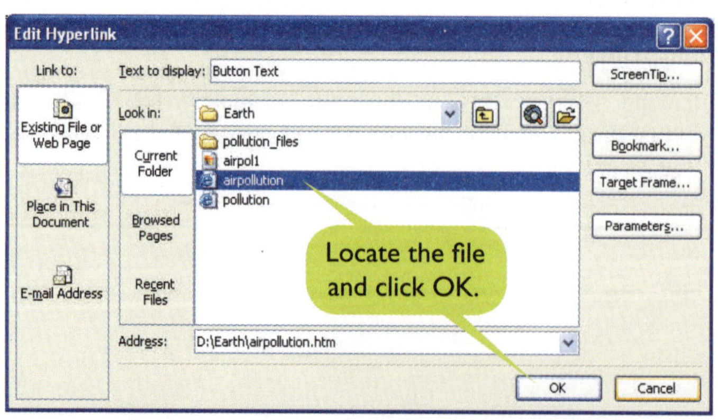

Fig 6.11 *Edit Hyperlink dialog box*

Step 7 Select the **Font Color**, **Hovered Font Color** and **Pressed Font Color**. When the user moves the mouse pointer over the button, the colour of the button changes to the specified **Hovered Font Color**. When the user clicks the button, the colour of the button changes to the specified **Pressed Font Color**.

Step 8 Click the **Image** tab in the **Interactive Buttons dialog box** (**Fig. 6.13**).

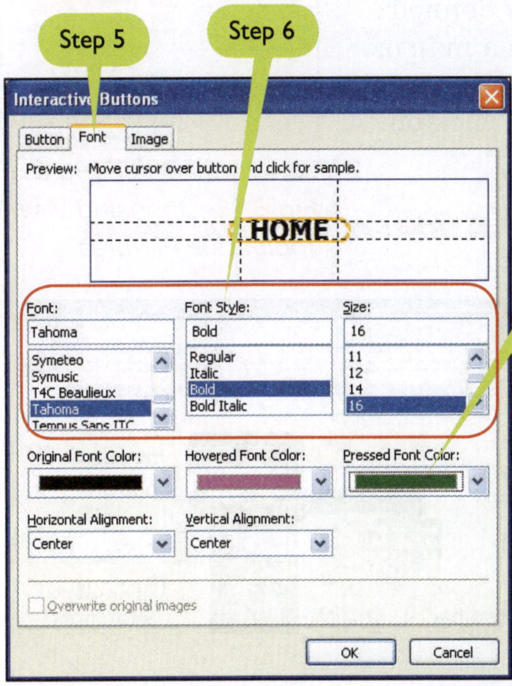

Fig 6.12 *Interactive Buttons dialog box (Font tab)*

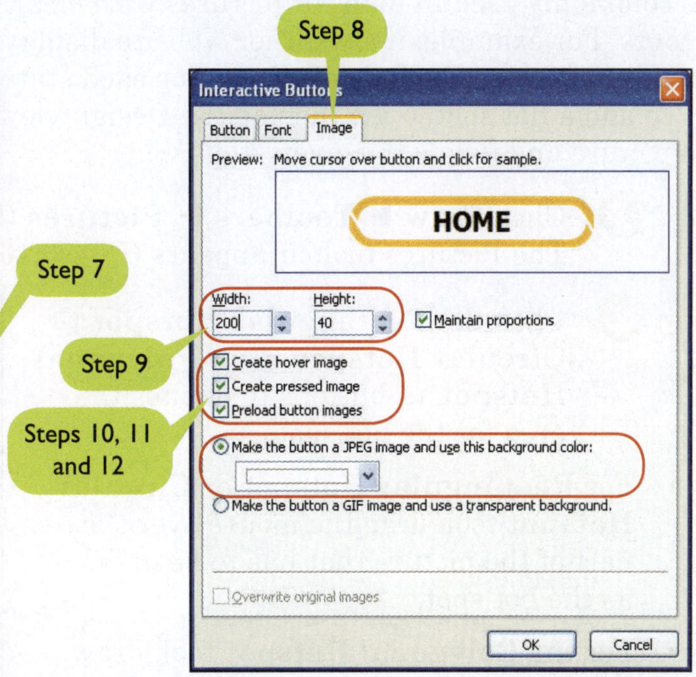

Fig 6.13 *Interactive Buttons dialog box (Image tab)*

Step 9 Set the **Width** and **Height** for the button.

Step 10 Select the **Create hover image** check box to display the button differently when a user rests the mouse pointer on it.

Step 11 Select the **Create pressed image** check box to display the button differently when a user clicks it.

Step 12 Select the **Preload button images** check box to load the images for the hover and pressed states of the button while the rest of the page loads.

Step 13 Click **OK**.

The interactive button gets inserted on the webpage (**Fig. 6.14**).

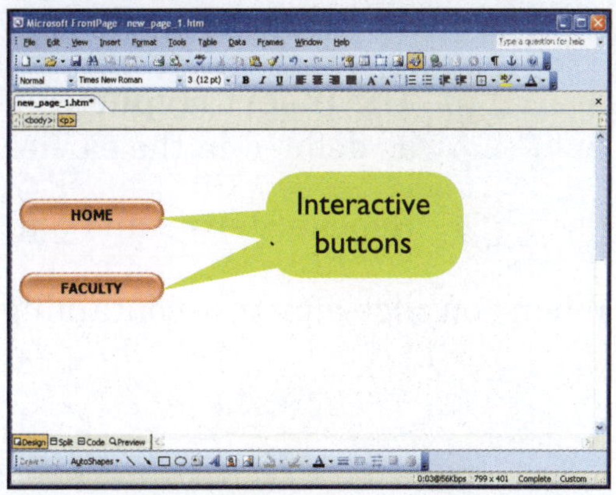

Fig 6.14 *Webpage showing the interactive buttons*

Quick Tip

You can edit the properties of an inserted button by right-clicking and choosing **Buttons Property** from the shortcut menu.

➤ Hot Spots and Image Maps

A **hot spot** is a text, an image or any other object that acts as a hyperlink. A picture with many hotspots is referred to as an **image map**. Image maps provide another way of implementing hyperlinks. Different parts of the same image can be linked to different webpages or URLs. The hot spots are commonly used in maps or pictures with clearly defined borders. For example, if a weather website displays a map of a country, it might include a hotspot for each state.

To add a hot spot, open the page in Design view, click on the picture and follow the given steps.

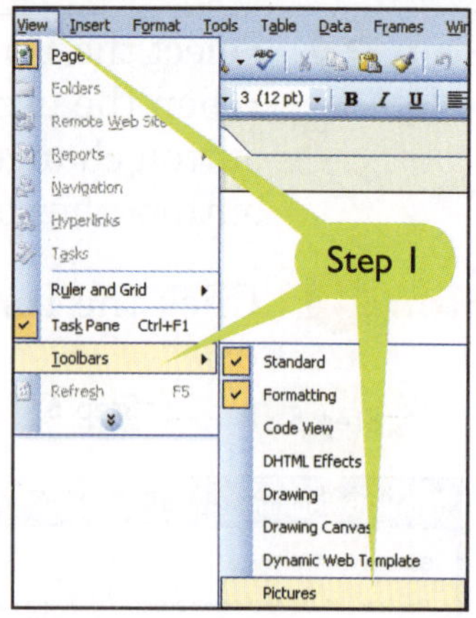

Fig 6.15 *Choosing View ▶ Toolbars ▶ Pictures*

Step 1 Click **View ▶ Toolbars ▶ Pictures** (**Fig. 6.15**). The Pictures toolbar appears (**Fig. 6.16**).

Step 2 Click the **Rectangular Hotspot** ▭, **Circular Hotspot** ◯ or **Polygonal Hotspot** buttons to defines the area for the hot spot.

- For **Rectangular Hotspot** or **Circular Hotspot** tool, drag the mouse over the part of the picture that has to be defined as the hot spot.
- For the **Polygonal Hotspot** tool, draw a polygon by clicking the mouse pointer at each corner of the shape you want. Double-click to close the polygon.

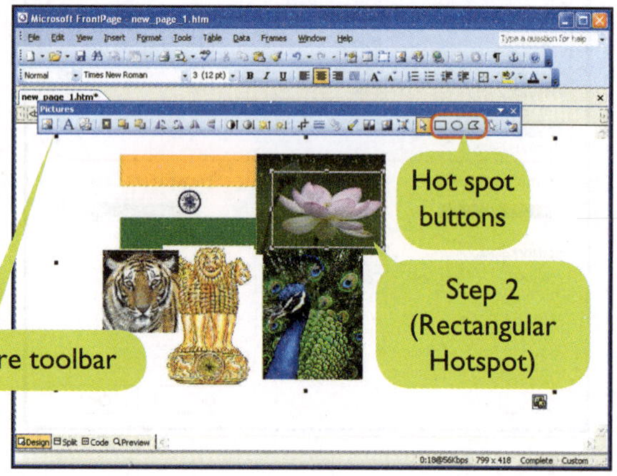

Fig 6.16 *Using the Picture toolbar*

Step 3 The **Insert Hyperlink** dialog box appears (**Fig. 6.17**). Define the hyperlinks as defined in the earlier sections. Click **OK**.

Step 4 Repeat Steps 2 and 3 to create more hotspots on the picture.

When you click a picture containing hot spots, MS FrontPage displays the clickable areas (**Fig. 6.18**).

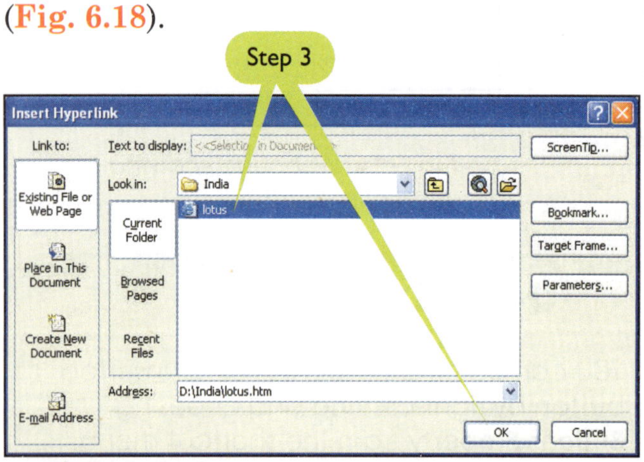

Fig 6.17 *Insert Hyperlink dialog box*

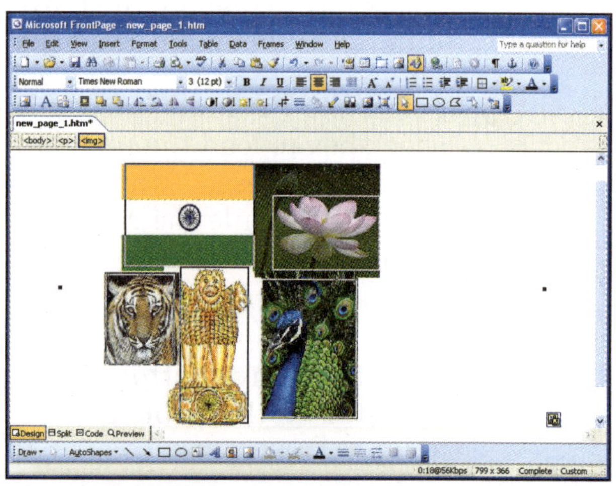

Fig 6.18 *Picture with clickable areas*

CHECK YOUR PROGRESS

2. **Create two webpages containing information about any two states of India. Incorporate the map of India a webpage and create hot spots for the two states that are linked to the two pages.**

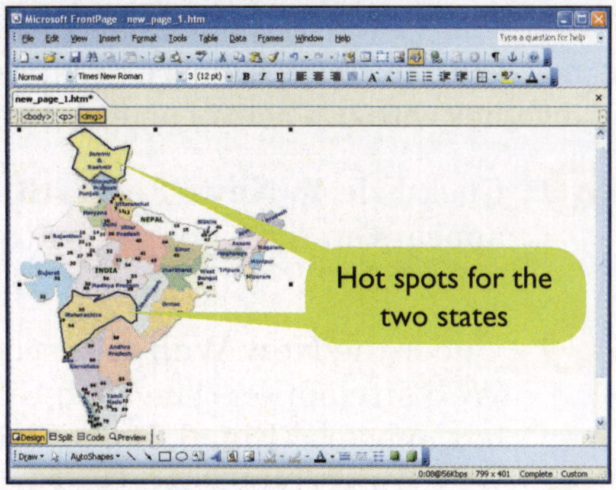

WEBSITE VIEWS IN MS FRONTPAGE

FrontPage offers various views for developing websites. Table 6.1 lists the various website views in MS FrontPage.

Table 6.1 *Various website views in MS FrontPage*

Views	Description
Folders	This view lets you see the files and folders that make up your FrontPage website.
Remote Web site	This view lets you publish a FrontPage website to a remote location.
Reports	This view enables you to run reports for information such as broken hyperlinks and pages that might be slow to load. In short, it lets you run many diagnostic reports on your website.
Navigation	This view shows hierarchical structure of a website. It allows you to rearrange the webpages by clicking and moving them.
Hyperlinks	This view shows a visual map of hyperlinks. When you click on a page in the Folders view, Hyperlinks view will show all the pages in your website that link to that page, as well as the pages linked from that page.
Tasks	This view allows you to maintain a list of tasks related to your website. This view is helpful if you have many things that need to be done on a website and want to keep track of them. This view lists the name, priority, status and other information about each task in the current website.

CREATING A WEBSITE

You have learnt to design the webpages and create hyperlinks. Let us now learn to create a website containing multiple webpages linked together with the help of an example.

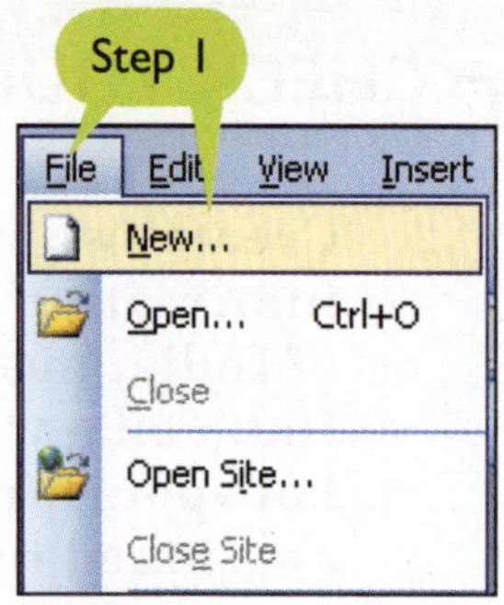

Fig 6.19 *Choosing File ▶ New*

Step 1 Click **File ▶ New** (**Fig. 6.19**). The **New** task pane appears on the right side of the FrontPage window (**Fig. 6.20**).

Step 2 Under the **New Web site** section, click **One page Web site** option. The **Web Site Templates** dialog box appears (**Fig. 6.21**).

Step 3 Choose the **One Page Web Site** option.

Step 4 Click the **Browse** button to specify the location of the website.

Step 5 Click **OK**. A new website is created with two folders and one webpage called **index.htm**. This is the main page of the website. Just like a webpage, a website also has several views. We will work in the **Folders** view (**Fig. 6.22**). The images folder should be used to store any pictures or graphics that are being used in the website. The private folder is managed by FrontPage to store information related to the website.

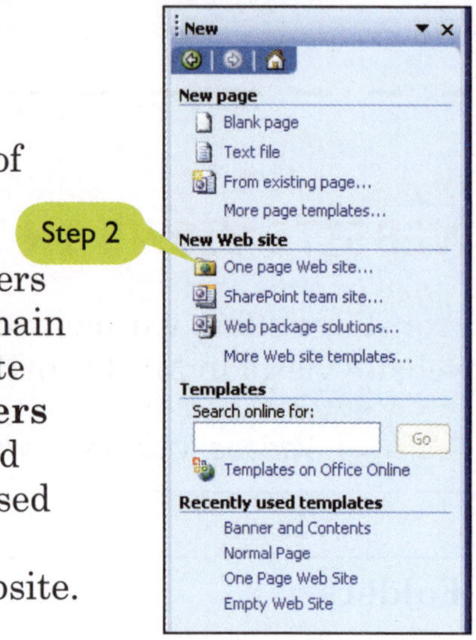

Fig 6.20 *New task pane*

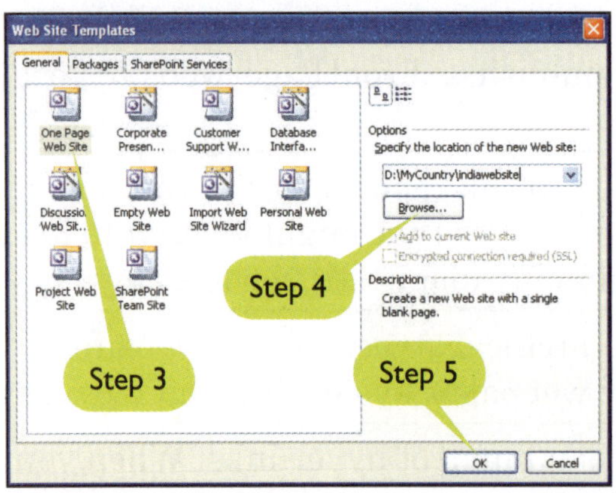

Fig 6.21 *Web Site Templates dialog box*

QUICK TIP

You can create an empty website by choosing the **Empty Web site** option in the Web Site Templates dialog box.

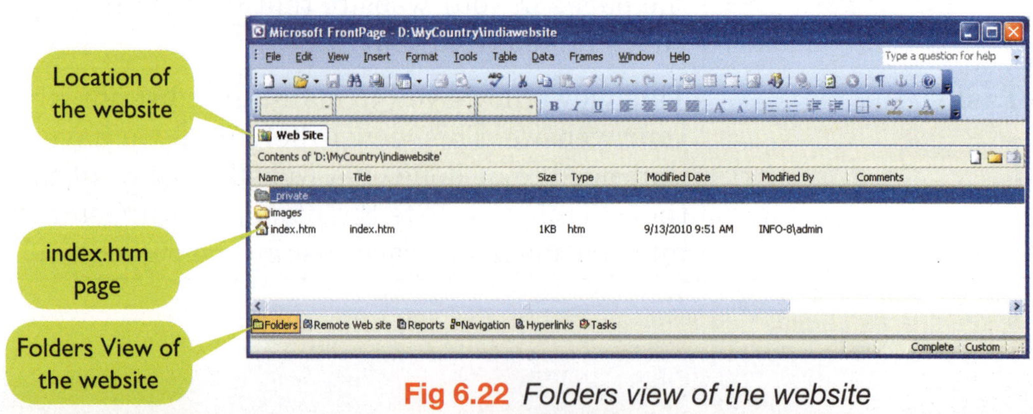

Fig 6.22 *Folders view of the website*

Step 6 Double-click the **index.htm** file and design the webpage (**Fig. 6.23**).

Step 7 Click the **New** button on the toolbar and choose the **Blank Page** option to add more pages to the website (**Fig. 6.24**).

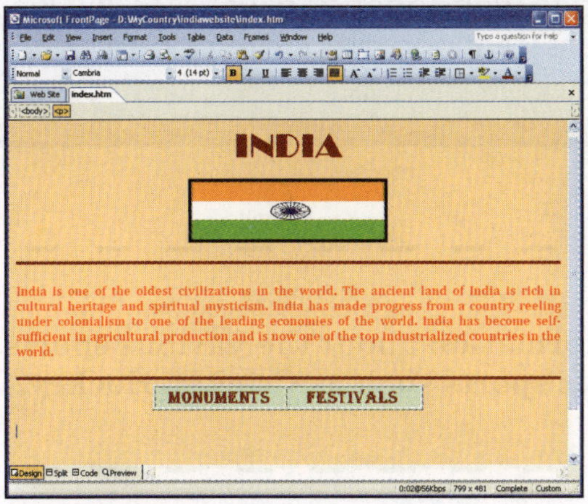

Fig 6.23 *Design of index.htm*

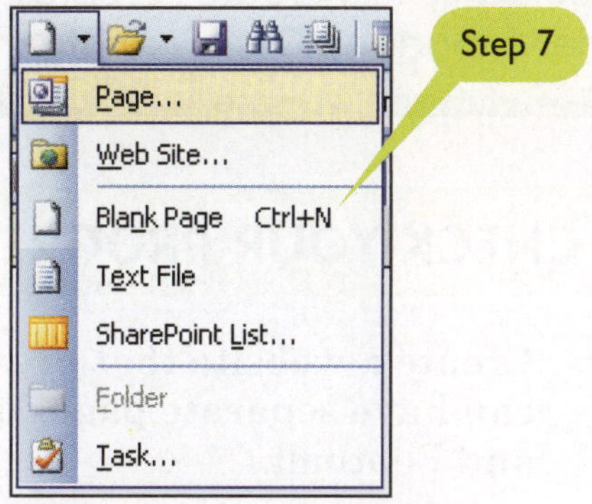

Fig 6.24 *Choosing the Blank Page option*

Step 8 Design the pages and save them. In the given example, the webpages have been saved with the name **monuments.htm** (**Fig. 6.25**) and **festivals.htm** (**Fig. 6.26**).

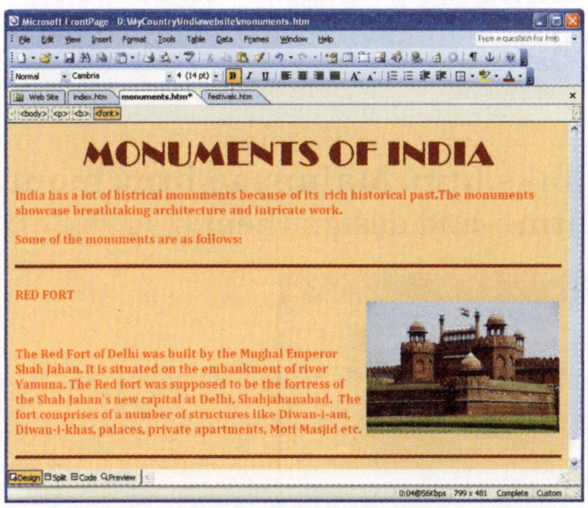

Fig 6.25 *Design of monuments.htm*

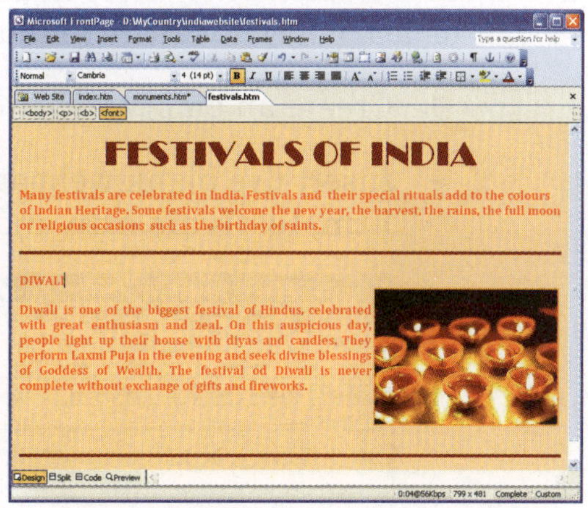

Fig 6.26 *Design of festivals.htm*

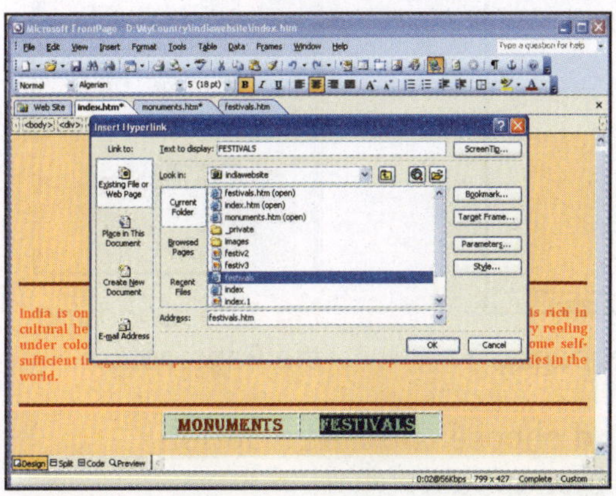

Fig 6.27 *Creating hyperlinks to connect the webpages in a website*

Step 9 Link the different webpages. In this example, **index.htm** is being linked to two other pages—**monuments.htm** and **festivals.htm**—by creating hyperlinks (**Fig. 6.27**).

Quick Tip

A theme is a set of professionally designed graphics, color schemes, design elements and formatting rules that can be applied to webpages and websites. By using themes, you can easily create websites with a consistent and attractive appearance across the webpages. Click **Format ▶ Theme** to apply themes.

CHECK YOUR PROGRESS

3. Create a website that provides information about the various sports. You can have separate pages on various sports such as Cricket, Hockey, Tennis and Football.

➤ Creating a Website with Frames

You can create website with frames in MS FrontPage. The advantage of using frames is that you can display more than one HTML document in the same browser window. The frames are generally used so that a list of links or menus are in one frame and content is in the other frame. When these links are clicked, all the pages open in the content frame.

Let us learn how to create and use frames by following the given steps.

Step 1 Create an empty website.

Step 2 Insert five blank webpages— **links.htm, Mainpage.htm, monument.htm, festivals.htm** and **top.htm**—and design them (Fig. 6.28).

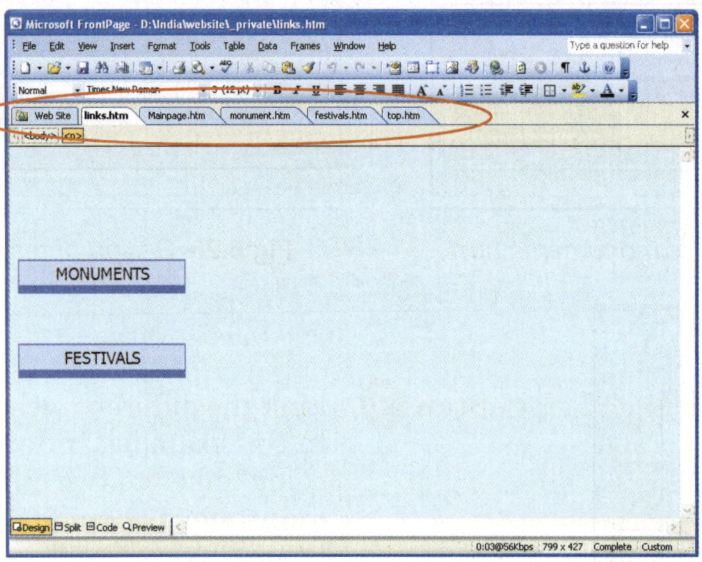

Fig 6.28 An empty website with five blank webpages

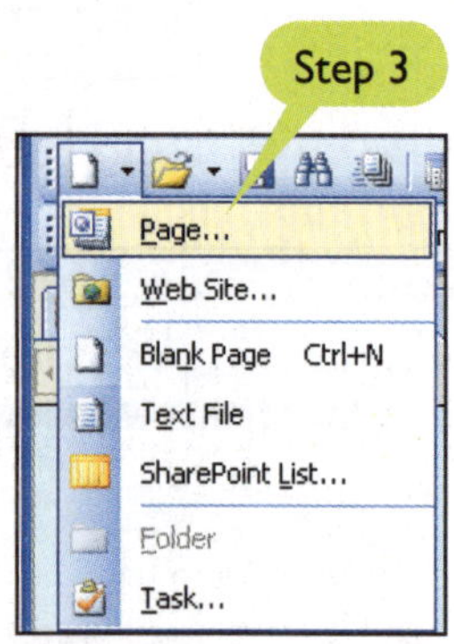

Fig 6.29 Choosing the Page option

Step 3 Click the **New** button on the toolbar and choose the **Page** option. (Fig. 6.29). The **Page Templates** dialog box appears (Fig. 6.30).

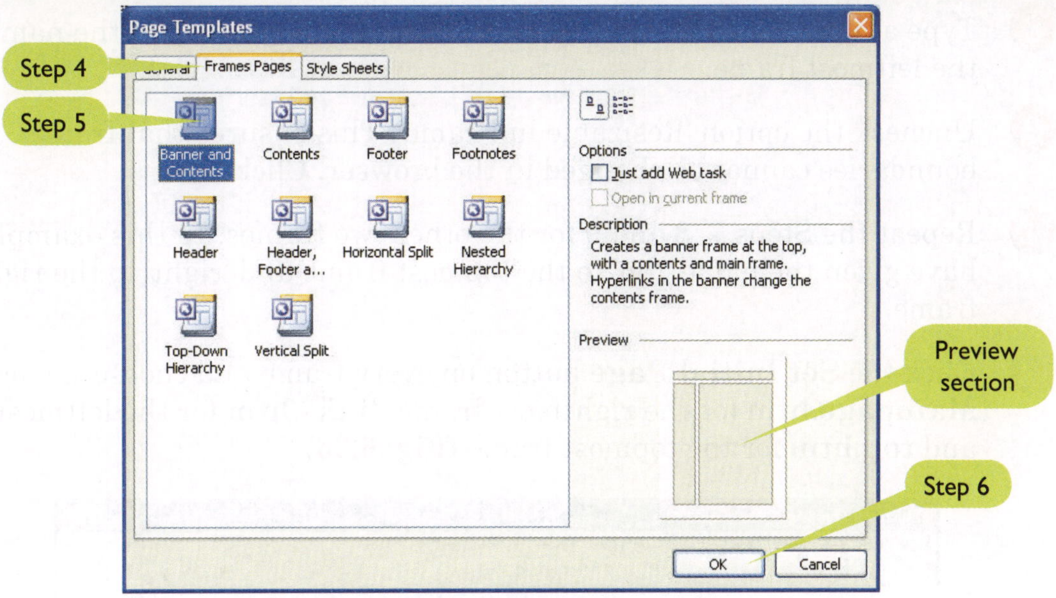

Fig 6.30 *Page Templates dialog box*

Step 4 Click the **Frames Pages** tab.

Step 5 Select a suitable frame layout. The preview of the document can be seen in the **Preview** section.

Step 6 Click **OK**. The document with the selected frame layout appears (**Fig. 6.31**). In this example, the document has three frames.

Step 7 Right-click in the leftmost frame window and choose **Frame Properties**. The **Frame Properties** dialog box appears (**Fig. 6.32**).

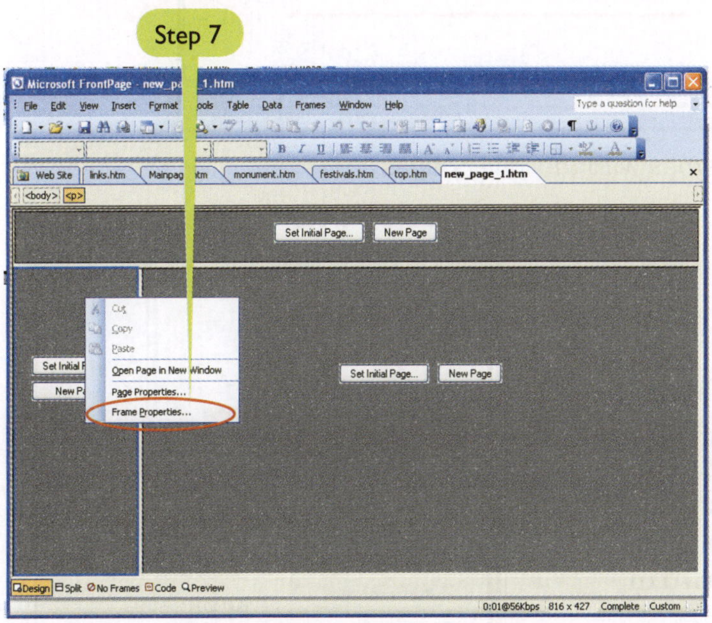

Fig 6.31 *Frame layout*

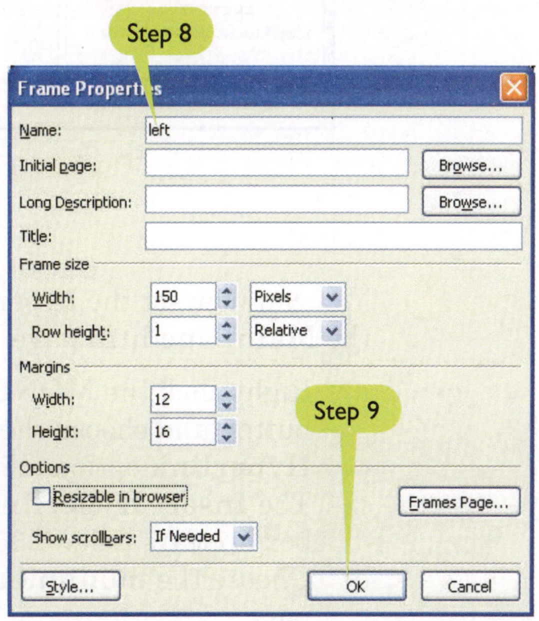

Fig 6.32 *Frame Properties dialog box*

Step 8 Type a name for the frame. In this example, we have given the name 'left' to the leftmost frame.

Step 9 Uncheck the option 'Resizable in Frame'. This ensures that frame boundaries cannot be changed in the browser. Click **OK**.

Step 10 Repeat the Steps 7, 8 and 9 for the other two frames. In this example, we have given the name 'top' to the topmost frame and 'right' to the rightmost frame.

Step 11 Click the **Set Initial Page** button on every frame and choose the pages **Mainpage.htm** for the rightmost frame, **links.htm** for the leftmost frame and **top.htm** for the topmost frame (Fig. 6.33).

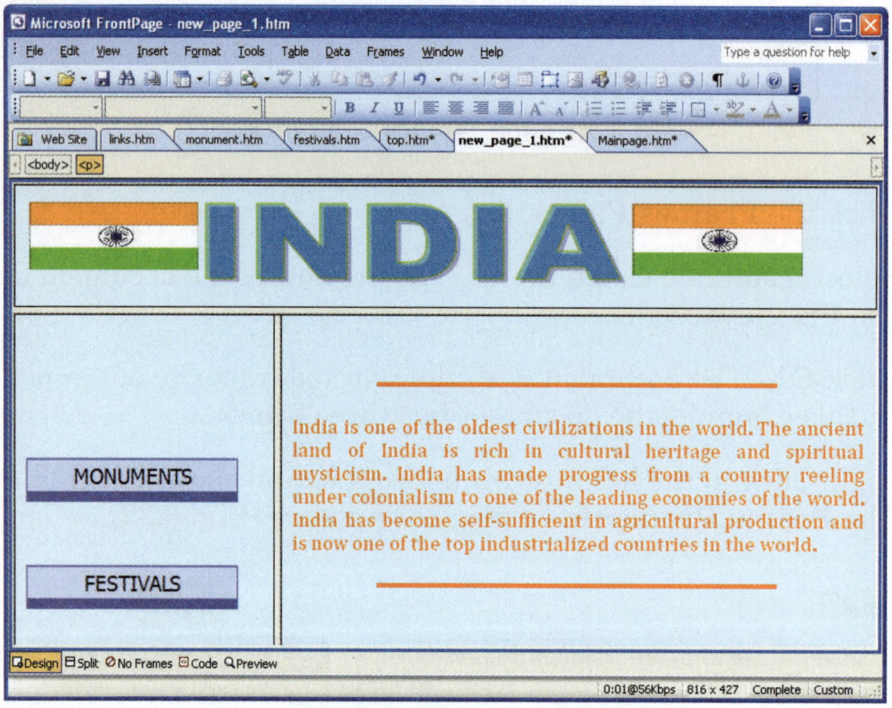

Fig 6.33 *Frames with the initial pages*

Step 12 You can now set the hyperlinks in the **Mainpage.htm** page.

a) Right-click the **MONUMENTS** button and choose the **Hyperlink** option (Fig. 6.34). The **Insert Hyperlink** dialog box appears (Fig. 6.35).

b) Choose the **monument.htm** page.

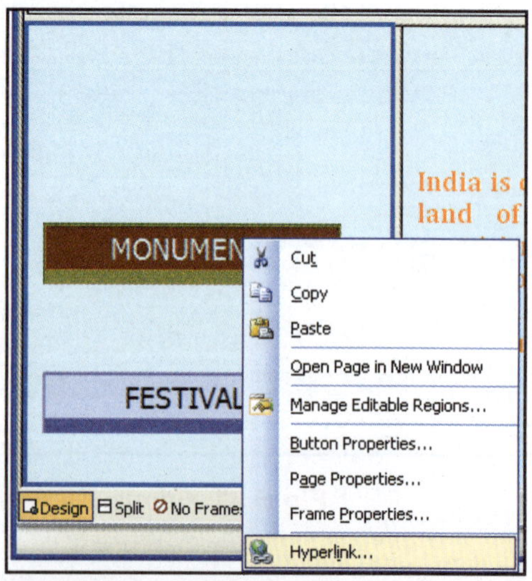

Fig 6.34 *Choosing the Hyperlink option*

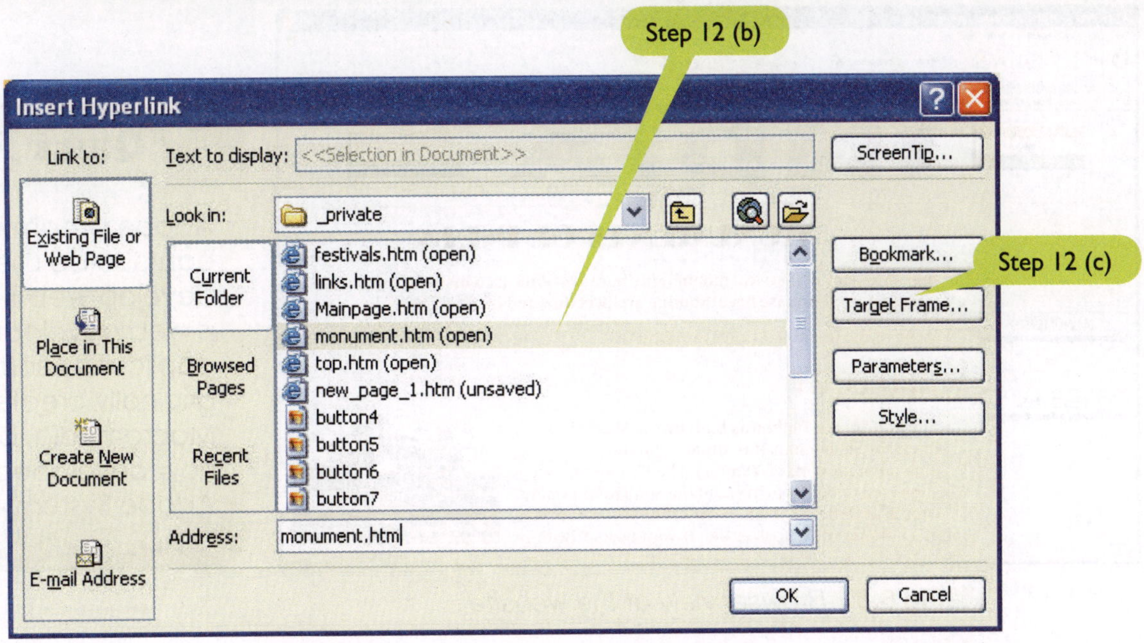

Fig 6.35 *Choosing the Hyperlink option*

c) Click the **Target frame** button. The **Target Frame** dialog box appears (**Fig. 6.36**).

d) Type the name of the frame in which you want the page to open. In this example, the target frame name is 'right'.

Click **OK**.

Fig 6.36 *Target Frame dialog box*

Step 13 Repeat Step 12 for the **festivals.htm** page also.

Step 14 Save the page with the name **index.htm**.

Preview the pages in the browser window (**Fig. 6.37**).

Fig 6.37 *Browser view of the website*

> **QUICK FACT**
>
> Adobe Dreamweaver can also be used to develop websites. It is web development application software originally created by Macromedia, but is now developed by Adobe Systems.

Recap Time

- Hyperlinks can be used to link two documents or different parts of the same document.
- You can create hyperlinks in Microsoft FrontPage by using Insert ▶ Hyperlink option or by clicking the Hyperlink button on the Standard toolbar.
- Interactive buttons as hyperlinks improve the appearance of a webpage.
- A hot spot is a text, an image or any other object that acts as a hyperlink.
- The image map is an image in which areas within the image act as hyperlinks.
- Frames let you display more than one document in the same browser window.

Assessment Time

1 Choose the correct answer.

a) To create internal links in MS FrontPage, different sections of the same page are identified using the

i) flag. ii) bookmark. iii) name tag. iv) None of these

b) Find the odd one out.

i) Rectangular hotspot ii) Circular hotspot

iii) Polygonal hotspot iv) Regular hotspot

c)  button is used to

i) create frames. ii) create hyperlinks. iii) insert pictures. iv) None of these

d) For an interactive button, the colour specified using the 'Hovered Font Color' option is used

i) when the mouse is over the button. ii) when the button is pressed or clicked.

iii) when the button is loaded on the webpage. iv) None of these

2 Fill in the blanks using the words given below.

Frames	Image map	Hyperlinks	Pictures	Bookmarks

a) ______________ are be used to link two documents or different parts of the same document.

b) ______________ are inserted on the page to create internal links.

c) You should create ______________ to view multiple documents in the same browser window.

d) An ______________ is a picture with areas that are linked to the files.

e) The Circular Hotspot button is present on the ______________ toolbar.

3 Answer the following questions.

a) Write the steps for inserting internal links in a webpage.

b) How can you add interactive buttons to a webpage?

c) What are hot spots?

d) What is an image map?

e) Give the use of frames.

Activity Time

1 Create a website giving details about your city such as history, culture and places of interest. You can include an image map of the city and give details about important places that a tourist can visit.

2 Your uncle has opened a car showroom. Create a website for him giving details about the various cars.

Notes for the Teacher

The teacher should encourage the students to be creative and to explore more options of Microsoft FrontPage such as incorporating Flash files.

INTRODUCTION TO VISUAL BASIC

Chapter 7

OBJECTIVES

After having studied this lesson, you will be able to:

- start Visual Basic.
- describe the elements of Visual Basic Integrated Development Environment (IDE).
- state the properties, methods and events of Form object.
- define the uses of common controls.
- add controls on the form.
- create a calculator in Visual Basic.

A **programming language** is a set of grammatical rules used for giving instructions to a computer. The two broad categories of programming languages are—low-level languages and high-level languages.

You have already learnt about one of the high-level languages called QBASIC. In this chapter, you will learn about another high-level programming language called **Visual Basic**.

INTRODUCTION TO VISUAL BASIC

Visual Basic is a high-level programming language that offers a Graphical User Interface for designing and developing programs as compared to QBASIC that offers a text-only environment.

Visual Basic offers an **Integrated Development Environment (IDE)** for writing programs. An IDE provides a common environment for designing, editing and removing errors in the programs.

Visual Basic is also referred to as an event-driven programming language. An event is the occurrence of some user-generated actions such as click and keypress. In Visual Basic, the code statements are executed in response to events. Let us learn more about Visual Basic.

STARTING VISUAL BASIC

To start Visual Basic, click **Start ▶ Programs ▶ Microsoft Visual Studio 6.0 ▶ Microsoft Visual Basic 6.0** (Fig. 7.1). The **Microsoft Visual Basic** window with the **New Project** dialog box appears (Fig. 7.2).

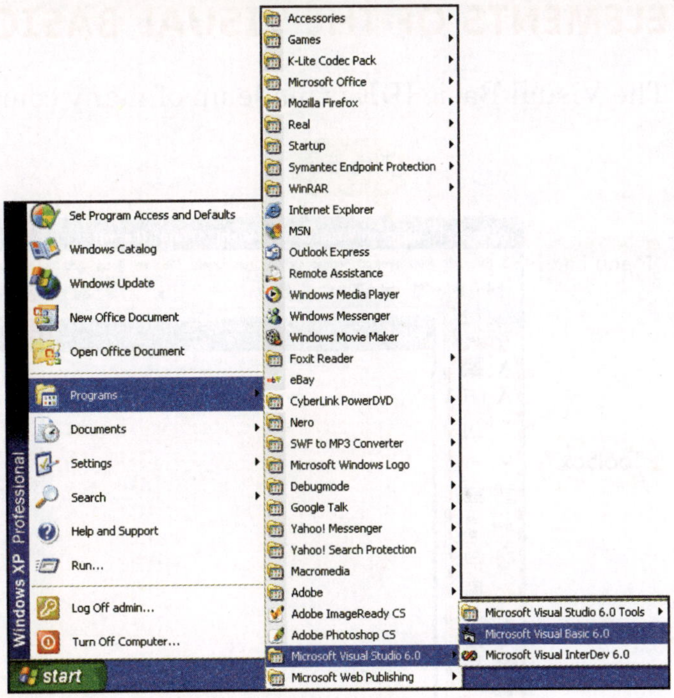

Fig 7.1 *Starting Visual Basic*

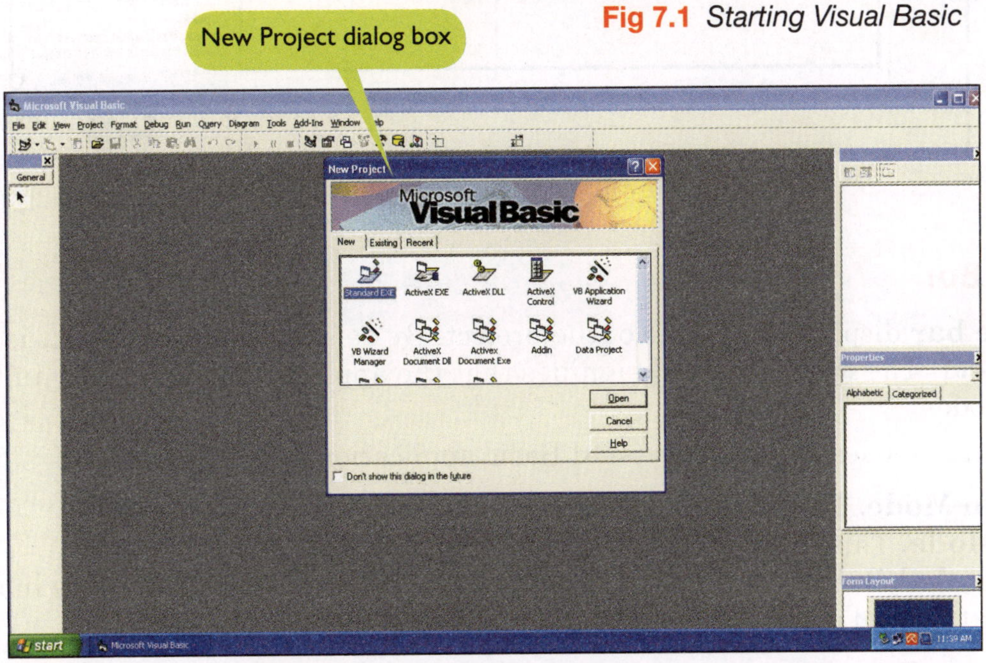

Fig 7.2 *Microsoft Visual Basic window*

In the **New Project** dialog box, you can choose to start a new project, open an existing project or select a list of recently opened programs using the different tabs. A **project** is a collection of files that make up an application. You can create various types of applications such as Standard EXE and ActiveX EXE.

In this chapter, we will be creating Standard EXE programs. **EXE** stands for **executable program**. An executable program is one that can be launched by double-clicking on its **.exe** file. To start with, choose **Standard EXE** in the New Project dialog box and click the **Open** button (Fig. 7.2) to develop an application in Visual Basic. The Visual Basic IDE appears as shown in Fig. 7.3.

ELEMENTS OF THE VISUAL BASIC IDE

The Visual Basic IDE is made up of many components (**Fig. 7.3**).

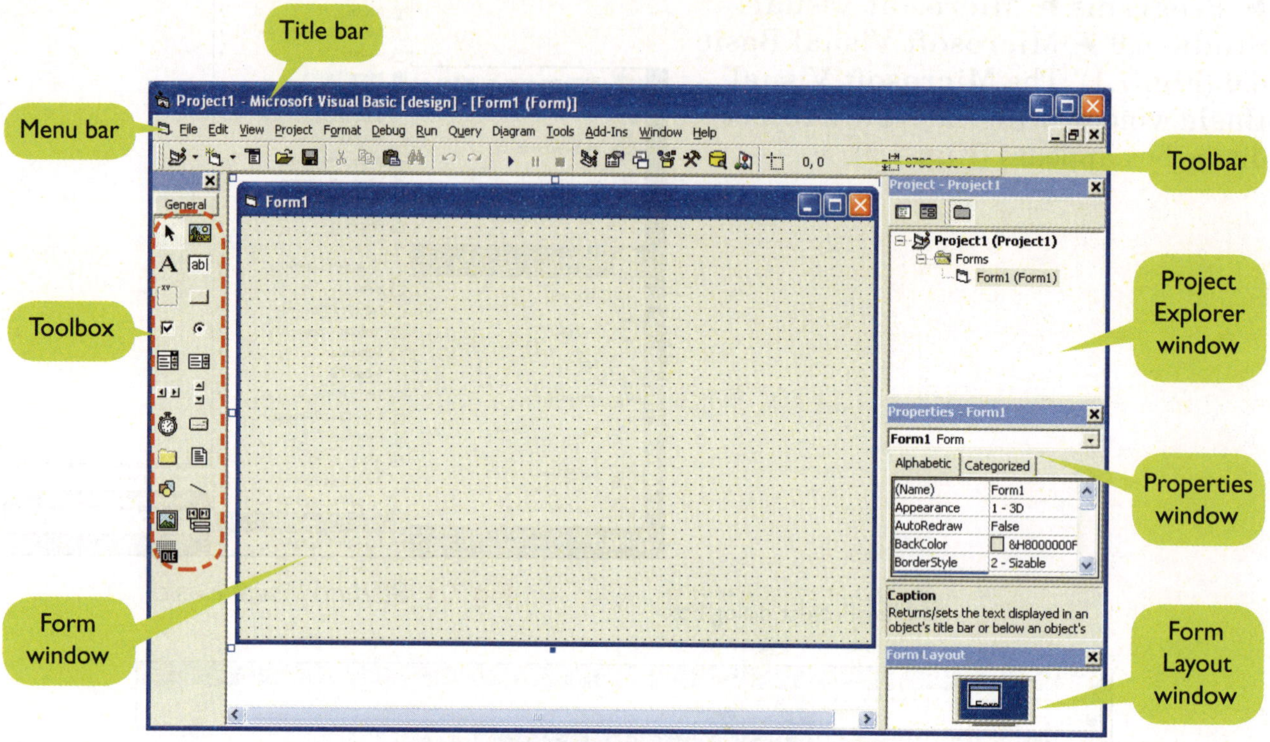

Fig 7.3 *Microsoft Visual Basic IDE*

➤ Title Bar

The **Title bar** displays the name of the project. By default, the first project is named as **Project1**. The word **[design]** signifies that the application is currently in the design mode.

The three modes in which a Visual Basic application works are:

1. **Design Mode.** This is the mode in which an application is designed.
2. **Run Mode.** This is the mode in which an application is executed.
3. **Suspended/Break Mode.** This mode pauses the execution of any code in an application and allows you to edit it.

➤ Menu Bar

The **Menu bar** offers commands for working in Visual Basic environment. Apart from the standard menus like File and Edit, menus such as Project, Format and Debug provide commands that are specific to programming.

➤ Toolbar

The **Toolbar** comprises buttons that provide shortcuts to various menu options.

➤ Form Window

The **Form window** is the basic building block on which you place various objects for designing a user interface. It is through form that a user interacts with an application.

➤ Toolbox

The **Toolbox** offers various tools (Fig. 7.4), which can be used on the forms for creating an interface. These tools are referred to as **controls** in Visual Basic. You will learn the use of some of the controls later in the chapter.

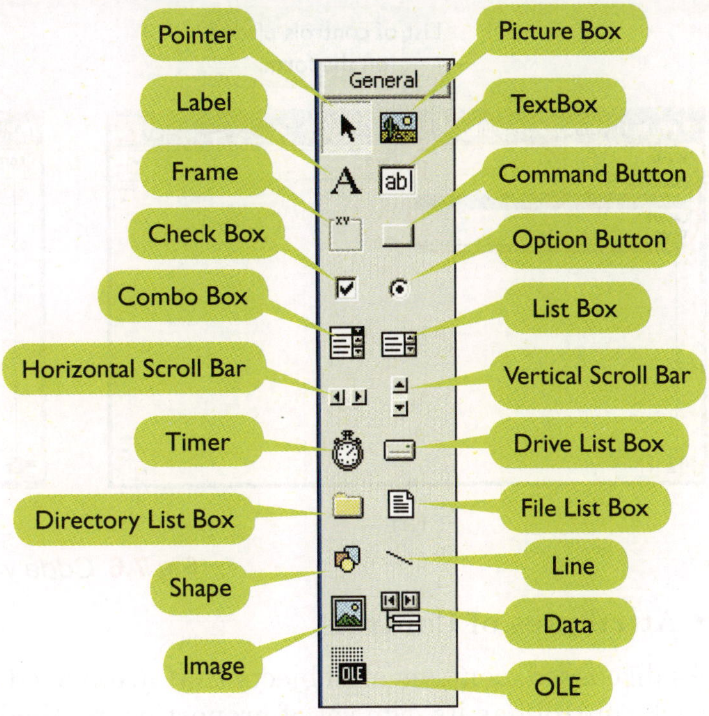

Fig 7.4 *Toolbox*

➤ Project Explorer Window

This window displays a list of various elements of a project, viz, forms, classes and modules. All the objects that make up an application are packed in a project. The Project Explorer window has the View Code and View Object buttons on the top-left (Fig. 7.5).

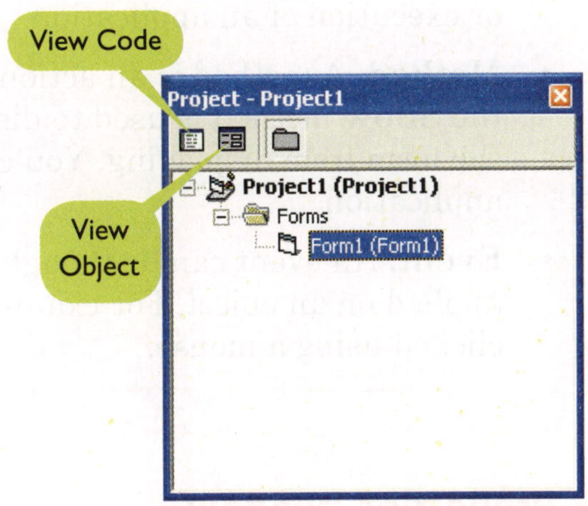

Fig 7.5 *Project Explorer window*

• View Code and View Object

You can switch between the two views to develop applications in Visual Basic.

1. **View Object.** In this view you can design the interface of an application by placing various controls on the form.
2. **View Code.** This is the view that lets you type code statements inside the form's or other control's event handlers. In the code view, the drop-down box to the left provides a list of all controls used on the current form including the form itself. The drop-down box on the right displays a list of all events related to the control selected in the left-side drop-down box (Fig. 7.6).

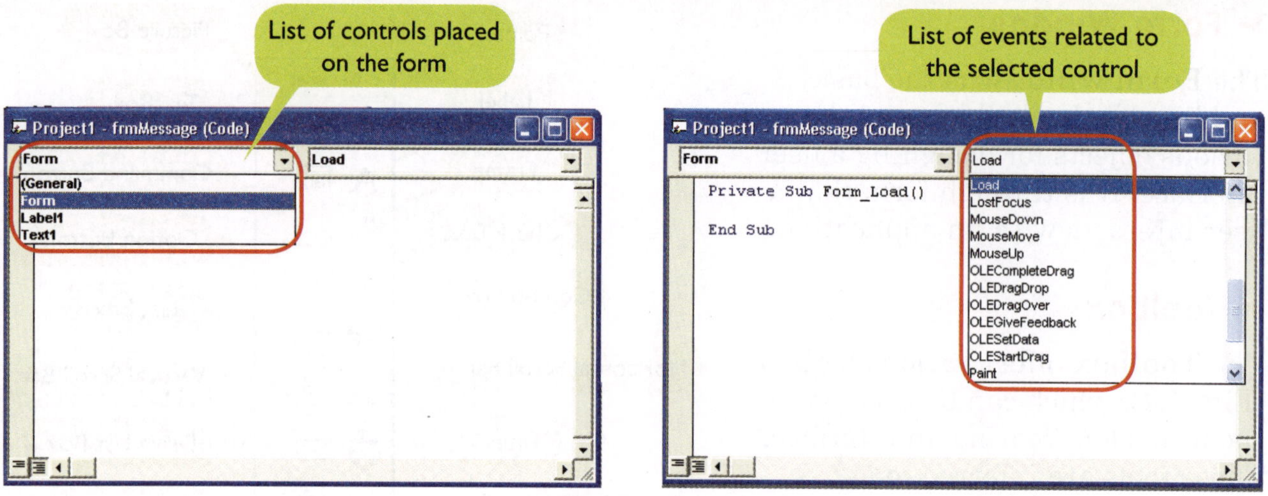

(a) (b)

Fig 7.6 *Code view*

• Attributes of Controls

As discussed, controls are objects that are placed on the form. Every form as well as each control has its own set of properties, methods and events.

- **Property.** A property refers to the characteristics of an object such as colour and size. For example, the **BackColor** property lets you change the background colour of an object. You can change the properties either at the time of designing or execution of an application.
- **Method.** A method is an action that can be performed on an object. For example, the **Show** method is used to display the form and **Hide** method is used to hide the form from displaying. You can call the methods at the time of execution of an application.
- **Event.** An event can be thought as an occurrence of some user-generated action applied on an object. For example, **click** event is triggered when an object is clicked using a mouse.

➤ Properties Window

The Properties window (Fig. 7.7) lists the property settings of the currently selected form or controls either alphabetically or category-wise. These properties define the different characteristics such as size, caption or colour of an object.

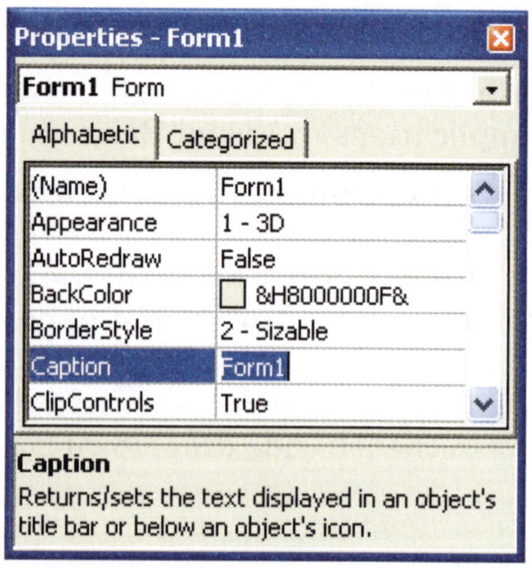

Fig 7.7 *Properties window*

➤ Form Layout Window

The Form Layout window (Fig. 7.8) lets you specify the position of a form with respect to the display area of the screen when you run an application.

Fig 7.8 *Form Layout window*

In the following discussion, we will learn about the basic concepts of working with forms, controls and their associated properties, methods, and events.

FORM OBJECT

As discussed earlier, forms are used for designing an interface with which the user interacts. A form has its own properties, events and methods with which you can control its appearance and behaviour. The following tables list the important form properties, events and methods.

Table 7.1 *Form properties*

Properties	Description
Name	Sets the name of the form. The default name of the first form is 'Form1'. You can change the properties of the form or call its methods by referring its name at the time of event handling.
BackColor	Sets the background colour of the form.
Caption	Specifies the text that appears in the form's Title bar.
Font	Sets the font, font size and font style of the text to be displayed on the form.
ForeColor	Sets the foreground colour for displaying text and graphics on the form.
WindowState	Specifies whether the form should be started in a maximized, minimized, or normal state. You specify the value '0' for normal, '1' for minimized and '2' for maximized state.

Table 7.2 *Form methods*

Methods	Description
Show	displays the form on the screen
Hide	hides the form from the screen
Print	displays a message on the form window

Table 7.3 *Form events*

Events	Description
Form_Load	This event is triggered when the form is loaded and displayed on the screen at the time of execution.
Form_ Unload	This event is triggered when the form is closed and removed from the memory.

Let us use some of the properties, methods and events of the form to print a message on the Form window by following the given steps.

Step 1 Choose **Start ▶ Programs ▶ Microsoft Visual Studio 6.0 ▶ Microsoft Visual Basic 6.0** (**Fig. 7.1**).

Step 2 The **New Project dialog box** gets displayed (**Fig. 7.2**).

Step 3 Double-click the **Standard EXE** icon. The **Visual Basic Project** window with the default form is displayed (**Fig. 7.3**).

Step 4 Select the form and set the following properties in the **Properties window** (**Fig. 7.9**).

a) Name: **frmMessage**

b) Caption: **Output**

c) Backcolor: **Any colour of your choice under the Palette tab**

d) Font: Font as **Comic Sans MS**, Font Style as **Bold**, and Size as **22**.

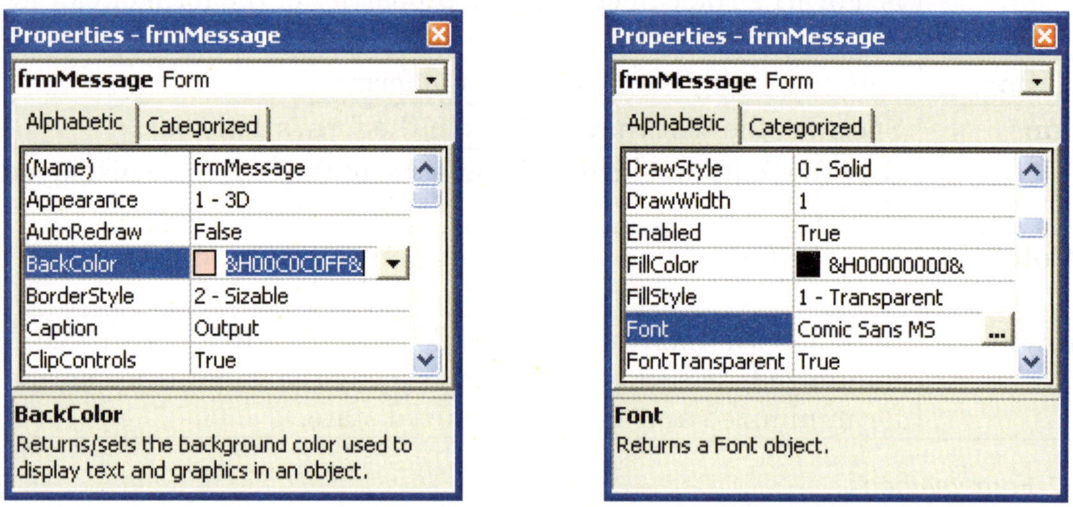

(a) (b)

Fig 7.9 *Properties window displaying various form properties*

Step 5 Switch to the Code view by clicking the **View Code** button in the Project Explorer window.

Step 6 The Code window of the project appears. Write the given lines of code inside the **Form_Load** event handler as shown in **Fig. 7.10**.

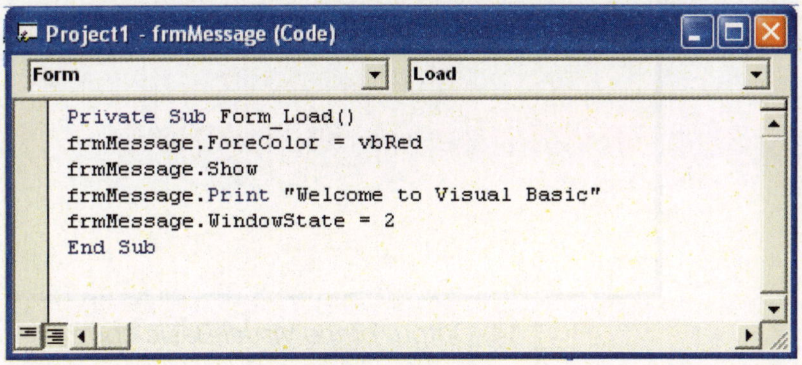

Fig 7.10 *Writing code statements in Form_Load event handler*

> **QUICK TIP**
>
> You can switch to the Code window by double-clicking on the form or any other control on the form. Alternatively, choose **View ▶ Code** or **View ▶ Object**.

Step 7 Choose **File ▶ Save**. The **Save File As** dialog box (**Fig. 7.11**) appears followed by the **Save Project As** dialog box (**Fig. 7.12**). First specify a name for the form and save it. Then name and save the project.

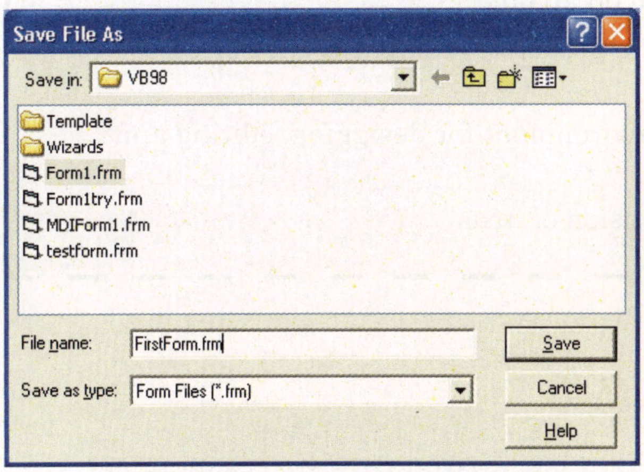

Fig 7.11 *Save File As dialog box*

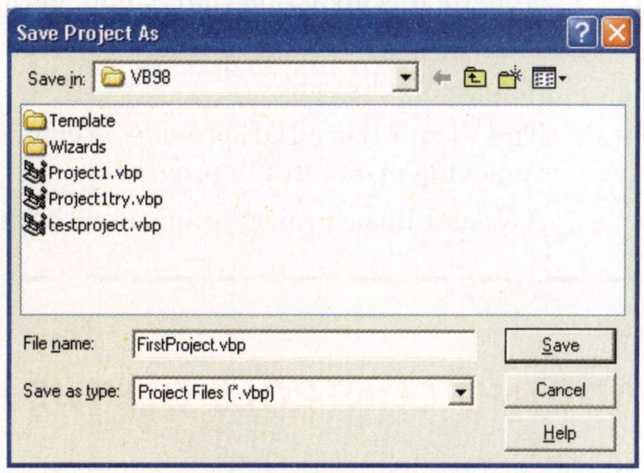

Fig 7.12 *Save Project As dialog box*

The form gets saved with the **.frm** extension and the project is saved with the **.vbp** extension.

Step 8 To run the project, use any one of the following ways.

- Press **F5**, or
- Click the **Start** button on the Toolbar (**Fig. 7.13**), or

Fig 7.13 *Toolbar*

- Choose **Run ▶ Start**.

When you run the application, the form appears in the maximized state with the message **Welcome to Visual Basic** displayed in red colour on the Form window as shown in **Fig. 7.14**.

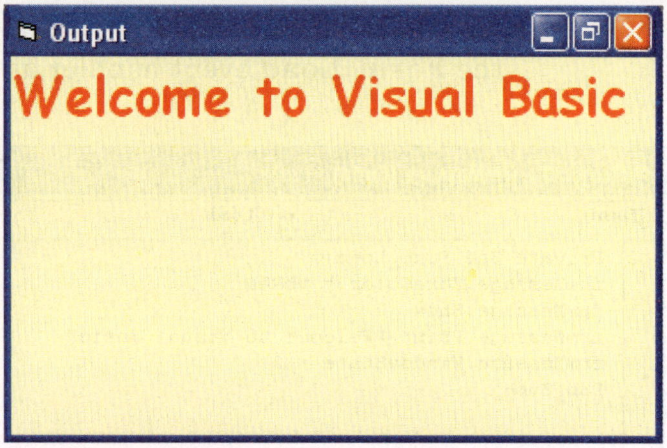

Fig 7.14 *Output of the Visual Basic code*

QUICK QUESTION

1. State whether the following statements are true or false.

a) You cannot change the properties of the form in the Run mode.

b) A method is an action that can be performed on an object.

c) The Form Layout window lets you change the properties related to the object currently selected.

d) The Visual Basic IDE provides a common environment for designing, editing and removing errors in the programs.

e) A Visual Basic project is saved with an extension of .frm.

ADDING CONTROLS ON THE FORM

Before we discuss some of the commonly used controls available in the Toolbox, let us first learn how to add controls to the form. There are two ways in which you can add controls to the form.

- Select the control in the Toolbox and then drag the control onto the form (**Fig. 7.15**).

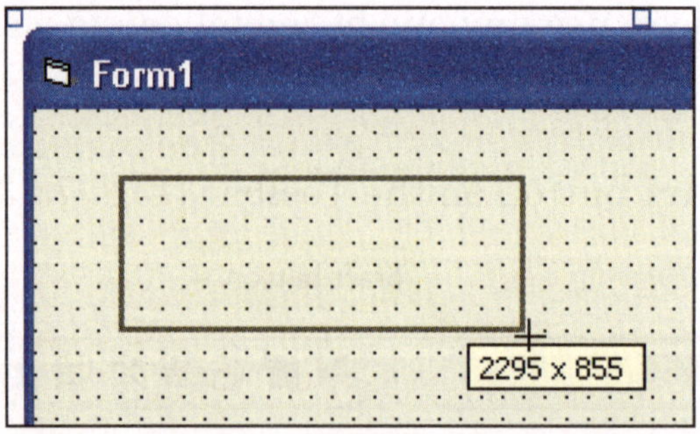

Fig 7.15 *Adding controls on the Form window*

Or

- Double-click the control in the Toolbox. The control gets added in the centre of the form. Drag the control to the desired location on the form. If required, resize the control by dragging its borders.

➤ Common Controls

Let us now learn about some of the common controls in Visual Basic.

- **Pointer Control**

The **Pointer control** is used to move and resize the controls on the form window.

- **Label Control** A

The **Label control** is used to display text on the form. You can use labels for identifying a Textbox or for displaying instructions to the user on the form. **Tables 7.4** and **7.5** list some of the common properties and events associated with the Label control.

Table 7.4 *Label control properties*

Properties	Description
Name	Sets the name of a label.
Backcolor	Sets the background colour of a label.
Caption	Specifies the text that appears on a label.
Font	Sets the font, font size and font style of the text to be displayed.
ForeColor	Sets the foreground colour for the displayed text.

Table 7.5 *Label control events*

Events	Description
Change	This event is triggered when the text on a label is changed.
Click	This event is triggered when the user clicks on a label.
Dblclick	This event is triggered when the user double-clicks on a label.
MouseMove	This event is triggered when the user moves the mouse on a label.

Let us use some of the properties and events of the Label control to change the caption and the foreground colour of the text when the mouse is moved over the surface of the label. To do this, follow the given steps.

Step 1 Double-click on the Label control in the Toolbox. The **Label1** gets inserted in the middle of the form (**Fig. 7.16**).

Step 2 Drag **Label1** to an appropriate location at the top of the form and resize it.

Fig 7.16 *Form with Label1*

Step 3 Change the following properties of the Label control.

a) Name: **lblMessage**

b) Caption: **Move the mouse over the surface of the following message**

c) Backcolor: **Any colour of your choice under the Palette tab**

d) Font: Font as **Comic Sans MS**, Font Style as **Regular**, and Size as **14**.

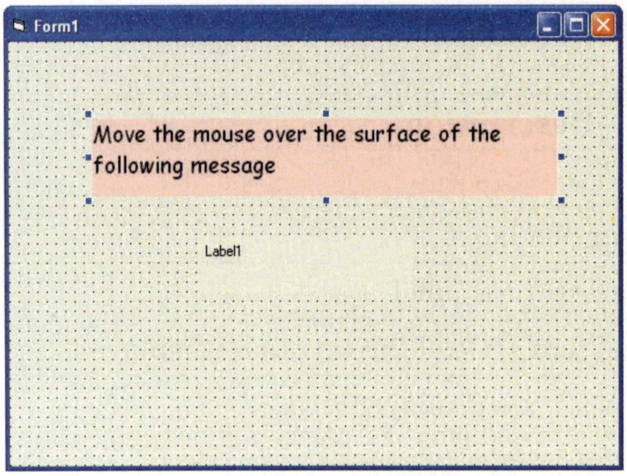

Fig 7.17 *Form with two labels*

Step 4 Add one more label on the form. Drag the new label at a position below the first label as shown in Fig. 7.17.

Step 5 Resize the second label control and change its following properties (Fig. 7.18).

a) Name: **lblChange**

b) Caption: **Secret to Success**

c) Backcolor: **Any colour of your choice**

d) Font: Font as **MS Sans Serif**, Font Style as **Bold**, and Size as **12**.

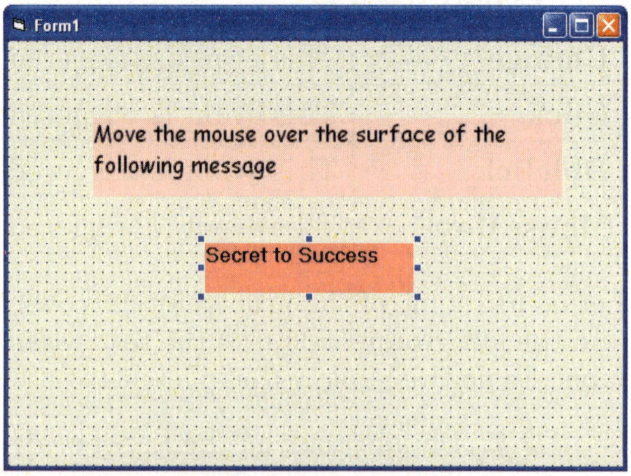

Fig 7.18 *Form after setting various label properties*

Step 6 Double-click on the **lblChange** control to open the Code view. The Code view gets displayed. Make sure that the label **lblChange** is selected in the first drop-down list. Select the **MouseMove** event from the second drop-down list as shown in **Fig. 7.19**.

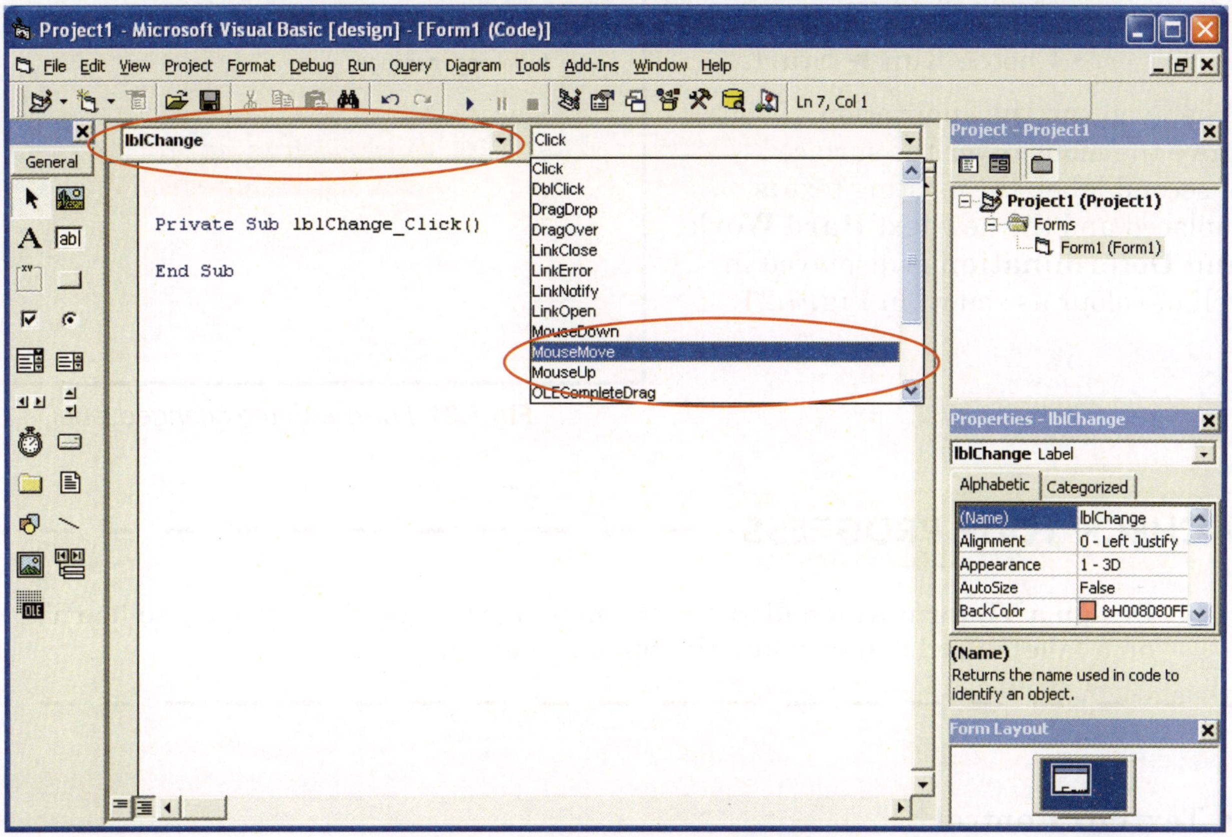

Fig 7.19 *Code view of the application*

Step 7 The **MouseMove** event handler for the label **lblChange** gets inserted. Enter the lines of code (as shown in **Fig. 7.20**) in the **MouseMove** event handler for the label.

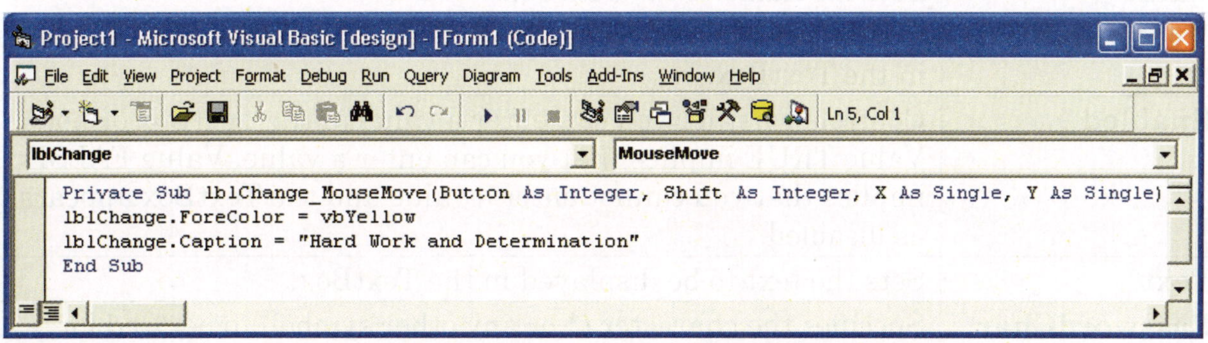

Fig 7.20 *Typing code in the MouseMove event handler*

Step 8 To run the application, use any one of the following ways.

- Press **F5**, or
- Click the **Start** button on the Toolbar, or
- Choose **Run ▶ Start**.

When you run the application, if you move the mouse over the surface of second label, the existing text is replaced and the new text **Hard Work and Determination** is displayed in yellow colour as shown in **Fig. 7.21**.

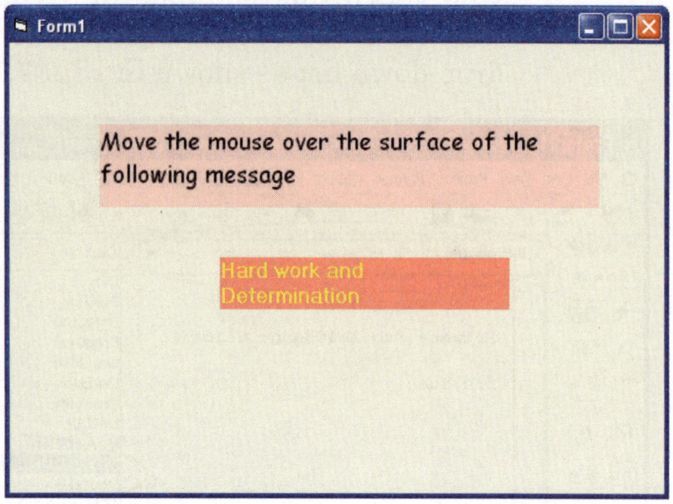

Fig 7.21 *Form with the changed label*

CHECK YOUR PROGRESS

1. **Design a VB form which displays the message 'Visual Basic is easy to learn' on a label in red colour when the form is loaded.**

• TextBox Control

The **TextBox control** is used for accepting text or numeric values from the user. **Tables 7.6** and **7.7** list some of the common properties and events associated with the TextBox control.

Table 7.6 *TextBox control properties*

Properties	Description
Name	Sets the name of the TextBox.
MaxLength	Controls the maximum number of characters that can be entered in the TextBox.
Enabled	Controls whether you can enter a value in the TextBox or not. Value TRUE implies that you can enter a value. Value FALSE implies that you cannot enter a value and the TextBox appears as disabled.
Text	Sets the text to be displayed in the TextBox.
PasswordChar	Specifies the character (* or any other symbol) to be used for accepting password values in a TextBox.

Table 7.7 *TextBox control events*

Events	Description
Change	This event is triggered when the value in the TextBox is changed.
Click	This event is triggered when the user clicks on the TextBox.
DblClick	This event is triggered when the user double-clicks on the TextBox.

- **Command Button Control**

The **Command Button control** is similar to push buttons used for initiating some action on the form. **Tables 7.8** and **7.9** list some of the common properties, and events associated with the Command Button control.

Table 7.8 *Command Button properties*

Properties	Description
Name	Sets the name of the Command Button.
Caption	Specifies the text that appears on the Command Button.
Enabled	Controls whether command button can respond to user-generated actions or not. Value TRUE implies that you can click the button. Value FALSE implies you cannot click the button and the button appears as disabled.
Font	Sets the font, font size and font style of the text to be displayed.

Table 7.9 *Command Button events*

Events	Description
Click	This event is triggered when the Command Button is clicked at the time of running an application.

Let us use some of the properties and events of the TextBox and the Command Button control to accept the **First Name** and **Last Name** of a user in two TextBoxes, and display the **Full Name** in the third TextBox when the Command Button is clicked. One more Command Button has been added to stop the execution of the form. To do this, follow the given steps.

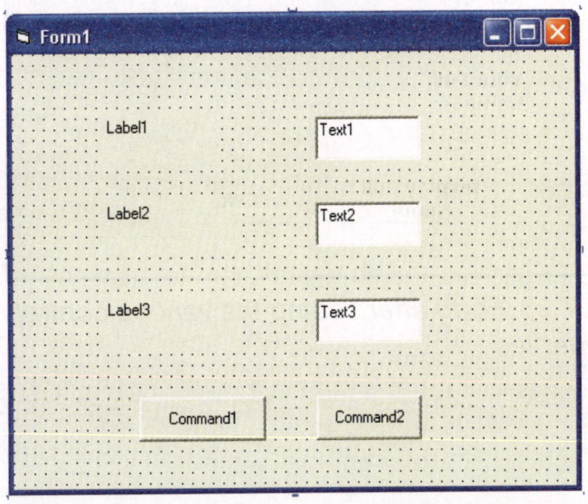

Fig 7.22 *Adding Controls to the Form*

Step 1 Add the Label, TextBox, and Command Button controls to the form as shown in **Fig. 7.22**.

Step 2 Change the properties of the controls as given in **Table 7.10**.

Table 7.10

Control	Properties
Label1	Caption: **Enter First Name:** Font: Font as **Verdana**, Font Style: **Bold**, Font size: **10**
Label2	Caption: **Enter Last Name:** Font: Font as **Verdana**, Font Style: **Bold**, Font size: **10**
Label3	Caption: **Your Full Name is:** Font: Font as **Verdana**, Font Style: **Bold**, Font size: **10**
Text1	Name: **txtFirst** Text: **blank**
Text2	Name: **txtSecond** Text: **blank**
Text3	Name: **txtFull** Text: **blank** Enabled: **False**
Command1	Name: **cmdDisplay** Caption: **Display Full Name** Font: Font as **Verdana**, Font Style: **Bold**, Font size: **10**
Command2	Name: **cmdExit** Caption: **Exit** Font: Font as **Verdana**, Font Style: **Bold**, Font size: **10**

The design of the form looks as shown in **Fig. 7.23**.

Step 3 Double-click on **the Display Full Name** Command button and type the given code in the **cmdDisplay_Click()** event handler.

```
Private Sub cmdDisplay_
Click()
txtFull.Text = txtFirst.
Text + " " + txtLast.
Text
End Sub
```

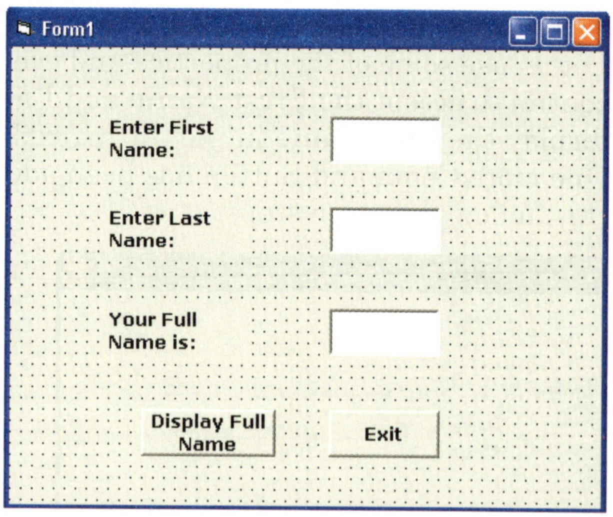

Fig 7.23 *Form after setting the various control properties*

The user enters the first name and the last name in the text boxes and clicks the **Display Full Name** Command Button. The click event handler of the cmdDisplay Command Button retrieves the value of the first name and last name textboxes by using the **Text property** and then concatenates (that is, joins the two strings) it. In order to include space between the first name and the last name, the first name is concatenated with space and then with the last name. The full name is then displayed in the **txtFull** TextBox using its Text property.

Step 4 Double-click on the **Exit** Command button and type the given code in the **cmdExit_Click()** event handler.

```
Private Sub cmdExit_Click()
End
End Sub
```

The **End** keyword stops the execution of the program.

Step 5 Run the application by pressing **F5**. When you click the **Display Full Name** Command button, the **Full Name** of the user is displayed in the third TextBox as shown in **Fig. 7.24**.

Note that the **Full Name** text box appears disabled. When you click the **Exit** button, the application stops executing.

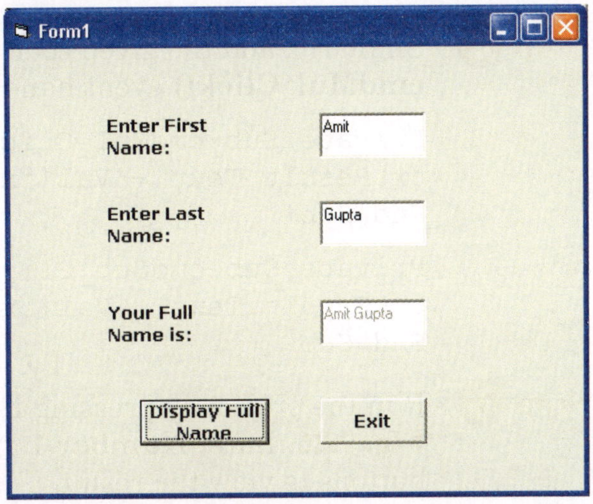

Fig 7.24 *Application in the Run mode*

CREATING A CALCULATOR IN VISUAL BASIC

Follow the given steps to create a calculator in Visual Basic that adds, subtracts, and multiplies two numbers accepted from the user and displays the result in the third TextBox when the respective buttons are clicked.

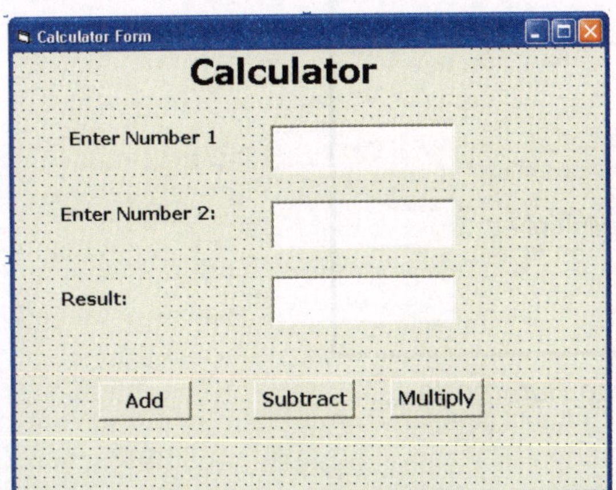

Fig 7.25 *Calculator Form*

Step 1 Design the form interface as shown in **Fig. 7.25**.

Step 2 Change the Name property of the controls as given here.

a) Number1 TextBox: **txtNum1**

b) Number2 TextBox: **txtNum2**

b) Result TextBox: **txtResult**

c) Add Command Button: **cmdAdd**

d) Subtract Command Button: **cmdSub**

e) Multiply Command Button: **cmdMul**

Step 3 Double-click on the **Add** Command button and type the given code in the **cmdAdd_Click()** event handler.

```
Private Sub cmdAdd_Click()
txtResult.Text = Val(txtNum1.Text) + Val(txtNum2.Text)
End Sub
```

The above code retrieves the value of the **txtNum1** and **txtNum2** textboxes by using the **Text property** and then adds it. A predefined function **Val** has been used to convert the values in textboxes to numeric values for the purpose of addition; otherwise the values inside the textboxes are treated as text values and are concatenated. The addition of two numbers is then shown in the **txtResult** TextBox by using its Text property.

Step 4 Similarly, add the given code in the **cmdSub_Click()** event handler and **cmdMul_Click()** event handler.

```
Private Sub cmdMul_Click()
txtResult.Text = Val(txtNum1.Text) * Val(txtNum2.Text)
End Sub

Private Sub cmdSub_Click()
txtResult.Text = Val(txtNum1.Text) - Val(txtNum2.Text)
End Sub
```

Step 5 Run the project by pressing **F5**. The Calculator Form appears as shown in Fig. 7.26. Enter **Number 1** and **Number 2**. Click on different Command buttons to view the result.

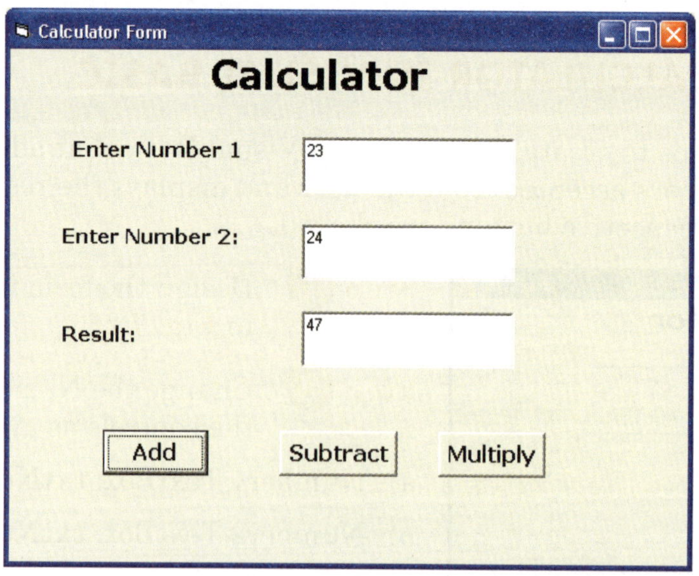

Fig 7.26 *Calculator Form in the Run mode*

Recap Time

- Visual Basic is a programming language that offers an Integrated Development Environment (IDE) for writing programs.
- An IDE provides a common environment for designing, editing and removing errors in the programs.
- Visual Basic is also referred to as an event-driven programming language.
- The different elements of Visual Basic IDE are Title bar, Menu bar, Toolbar, Form window, Toolbox, Project Explorer, Properties window and Form Layout Window.
- Every form as well as control has its own set of properties, methods and events.
- A property is a characteristic such as colour and size of an object.
- A method is an action that can be performed on an object.
- An event can be thought as an occurrence of some user generated action applied on an object.
- You can run the application by pressing F5, or by choosing Run ▶ Start.

Answers to Quick Questions

1. a) False b) True c) False d) True e) False

Assessment Time

1 Choose the correct answer.

a) Which of the following is not a property of Textbox control?

i) Caption ii) Text iii) Name iv) Enabled

b) Which one of the following elements of the Visual Basic IDE is used for specifying the position of the form with respect to the display area of the screen when you run the application?

i) Properties window ii) Project Explorer iii) Form Layout iv) Form

c) Which of the following best describes a property related to a control?

i) A property is a characteristic such as colour and size of an object.

ii) A property is an action that can be performed on an object.

iii) A property can be thought as an occurrence of any activity related to an object.

iv) None of these

d) Which of the following methods belong to the Form object?

i) Show ii) Hide iii) Print iv) All of these

2 **Fill in the blanks using the words given below.**

Project Explorer	**Object**	**MaxLength**	**Method**	**IDE**

a) An ______________ provides a common environment for designing, editing, and removing errors in the programs.

b) A ______________ is an action that can be performed on an object

c) This ______________ window displays a list of various elements of a project, viz, classes and modules.

d) The ______________ property of the TextBox control can be used to control the maximum number of characters that can be entered in the TextBox.

e) You can use the ______________ view to design the interface of the application by placing various controls on the form.

3 **Answer the following questions.**

a) Why is it easy to write programs using Visual Basic as a language?

b) Name the different elements that make up the Visual Basic IDE.

c) Define property, method and event in relation to controls.

d) Discuss the two ways in which you can add controls on a form.

e) Discuss the various ways to run an application.

f) How is Label control different from TextBox control?

g) When do you use Command Button control? Name some of its properties.

Activity Time

1 Write a Visual Basic program to calculate the Simple Interest after accepting the values for Principal, Rate and Time (in years) from the user in respective textboxes. The TextBox Interest should appear as disabled.

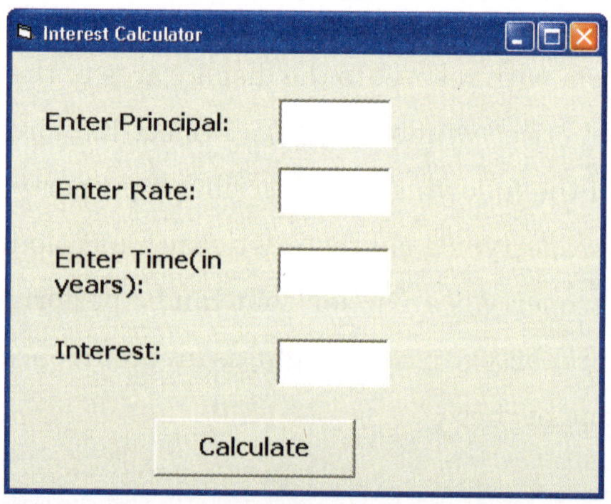

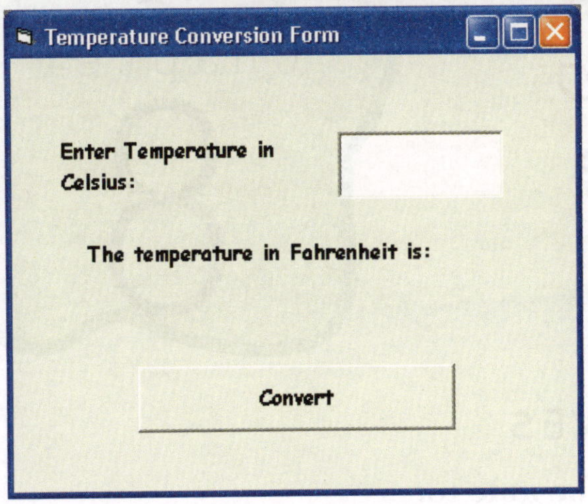

2. Write the Temperature Conversion program in Visual Basic that accepts the temperature in Celsius and displays the temperature in Fahrenheit on a label.

   Note: *The formula for converting Celsius (C) into Fahrenheit (F) is* F=(9/5 × C) + 32.

3. Write a Visual Basic program that accepts the 'Price Per Unit' and the 'Quantity Purchased' of a product and then calculates the 'Total Amount Due' when the 'Calculate' button is clicked.

   Note: *Total Amount = Price per unit * Quantity purchased*

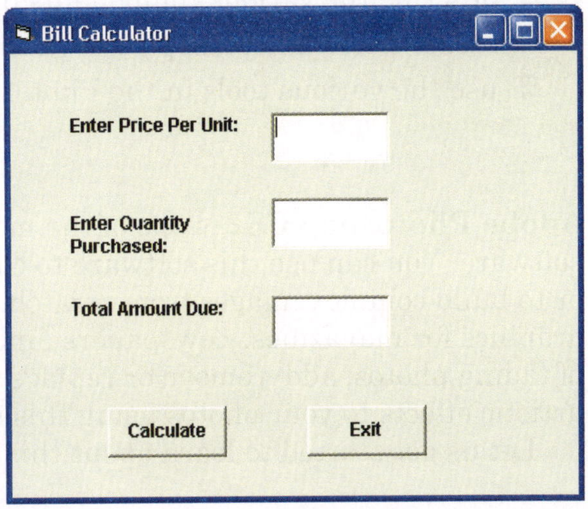

Notes for the Teacher

- Teachers can discuss the advantages of Visual Basic over other programming languages. Some application areas wherein Visual Basic programming language can be used for developing applications can also be discussed.
- Students can be given various hands-on-practice questions to make them comfortable with the Visual Basic programming environment.

INTRODUCTION TO ADOBE PHOTOSHOP

Chapter 8

OBJECTIVES

After having studied this lesson, you will be able to:

- start Photoshop.
- describe the various components of Photoshop work area.
- create a new Photoshop file.
- use the various tools in the Photoshop Toolbox.

Adobe Photoshop CS2 is one of the most powerful image editing and creation software. You can use this software to correct errors in photos, to add effects to images or to build complex images from scratch. This software is widely used for creating graphics for magazines, newspapers and websites. You can improve or change colours of fading photos; add, remove or replace people to and from the photos; and apply artistic effects to your photos using this software.

Let us get started to learn about this exciting and versatile software program.

STARTING PHOTOSHOP

To open Adobe Photoshop CS2, select **Start ▶ Programs ▶ Adobe Photoshop CS2**. The startup screen of the Photoshop appears as shown in **Fig. 8.1**.

While working in Photoshop, you can choose to create a new image or open an existing image for editing. To open an existing image, choose **File ▶ Open**. The Photoshop work area appears as shown in **Fig. 8.2**.

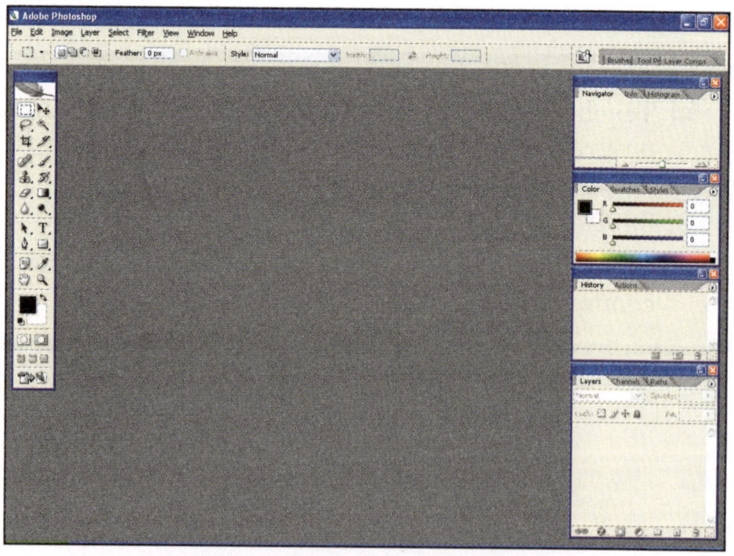

Fig 8.1 *Adobe Photoshop CS2 startup screen*

Fig 8.2 *Components of Photoshop work area*

COMPONENTS OF THE PHOTOSHOP WORK AREA

The Photoshop work area consists of the various components (**Fig. 8.2**). They are:

- **Title Bar.** The **Title bar** displays the name of an application.

- **Menu Bar.** The **Menu bar** provides menu commands for performing various tasks in Photoshop. The Photoshop menus are arranged by topic. For example, the Layer menu provides options for working with layers.

- **Options Bar.** The **Options bar** provides options related to the tool currently selected in the Toolbox. For example, to choose the thickness of the Brush Tool selected in the Toolbox, you use the Options bar.

- **Toolbox.** The **Toolbox** offers various tools that let you select, edit, draw, paint and view images (**Fig. 8.3**). To use any tool, you need to click its icon in the Toolbox. Most of the tools in the Toolbox show a small triangle at the lower-right corner. Click and hold the mouse on these tools to view more tools of the same category.

- **Palettes.** Photoshop offers various **palettes** that help you monitor and change various properties of an image.

- **Image Area.** It is the area that displays the image file that you will work on. This window containing the open image file is also called the **document window**.

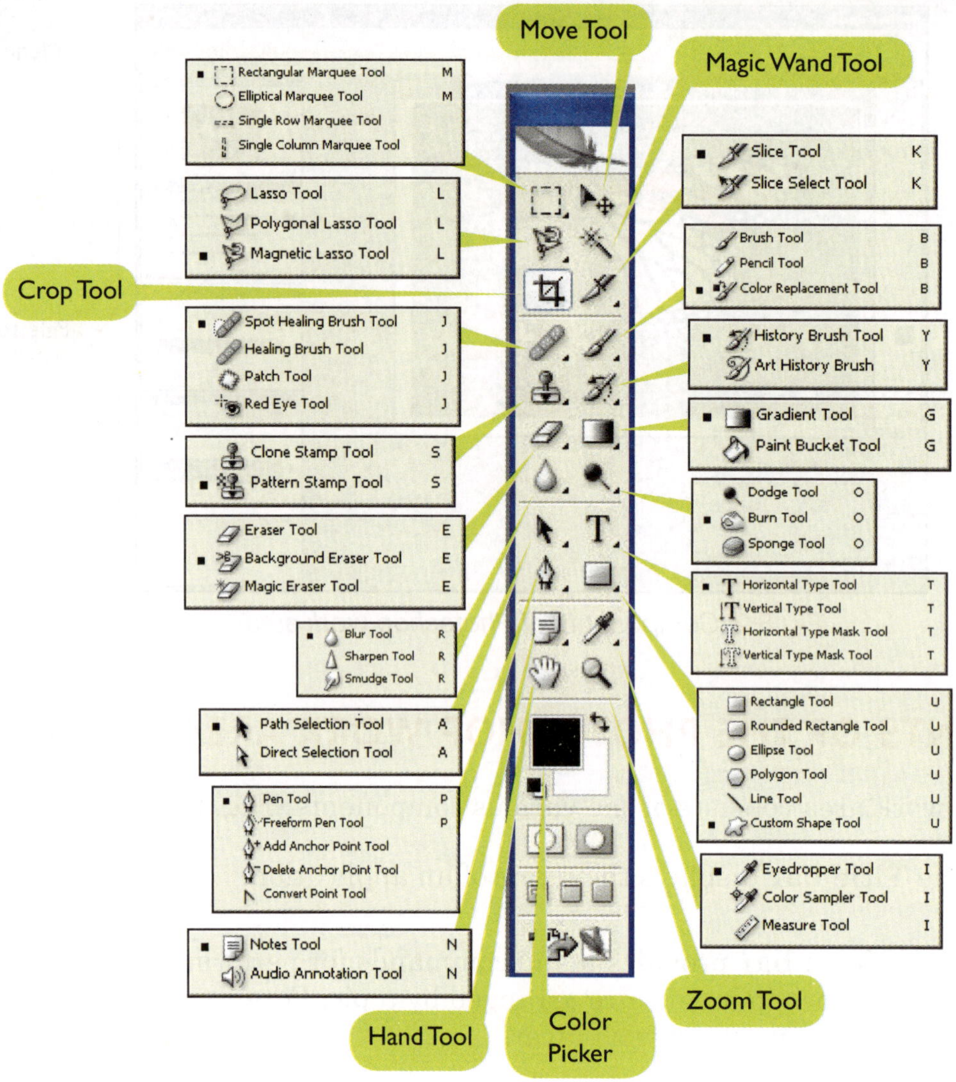

Fig 8.3 *Toolbox*

CREATING A NEW PHOTOSHOP FILE

You can create a new image by choosing the **File ▶ New** menu option. This displays the **New dialog box** wherein you can set properties related to the new file (Fig. 8.4).

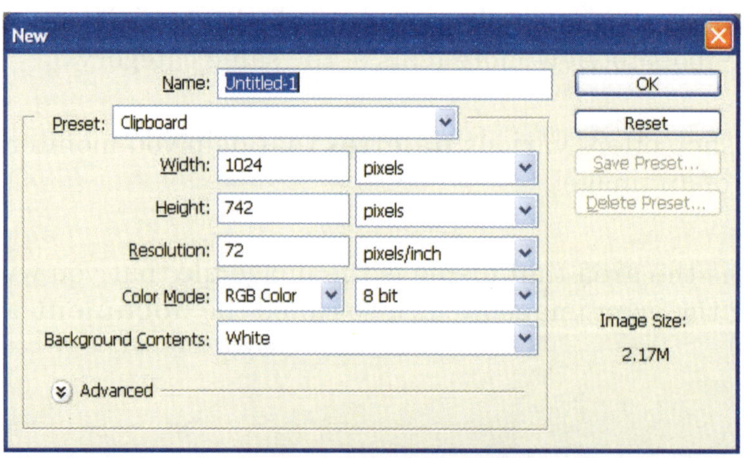

Fig 8.4 *New dialog box*

In the New dialog box, you can change the following properties:

- **Name.** To specify the name of an image file.
- **Width and Height.** To specify the size of an image file in different units of measurement such as pixels, inches, centimeters and points.
- **Resolution.** To specify the number of pixels to be displayed per inch or per cm. Resolution determines the sharpness and clarity of an image. Higher the resolution, better will be the clarity of an image.
- **Color Mode.** To specify the Color mode such as RGB, CMYK or Grayscale that has to be used for displaying and printing an image. Color mode determines the number of colours and the file size of an image.
- **Background Contents.** To provide information about the background of an image. You can choose from the three options—white, background colour and transparent.

SAVING A FILE

You can save the new Photoshop file using the **File ▶ Save** or **File ▶ Save As** menu option. Photoshop supports various types of file formats such as **PSD**, **TIFF**, **GIF**, **JPEG** and **PDF**. The default Photoshop file format is **.PSD**.

USING THE TOOLBOX

The Toolbox contains a collection of tools that let you work with different aspects of images. Some of the categories of tools that will be discussed in this class are—**Selection tools**, **Painting tools**, **Drawing tools**, **Type tools** and **Retouching tools**.

Before we proceed to learn about the different categories of tools, let us first learn about the Color Picker tool of the Toolbox.

➤ Color Picker 

Color Picker lets you select a colour for setting the **foreground** and the **background colour**. The currently selected foreground colour gets displayed in the upper box and the currently selected background colour is displayed in the lower box. The default foreground colour is **black** and the default background colour is **white**.

The foreground colour is used for painting, filling shapes, and drawing strokes (lines). The background colour is used to fill the erased areas of an image.

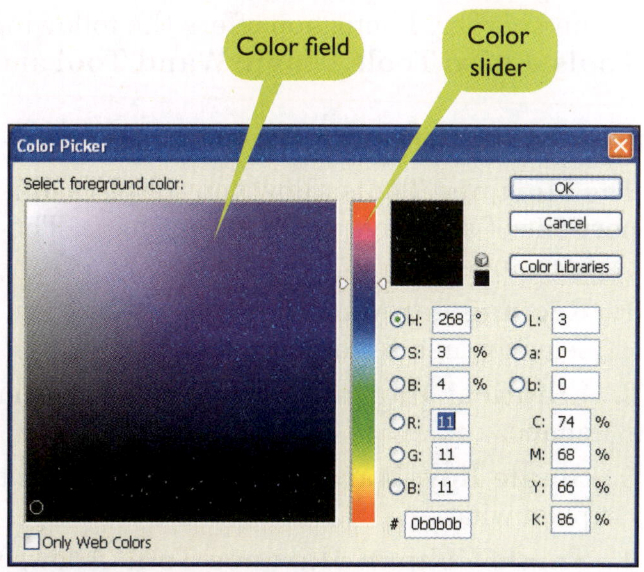

Fig 8.5 *Color Picker dialog box*

The steps to change the foreground or the background colour using the Color Picker are:

Step 1 Click the upper box or the lower box of the Color Picker in the Toolbox. The **Color Picker** dialog box appears (**Fig. 8.5**).

Step 2 Select a colour by performing any one of the following tasks.
- Drag the white triangles along the color slider, or
- Click in the Color slider, or
- Click in the Color field.

Step 3 Click **OK**.

Quick Tip

You can also change the foreground and the background colour using the Color Palette located at the right of the Photoshop work area. The colours can be set either by dragging the R, G and B sliders or by choosing a colour from the color ramp at the bottom of the palette. If the Color Palette is not available, choose **Window ▶ Color**.

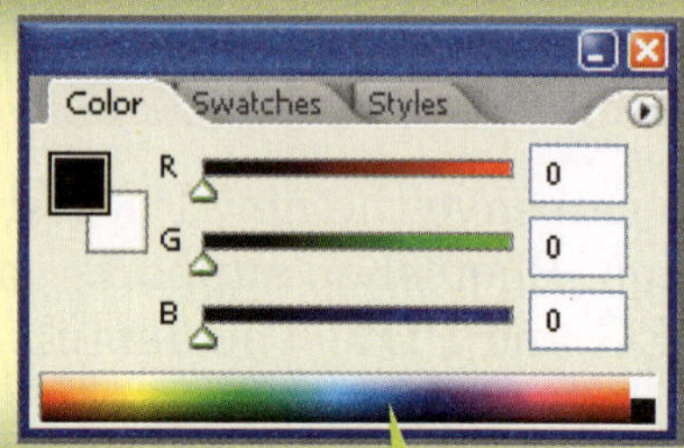

Color ramp

➤ Selection Tools

The Selection tools allow you to select a portion or subset of an image to work on. This helps you in editing and applying effects only to the selected portions of an image while leaving the unselected areas unaffected. The selected portions are highlighted using a dashed border. Photoshop offers the following categories of selection tools—**Marquee Tools**, **Lasso Tools**, **Magic Wand Tool** and **Crop Tool**.

- **Marquee Tools**

The **Marquee Tools** allow you to select different portions of an image in a specific shape. The marquee tools include:

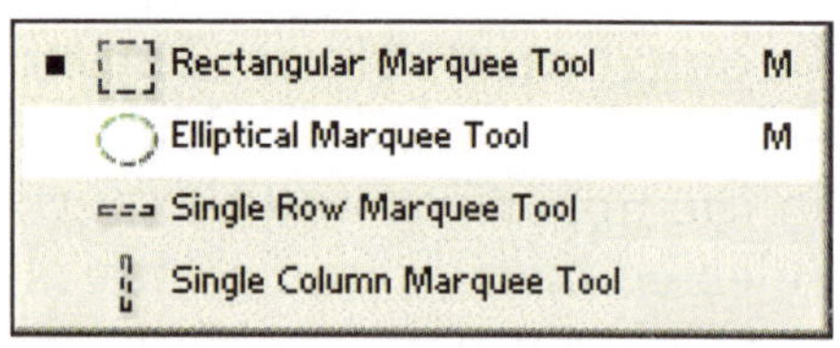

Fig 8.6 *Marquee Tools*

1. **Rectangular Marquee Tool.** Allows you to make a selection in a rectangular shape.
2. **Elliptical Marquee Tool.** Allows you to make a selection in an elliptical or circular shape.
3. **Single Row Marquee Tool.** Allows you to make a selection as a row that is one pixel wide.
4. **Single Column Marquee Tool.** Allows you to make a selection as a column that is one pixel wide.

The steps to be followed to select an area using the Marquee tools are:

Step 1 Open the image.

Step 2 Choose the required Marquee Tool.

Step 3 Drag the mouse over the surface of the image to mark the selection (**Fig. 8.7** and **Fig. 8.8**).

Fig 8.7 *Selection using Rectangular Marquee Tool*

Fig 8.8 *Selection using Single Column Marquee Tool*

- **Lasso Tools**

The **Lasso Tools** allow you to select different potions of an image by drawing a freehand or a straight-edged area.

The steps to be followed to select an area using the Lasso Tools are:

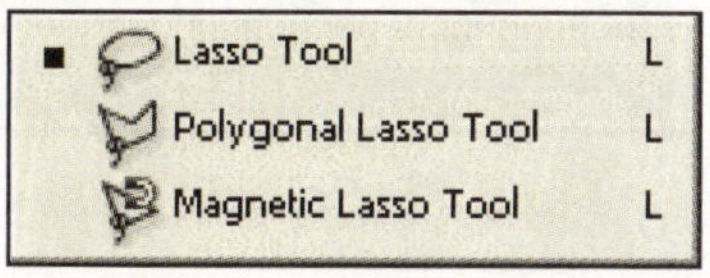

Fig 8.9 *Lasso Tools*

Step 1 Open the image.

Step 2 Choose the required Lasso Tool and follow the given steps to use it:

1. **Lasso Tool.** Allows you to make selections by drawing a freehand area. To use this tool, drag the mouse around the portion of the image to be selected (**Fig. 8.10**).
2. **Polygonal Lasso Tool.** Allows you to make selections by clicking specific points around an image. To use this tool, click anywhere in the image to mark the first starting point and then click at the position where you want

Fig 8.10 *Selection using the Lasso Tool*

the first straight segment to end. Continue clicking to mark endpoints for subsequent segments till the area you wish to select is enclosed forming a polygon. To close the selection, position the pointer over the starting point and click (**Fig. 8.11**).

3. **Magnetic Lasso Tool.** Allows you to select objects by sticking the selection border to the edges of an object. This tool is particularly useful when there is a huge contrast between the foreground objects or the background objects of an image. Magnetic Lasso Tool identifies this contrast and draws points to create a selection area as you drag the mouse around the edges of the object to be selected (**Fig. 8.12**).

Fig 8.11 *Selection using the Polygonal Lasso Tool*

Fig 8.12 *Selection using the Magnetic Lasso Tool*

- **Magic Wand Tool**

The **Magic Wand Tool** lets you select those areas of an image which share a similar colour. When using this tool, you can also set various options for specifying the exact selection in the Options bar (**Fig. 8.13**). These options include:

- **Tolerance.** Tolerance determines how closely the colours should be matched. Specifying a low value selects colours that are very similar to the pixel where you clicked. Specifying a higher value selects a wide range of colours.
- **Anti-aliased.** This option lets you define a smooth edge for the selection.
- **Contiguous.** This option lets you select only adjacent areas that share the same colours.

Fig 8.13 *Magic Wand Tool's Options bar*

The steps to use Magic Wand Tool are:

Step 1 Click the Magic Wand Tool.

Step 2 Set the **Tolerance**, **Anti-aliased**, and **Contiguous** options in the Options bar.

Step 3 Click on the colour you want to select in the image.

All the contiguous areas having the similar colour get selected.

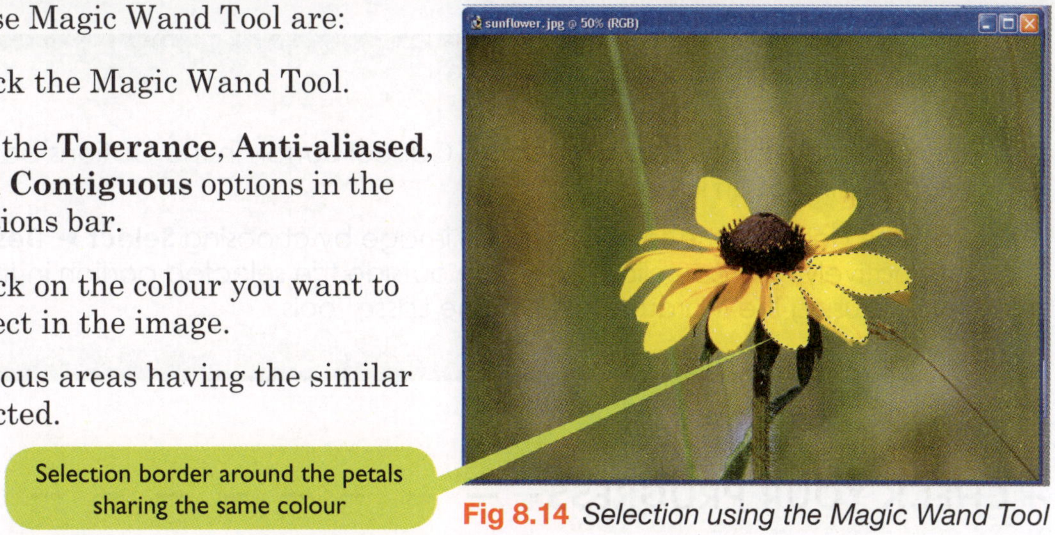

Fig 8.14 *Selection using the Magic Wand Tool*

- **Crop Tool**

The **Crop Tool** is used to discard the portions of an image that are not required. The steps to use this tool are:

Step 1 Open the image and select the **Crop Tool**.

Step 2 Drag the mouse over the part of the image you want to retain. The area outside the cropped area appears dark.

Step 3 Click **Enter**, or click the **Commit** button ✓ in the Options bar to crop the image.

Fig 8.15 *Selection using the Crop Tool*

- **Move Tool**

The **Move Tool** is used to drag a selected part of the image to a new location in the image.

To use this tool, follow the given steps.

Step 1 Select the portion of the image to be moved using one of the selection tools.

Step 2 Select the **Move Tool**.

Step 3 Place the mouse pointer inside the selection area and drag the selection to a new location.

Fig 8.16 *Using the Move Tool*

QUICK TIP

- You can press the Esc key or click the Cancel button in the Options bar to cancel the cropping of an image.
- You can deselect the selections in an image by choosing **Select ► Deselect**. Alternatively, you can click anywhere outside the selected portion in the image if you are using the Marquee Tools or the Lasso Tools.

CHECK YOUR PROGRESS

1. **Take a picture of your choice. Select any object in the picture and create its multiple copies. For example, in Picture 1, the lotus flower is selected using an appropriate Selection tool, and multiple copies of it are placed at different locations in the pond as shown in Picture 2. (*Note: To create multiple copies of the flower, you can use the Copy and Paste commands*)**

Picture 1

Picture 2

QUICK QUESTION

1. **Which tool will you use to**

a) select areas of an image which share a similar colour?

b) remove portions of an image, which are not required?

c) drag a selected part of an image to a new location?

d) to select a portion of the image by drawing a freehand area?

➤ Drawing Tools

You can use tools like Rectangle, Rounded Rectangle, Ellipse, Polygon and Line from the Toolbox for drawing various shapes in Photoshop. You can also draw other shapes such as blob, heart and arrows using the Custom Shape Tool.

• Shape Tools

The steps to draw shapes like Rectangle, Rounded Rectangle, Ellipse, Polygon and Line are:

Step 1 Select an appropriate **Shape Tool** from the Toolbox (**Fig. 8.17**). Alternatively, you can choose the desired shape from the Options bar after clicking the **Rectangle Tool** in the Toolbox (**Fig. 8.18**).

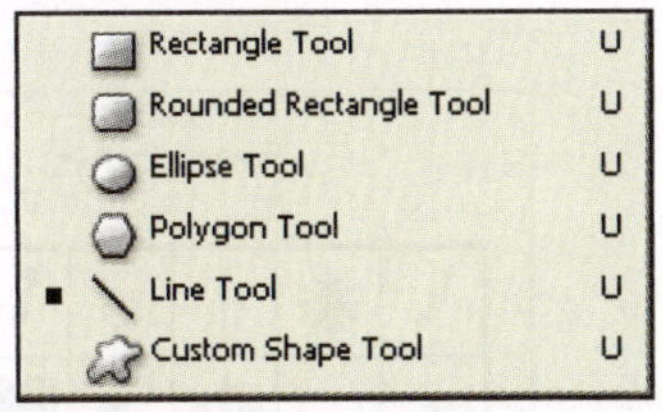

Fig 8.17 *Shape Tools*

Fig 8.18 *Shape Tools' Options bar*

Step 2 Choose the desired fill colour from the **Color pop-up palette** in the Options bar. Alternatively, you can click in the upper box of the Color Picker in the Toolbox to choose a colour.

Step 3 If required, choose an appropriate style from the **Style** pop-up palette in the Options bar.

Step 4 Click and drag the mouse to draw the required shape.

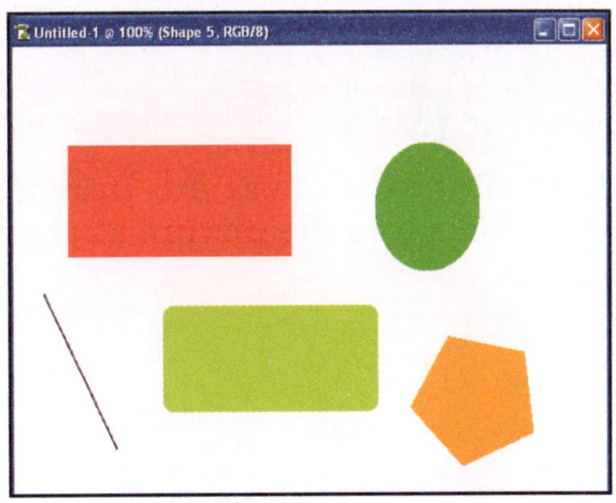

Fig 8.19 *Drawing shapes*

• Custom Shape Tool

The **Custom Shape Tool** lets you draw a variety of preset shapes like flowers and grids.

The steps to use the Custom Shape Tool are:

Step 1 Select the **Custom Shape Tool** from the Toolbox. Alternatively, select the Custom Shape button in the Options bar after clicking the Rectangle Tool in the Toolbox.

Step 2 Select a shape from the **Shape** pop-up palette in the Options bar (**Fig. 8.20**).

Step 3 Click and drag the mouse to draw the selected custom shape.

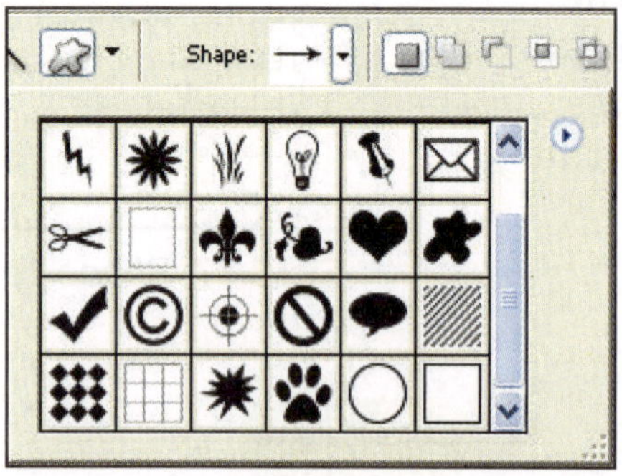

Fig 8.20 *Shape pop-up palette*

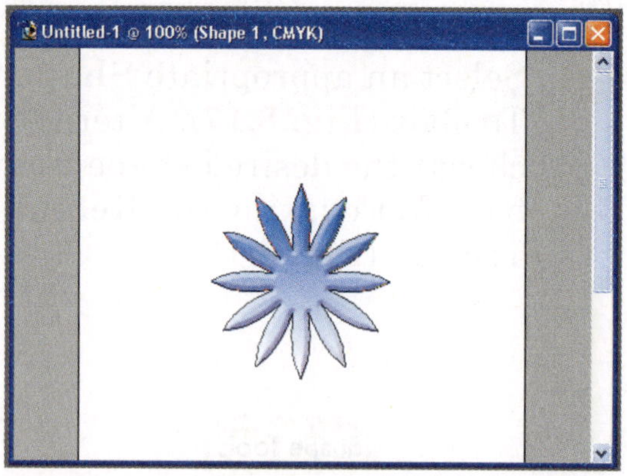

Fig 8.21 *Using the Custom Shape Tool*

CHECK YOUR PROGRESS

2. **Make use of various Drawing tools to create the picture as shown here.**

➤ Painting Tools

The Painting tools are used for changing the fill colour of an image. The Painting tools available in Photoshop are—**Brush Tool**, **Pencil Tool**, **Color Replacement Tool**, **History Brush Tool**, **Paint Bucket Tool** and **Gradient Tool**.

You can use the Brush Tool and the Pencil Tool to apply colour with brush strokes while the Gradient Tool and the Paint Bucket Tool can be used to apply colour to large areas. Let us discuss some of these tools.

- **Brush Tool**

The **Brush Tool** can be used to create soft strokes of colour in your images. You can set the various options while using the Brush Tool's Options bar (**Fig. 8.22**). These options are:

- **Brush.** It displays the Brush Preset Picker that lets you change the master diameter of the brush. The master diameter determines the size of the brush. You can change the size either by dragging the master diameter slider or by selecting a preset brush at the bottom of the menu.
- **Mode.** It allows you to set the painting mode such as darken and lighten when applying the brush strokes.
- **Opacity.** It allows you to set the level of transparency when applying brush strokes. Decreasing the opacity makes your brush more transparent while increasing the opacity makes it less transparent.
- **Flow.** It allows you to specify how quickly the paint will be applied.

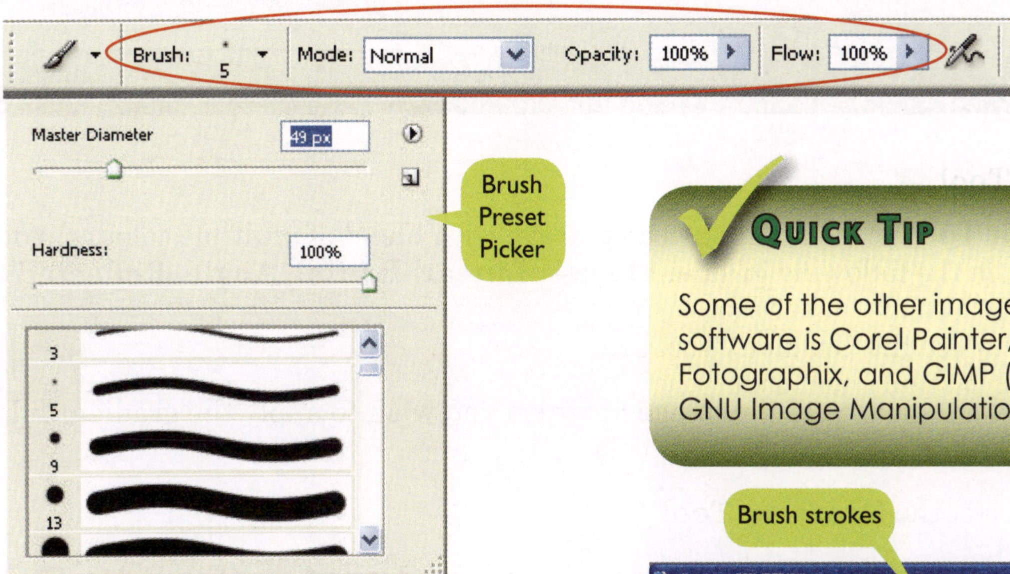

Fig 8.22 *Brush Tool's Option bar*

QUICK TIP

Some of the other image editing software is Corel Painter, Artweaver, Fotographix, and GIMP (short for GNU Image Manipulation Program).

To use the Brush Tool, follow the given steps.

Step 1 Open the image file.

Step 2 Choose an appropriate foreground colour from the Color Picker.

Step 3 Select the **Brush Tool**.

Step 4 Set the appropriate **Brush size**, **Mode**, **Opacity** and **Flow** for the Brush in the Options bar.

Step 5 Drag the mouse to paint strokes using the brush on the image.

Fig 8.23 *Creating strokes using the Brush Tool*

Quick Tip

You can use the Brush palette for setting various other brush properties such as Brush Tip Shape and Texture. To open the Brush palette, click on the **Brushes** tab in the **Palette Well** towards the top-right corner of the Photoshop work area.

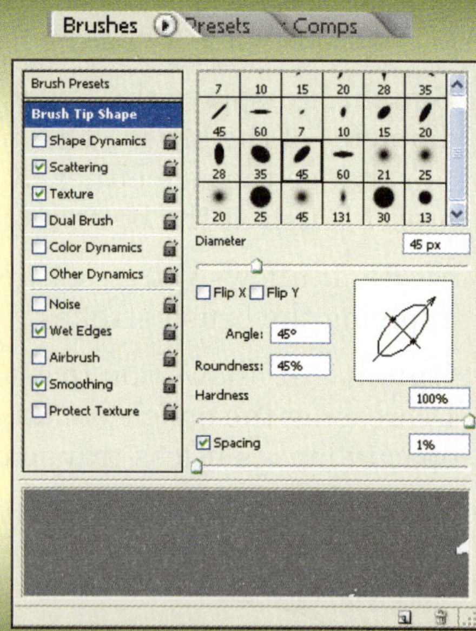

- ### Gradient Tool

The **Gradient Tool** is used to fill selected areas with blend of multiple colours. You can choose from the following gradient types—**Linear**, **Radial**, **Angle**, **Reflected** and **Diamond**.

The steps to use the Gradient Tool are:

Step 1 Select the area of the image in which you wish to apply the gradient fill using one of the Selection tools.

Step 2 Select the **Gradient Tool**.

Step 3 Click on the **Gradient Sample** box in the Options bar (**Fig. 8.24**). The **Gradient Editor** dialog box appears (**Fig. 8.25**).

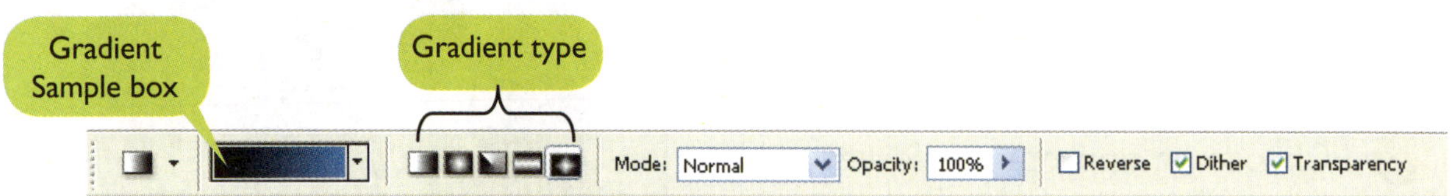

Fig 8.24 *Gradient Tool's Options bar*

Step 4 Select a Preset gradient fill or create a New gradient fill in the Gradient Editor dialog box. Click **OK** to close the dialog box.

Step 5 Choose an appropriate gradient type in the Options bar.

Step 6 Place the mouse pointer in the selected area where you want to set the starting point of the gradient and drag to define the end point.

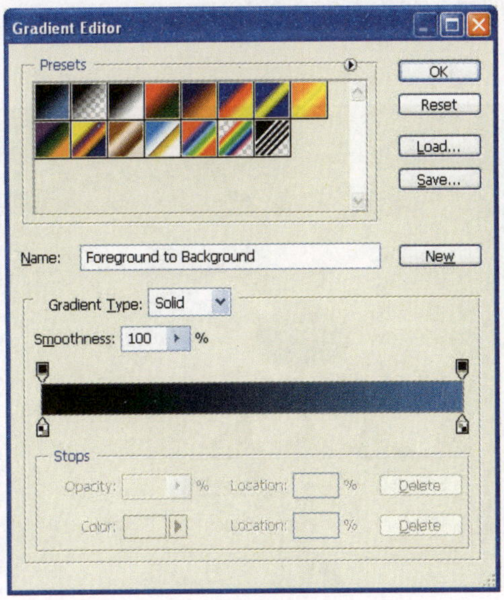

Fig 8.25 *Gradient Editor dialog box*

Fig 8.26 *Applying Gradient fill using the Gradient Tool*

- **Color Replacement Tool**

The **Color Replacement Tool** in Photoshop enables you to replace the original colour of an image with the foreground colour. When you choose this tool, the mouse pointer changes to the target symbol. As you drag the Color Replacement Tool, it picks up the sample of the original colour to be replaced. The sampled colour is then replaced with the currently selected foreground colour. You can also specify various settings to control the behaviour of the Color Replacement Tool in the Options Bar. Two of these settings include:

1. **Tolerance.** Tolerance determines how closely the colours should be matched for sampling. Specifying a low value selects colours that are very similar to the pixel where you clicked. Specifying a higher value selects a wide range of colours.
2. **Limits.** Allows you to specify whether only the colour of adjacent pixels containing the sample colour should be replaced or the colour of the non-adjacent areas should also be selected.

Fig 8.27 *Color Replacement Tool's Options bar*

The steps to use the Color Replacement Tool are:

Step 1 Set the foreground colour in the **Color Picker** in the Toolbox.

Step 2 Select the Color Replacement Tool. The pointer shape changes to a target symbol.

Step 3 Set the appropriate options for **Tolerance** and **Limits** in the Options bar.

Step 4 Drag the target symbol over the area of the image whose colour needs to be changed.

Fig 8.28 *Original image*

Fig 8.29 *Image after using the Color Replacement Tool*

QUICK QUESTION

2. State whether the following statements are true or false.

a) You cannot change the brush size when applying strokes.

b) The Gradient Tool can be used to fill selected areas by blending two or more colours.

c) The Opacity option of the Brush Tool can be used to specify how quickly the paint will be applied.

d) You can create preset shapes like flowers and grass using the Custom Shape Tool.

e) You cannot change the colour of the preset brushes.

Recap Time

- Photoshop is one of the most powerful image editing and creation software
- The various components of the Photoshop work area are—Title Bar, Menu Bar, Options Bar, Toolbox, Palettes and Image area.
- The Toolbox contains a collection of tools that let you work with different aspects of images.
- The various categories of tools in the Toolbox include Selection tools, Painting tools, Drawing tools, Type tools and Retouching tools.

- The Selection tools are used for selecting different portions of the image. The various selection tools present in the Toolbox include Marquee Tools, Lasso Tools, Magic Wand Tool and Crop Tool.
- The Drawing tools are used for drawing various shapes. The various drawing tools present in the Toolbox include Rectangle Tool, Rounded Rectangle Tool, Ellipse Tool, Polygon Tool, Line Tool and Custom Shape Tool.
- The Painting tools are used for changing the fill colour of an image. The various Painting tools are available in Photoshop include Brush Tool, Pencil Tool, Color Replacement Tool, History Brush Tool, Paint Bucket Tool and Gradient Tool

Answers to Quick Questions

1. a) Magic Wand Tool b) Crop Tool c) Move Tool d) Lasso Tool

2. a) False b) True c) False d) True e) False

Assessment Time

1 Choose the correct answer.

a) Which one of the following tools lets you fill selected areas of an image with a blend of multiple colours?

i) Custom Shape Tool ii) Gradient Tool

iii) Color Replacement Tool iv) Magic Wand Tool

b) Which of the following is not a type of Selection tool?

i) Magic Wand Tool ii) Polygonal Lasso Tool

iii) Elliptical Marquee Tool iv) Custom Shape Tool

c) Which of the following tool can be used for making selections around the edges of an image?

i) Rectangular Marquee Tool ii) Move Tool

iii) Magnetic Lasso Tool iv) Crop Tool

d) Which one of the following statements holds true for the Color Replacement Tool?

i) It can be used to replace a selected colour with the foreground colour.

ii) It can be used to replace a selected colour with the background colour.

iii) It can be used for creating soft strokes of colours in your images.

iv) It can be used for moving the selected coloured portion of the image to the new location.

2 **Fill in the blanks using the colours given below.**

Palette	**Move**	**Magic Wand**	**Marquee**	**.psd**	**Resolution**	**Color Picker**

a) The ______________ tools allow you to select different portions of an image in a rectangular or elliptical shape in Photoshop.

b) You can use the ______________ tool to place the selected area to a new location.

c) You can change the foreground and background colour using the ______________.

d) ______________ lets you monitor and change various properties related to an image.

e) The default Photoshop file format is ______________.

f) ______________ determines the sharpness and clarity of an image.

g) The ______________ Tool lets you select those areas of an image which share a similar colour.

3 **Answer the following questions.**

a) What is the purpose of the following in the Photoshop work area?

i) Options bar ii) Toolbox

b) How is Polygonal Lasso Tool different from Magnetic Lasso Tool?

c) What is the use of Magic Wand Tool?

d) Differentiate between Crop Tool and Move Tool.

e) How is Custom Shape Tool useful to us?

f) What is the purpose of Gradient Tool?

Activity Time

1. It is your best friend's birthday. Design a beautiful greeting card using various Shape and Painting tools.
2. Scan your photograph. Now place your photo into a landscape with beaches and mountains.
3. You are a big fan of cars. Create a collage or a picture gallery by placing your favourite cars alongside.

Notes for the Teacher

- The teacher can give ample hands-on practice on the various tools in Photoshop learnt as a part of this chapter.

EXPLORING MORE FEATURES OF ADOBE PHOTOSHOP

Chapter 9

OBJECTIVES

After having studied this lesson, you will be able to:

- use the Retouching tools in Photoshop.
- use the Type tools in Photoshop.
- understand the use of layers in Photoshop.
- apply Filters to images in Photoshop.

In the previous chapter, you learnt about the Selection tools, the Drawing tools and the Painting tools. In this chapter, you will learn about the Retouching tools and the Type tools. You will also learn about two interesting and useful features of Photoshop—Layers and Filters. **Layers** let you organise your work while **Filters** let you enhance the look of an image by adding various effects.

RETOUCHING TOOLS

The **Retouching tools** let you repair damaged images, apply repeated patterns or enhance the look of an image using various effects. Some of the Retouching tools available in Photoshop are—**Healing Brush Tool, Spot Healing Brush Tool, Patch Tool, Red Eye Tool, Blur Tool, Sharpen Tool, Smudge Tool, Dodge Tool, Sponge Tool, Burn Tool, Clone Stamp Tool** and **Pattern Stamp Tool**. Let us learn about some of these tools in detail.

➤ Healing Brush Tool

The **Healing Brush Tool** allows you to repair imperfections such as scratches, blemishes and marks in an image. While working with this tool, you pick up sample pixels (pixels to be used for repairing) from the adjoining portion of an image. The Healing Brush Tool matches the texture, lighting, transparency and shading of the sampled pixels and applies them to the pixels that are being repaired.

The steps to use the Healing Brush Tool are:

Step 1 Select the **Healing Brush Tool**.

Step 2 Select the appropriate options for the Healing Brush Tool in the Options bar (**Fig. 9.1**). These options include:

- **Brush Size.** To set the size of the brush tip.
- **Source.** To specify whether to pick up sampled pixels from the image (Sampled) or use pre-defined pattern (patterns).
- **Aligned.** To specify the sampling point to be used for repairing. If you select this option, you can release the mouse button without loosing the current sampling point. If you deselect this option, the sampled pixels are always taken from the initial sampling point.

Step 3 Hold down the **Alt** key. The cursor shape changes to a target ⊕ symbol. Click on the area close to the area to be repaired to pick up the sampled pixels.

Step 4 Click and drag over the area to be repaired. The image gets repaired.

Fig 9.1 *Healing Brush Tool's Options bar*

Fig 9.2 *Original Image*

Fig 9.3 *Image after applying the Healing Brush Tool*

➤ Spot Healing Brush Tool 

The **Spot Healing Brush Tool** works in the similar manner as the Healing Brush Tool except that it does not require the sampling point to be set. It automatically picks up the sampled pixels from around the area to be retouched. This tool can be used to quickly remove blemishes and other marks from the photos.
The steps to use the Spot Healing Brush Tool are:

Step 1 Select the **Spot Healing Brush Tool**.

Step 2 Select the appropriate options in the Options bar (**Fig. 9.4**). One of the options include choosing an appropriate **Type** option.

The **Type** options include:

a) **Proximity Match.** Choosing this option makes the Spot Healing Brush Tool to use the pixels around the edge of the selection to pick the patch for repairing the selected area.

b) **Create Texture.** Choosing this option uses all the pixels in the selection to create a texture that can be used to fix the area.

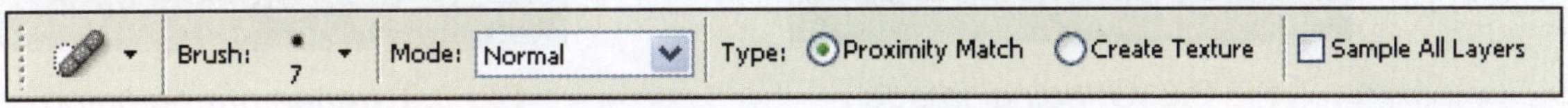

Fig 9.4 *Spot Healing Brush Tool's Options bar*

Step 3 Click on the area you want to fix.

Fig 9.5 *Original Image*

Fig 9.6 *Image after applying the Spot Healing Brush Tool*

➤ Clone Stamp Tool

The **Clone Stamp Tool** lets you duplicate the parts of an image by setting a sampling point in the image to be cloned. The cloned image can be drawn over another image or part of the same image.

The steps to use the Clone Stamp Tool are:

Step 1 Choose the **Clone Stamp Tool**.

Step 2 Click the appropriate settings in the Options bar (Fig. 9.7). These settings may include choosing a **Brush Size**, **Opacity** value or setting the **Aligned** checkbox.

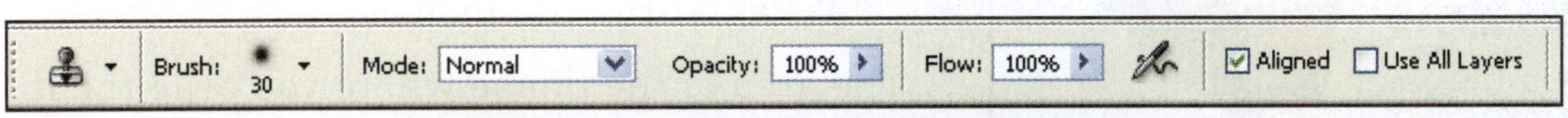

Fig 9.7 *Clone Stamp Tool's Options bar*

Step 3 Hold down the **Alt** key. The cursor shape changes to a target ⊕ symbol. Click on the image to be cloned to set the sampling point.

Step 4 Click and drag where you want the cloned image to appear. When you draw, a plus sign + appears on the original image while a corresponding circle ○ appears on the cloned image (Fig. 9.9).

Fig 9.8 *Oringinal image*

Fig 9.9 *Image after cloning*

➤ Pattern Stamp Tool

A **pattern** is a usually a design made up of an image that is repeated or tiled. The **Pattern Stamp Tool** lets you fill an area with a selected pattern. Photoshop comes with a variety of preset patterns. You can select a preset pattern from the Photoshop library or create your own pattern. The steps to use this tool are:

Step 1 Select the **Pattern Stamp Tool**.

Step 2 Set appropriate options such as Brush Size, Mode, Opacity and Flow for the Pattern Stamp Tool in the Options bar.

Step 3 Select a pattern from the Pattern pop-up palette in the Options bar (**Fig. 9.10**).

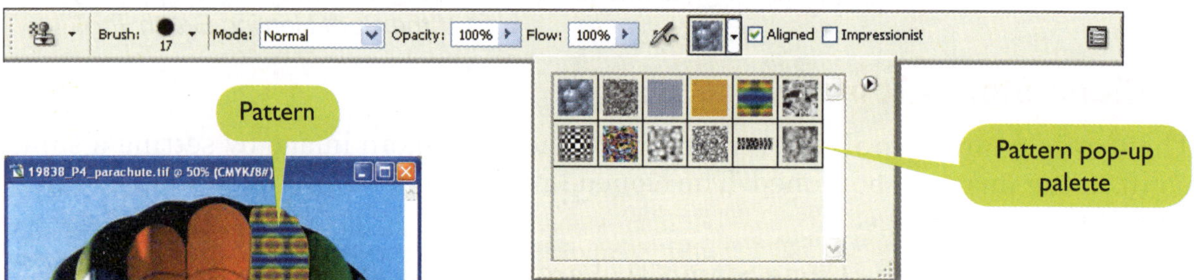

Fig 9.10 *Pattern Stamp Tool's Options bar*

Fig 9.11 *Image with the inserted pattern*

Step 4 Place the mouse pointer inside the area to be painted with pattern and drag the mouse.

The area of the image where you drag the mouse gets filled with the pattern (**Fig. 9.11**).

➤ Blur, Sharpen and Smudge Tools

Fig 9.12 *Blur, Sharpen and Smudge Tools*

These tools let you change the appearance or focus of selected portions of the image.

The **Blur Tool** softens the selected portions of an image giving it a blurred effect. This tool is useful in situations when you want to moderate or soften the focus of some areas of an image.

The **Sharpen Tool** is the opposite of the Blur Tool. This tool lets you improve the clarity of an image by sharpening the edges of selected portions of an image.

The **Smudge Tool** gives an effect of spreading the paint across the image as if you have dragged your finger through a wet paint. This tool picks up the colour from where the stroke begins and pushes it in the direction you drag your mouse.

The steps to use these tools are:

Step 1 Select the **Blur Tool**, **Sharpen Tool** or **Smudge Tool** from the Toolbox.

Step 2 Set the **Brush Size** and **Blending Mode** for the tool in the Options bar.

Step 3 Drag the mouse pointer over the portion of the image you want to blur, sharpen or smudge.

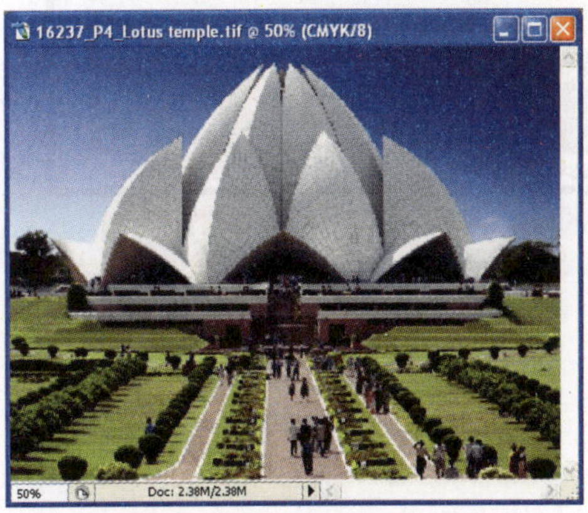

Fig 9.13 *Original Image*

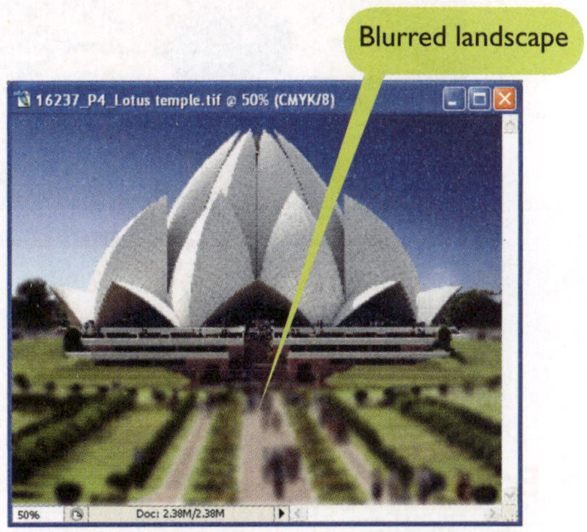

Fig 9.14 *Image after using the Blur Tool*

Fig 9.15 *Original Image*

Fig 9.16 *Image after using the Smudge Tool*

➤ Dodge and Burn Tools

The **Dodge Tool** is used to lighten the areas of an image whereas the **Burn Tool** is used to darken the areas of an image. The steps to use the Dodge or Burn Tool are:

Step 1 Select the **Dodge Tool** or the **Burn Tool**.

Step 2 In the Options bar, set the appropriate **Brush Size** and select an appropriate **Range** option and the **Exposure Level**.

Step 3 Drag the mouse pointer over the area of the image you want to lighten or darken.

Fig 9.17 *Original Image*

Fig 9.18 *Image after using the Burn Tool*

Fig 9.19 *Image after using the Dodge Tool*

➤ Eraser Tool

The **Eraser Tool** erases pixels as you drag it across the image. Pixels are erased to transparency or to the background colour if the layer is locked. There are three variants of this tool—Eraser Tool, Background Eraser Tool and Magic Eraser Tool.

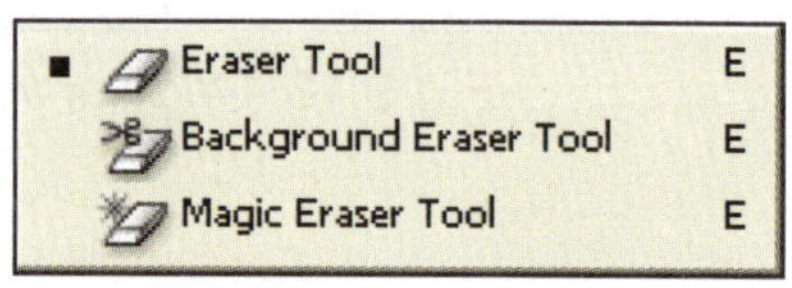

Fig 9.20 *Eraser Tools*

The **Background Eraser Tool** allows you to erase the background colour from an image or layer. You will learn more about layers later in this chapter. The Background Eraser Tool picks up the sample colour when you click on the image and erases this colour as you drag the mouse (**Fig. 9.21**).

On the other hand, the **Magic Eraser Tool** erases all areas that share similar colour pixels. When using this tool, click on the area containing the colour to be removed from the image. This erases all the coloured pixels within a set tolerance. You can associate the functionality associated with Magic Eraser Tool to using the Magic Wand Tool and then pressing Delete (**Fig. 9.22**).

The steps to use the Eraser Tools are:

Step 1 Select the **Eraser Tool**, the **Background Eraser Tool** or the **Magic Eraser Tool**.

Step 2 Set the appropriate options for the eraser tools in the Options bar.

Step 3 Drag over the area you want to erase when using Eraser or Background Eraser Tool. When using the Magic Eraser Tool, click in the part of the image you want to erase.

Fig 9.21 *Erasing the background using the Background Eraser Tool*

Fig 9.22 *Erasing the background using the Magic Eraser Tool*

QUICK QUESTION

1. **Which Photoshop tool will you use to**

a) duplicate a part of an image by setting the sampling point in the image?

b) quickly remove blemishes and other marks in photos without setting the sampling point?

c) remove all areas that share similar pixels in an image?

d) darken the areas of an image?

e) give an effect of spreading paint across the image?

f) moderate or soften the focus of some areas of an image?

CHECK YOUR PROGRESS

1. **Scan any of your old photographs. Make use of various Retouching tools to remove any scratches, marks, etc in your photos to give it a new and fresh look.**

TYPE TOOLS

The **Type Tools** are used for inserting text in Photoshop. You can format the text in many ways by changing its font family, size, style, colour, alignment, horizontal or vertical orientation, indentation, line spacing and much more. You can also warp the shape of the text in a number of interesting ways such as that of a wave, flag or arc.

Note: *When you insert text in Photoshop, it is created on a separate layer called the Type Layer. You will learn more about layers later in this chapter.*

Two of the Type Tools available in the Toolbox are:

- **Horizontal Type Tool** inserts text in the horizontal direction.
- **Vertical Type Tool** inserts text in the vertical direction.

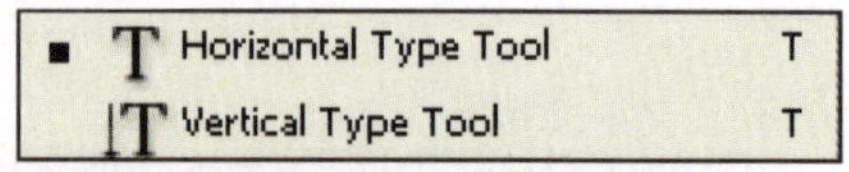

Fig 9.23 *Type Tools*

The steps to use the Type Tool are:

Step 1 Open the image.

Step 2 Select the **Horizontal Type Tool** or the **Vertical Type Tool**.

Step 3 Set the appropriate options such as font family, size, style, alignment and text colour for the Type Tool in the Options bar.

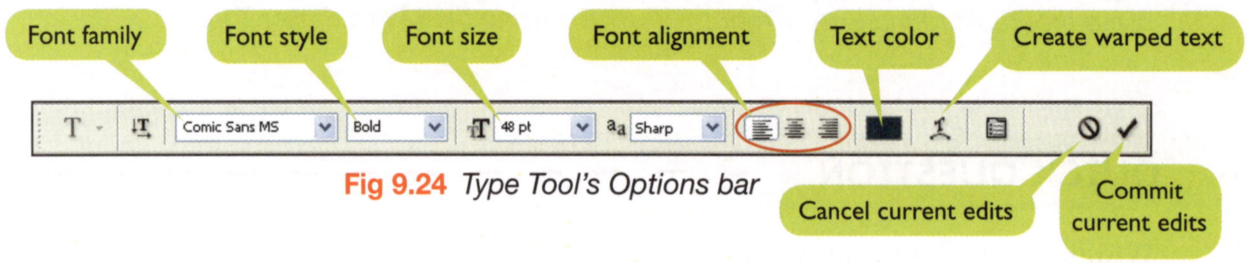

Fig 9.24 *Type Tool's Options bar*

Step 4 Click to set the insertion point anywhere on the image.

Step 5 Enter the desired text.

Step 6 Accept changes to the text by clicking the **Commit** button ✓ or cancel the operation by pressing the **Cancel** button in the Options bar.

Fig 9.25 *Using the Type Tool*

➤ Warping Text

The steps to be followed for warping the text are:

Step 1 Place the cursor anywhere in the already written text.

Step 2 Select the Type Tool.

Step 3 Click the **Create warped text** button in the Options bar. This displays the **Warp Text** dialog box (Fig. 9.26).

Step 4 Choose a warp style from the **Style** drop-down list.

Step 5 Select the orientation of the warp style—**Horizontal** or **Vertical**.

Step 6 If desired, specify values for additional options given in the **Warp Text** dialog box.

Step 7 Click **OK** to apply the warp style.

> **QUICK TIP**
>
> You can also select the text by selecting the Type Layer in the Layers palette. (You will more about Layers later in this chapter.)

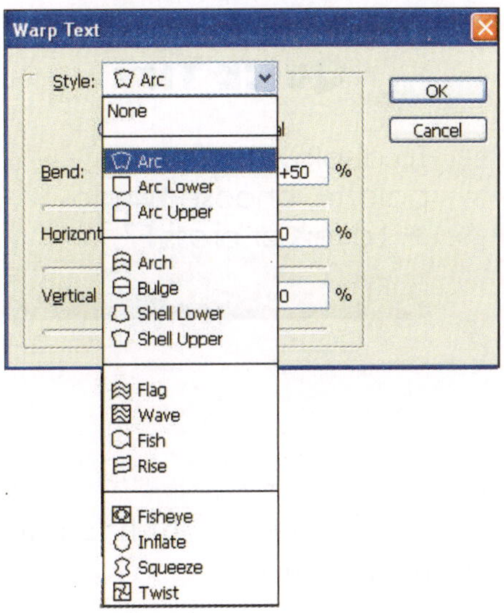

Fig 9.26 *Warp Text dialog box*

Fig 9.27 *Using the Warp Tool*

LAYERS

Layers can be thought of as transparent sheets mounted on the top of each other. Layers let you work on an individual part or element of an image without affecting the other parts or elements. You can change the composition of an image by changing the order and properties of layers. Elements placed on higher layers are displayed above the elements placed on lower layers.

Look at the graphic in Fig. 9.28. To you, it may look a single, flat graphic but is actually a combination of various elements placed on different layers. In the shown graphic, the bushes, leaves, text and background are all placed on different layers.

➤ Layers Palette

You can work with layers using Layers palette. For example, the Layers Palette of the image shown in **Fig. 9.28** looks like the one shown in **Fig. 9.29**.

Fig 9.28 *Image created using layers*

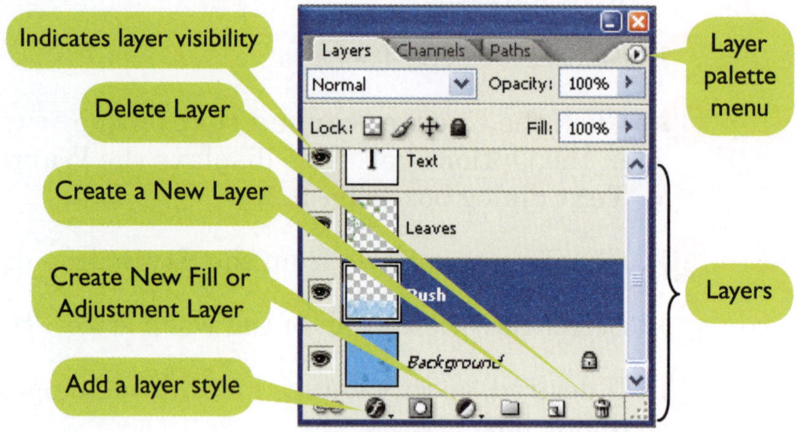

Fig 9.29 *Layers palette*

When you open a new image file with the white or the coloured background, the bottommost image in the Layers palette is called **Background**. An image can have only one background. You cannot change the order of the background layer.

You can add more layers, delete layers, show/hide layers, lock layers and use different layer styles to add sophisticated effects to your image. Let us learn more about working with layers.

> **QUICK TIP**
>
> To display the Layers palette, choose Window ► Layers or press F7.

➤ Working with Layers

Let us now learn about adding new layers, deleting layers, renaming layers, hiding and showing layers changing the order of layers and layer effects in this section.

• Adding a New Layer

You can add a new layer by using any one of the following methods.

Click the **New Layer** button in the Layers palette, or

Choose **Layer** ► **New** ► **Layer**, or

The new layer with the name **Layer1** gets inserted above the selected layer.

• Renaming a Layer

You can rename a layer by double-clicking on the layer name in the Layers palette and typing a new name.

- **Deleting a Layer**

You can delete one or more layers by using any one of the following methods.

Select the layer and click the **Delete Layer** button in the Layers palette, or

Choose **Layer ▶ Delete ▶ Layer**, or

Drag the layer to the **Delete Layer** button.

- **Showing and Hiding Layers**

To hide the layer contents, click the **Eye** icon next to a layer. Click in the **Eye** icon again to display the contents of the layer again.

- **Changing the Order of Layers**

The elements that are placed on the higher layers are displayed above the elements placed on the lower layers. To change the placement of elements in an image, you can rearrange the layers containing them in the Layers palette. To change the order of layers, drag the layer to an appropriate position in the Layers palette.

- **Layer Effects**

Photoshop offers various layer effects that allow you to enhance the look of the layer's contents. Some of these effects include shadow, glow, bevel, emboss and overlay. The steps to apply the layer effects are:

Step 1 Select a layer in the Layer palette (**Fig.9.30**).

Step 2 Click the **Layer Styles** button at the bottom of the Layers palette and choose an effect from the list, or Choose **Layer ▶ Layer Style** and then select the desired layer effect.

Step 3 The **Layer Style** dialog box appears. Choose the desired effect options by clicking the corresponding check boxes on the left side of the dialog box.

Step 4 Set appropriate options for the selected effect on the right side of the dialog box.

Step 5 Click **OK** to apply the effect.

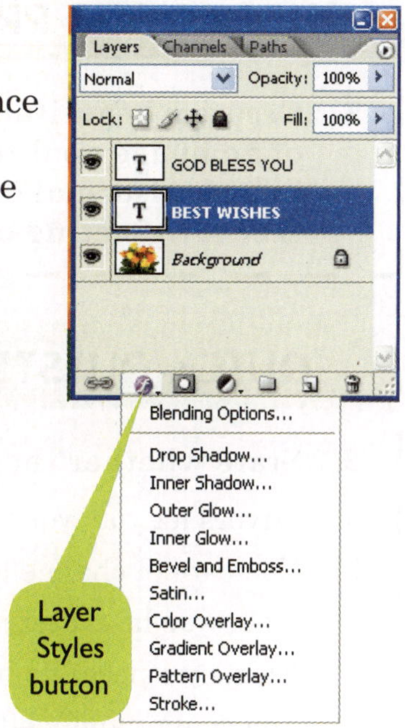

Fig 9.30 *Layers palette*

When you apply Layer effects, an 'f' icon appears to the right of the layer's name in the Layers palette. You can click on this icon to display the list of the effects applied on the layer.

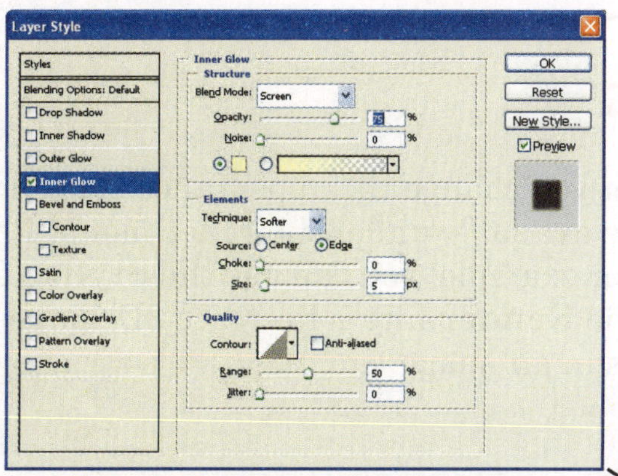

Fig 9.31 *Layer Style dialog box*

Fig 9.32 *Output of Color Overlay and Stroke Layer Effects*

Fig 9.33 *Output of Drop Shadow, Bevel and Shadow Layer Effects*

CHECK YOUR PROGRESS

2. Create a beautiful scenery/greeting card/collage by placing various elements of an image on different layers. Apply layer effect to various elements of the image. Also, make use of Type Tool to provide appropriate caption to your scenery/greeting card/collage.

QUICK QUESTION

2. State whether the following statements are true or false.

a) Layers let you work on an individual part of an image without affecting others.

b) You cannot change the stacking order of layers.

c) When you insert text in Photoshop, it is created on a separate layer called the Type Layer.

d) Elements placed on higher layers are displayed below the elements placed on lower layers.

e) You cannot apply effects on layers.

f) An image can have only one background.

FILTERS

Filters let you change the appearance of an image by adding special effects to it. Filters are available under the Filter menu. Photoshop offers various categories of Filters. For example, you can use the **Stylize** filters to give a painted effect to your images, the **Render** filters to create 3D shapes, cloud patterns and simulated light reflections in an image, etc.

✓ Quick Tip

Sometimes, some of the Filters may appear disabled in the Filter menu. In such a case, change the color mode of the image to RGB by choosing **Image ▶ Mode** menu option although some image data may be lost.

➤ Applying Filters

You can apply a filter to an entire layer, or a selected portion of a layer. The steps to be followed for applying a filter are:

Step 1 Select the entire layer or a particular portion of a layer.

Step 2 Choose the desired filter from the Filter menu (**Fig. 9.34**).

Step 3 Some filters have dialog box associated with them. If the dialog box appears, set the desired options in the dialog box to apply the filter (**Fig. 9.35**). If no dialog box appears, the selected filter is applied directly to the image (**Fig. 9.36**).

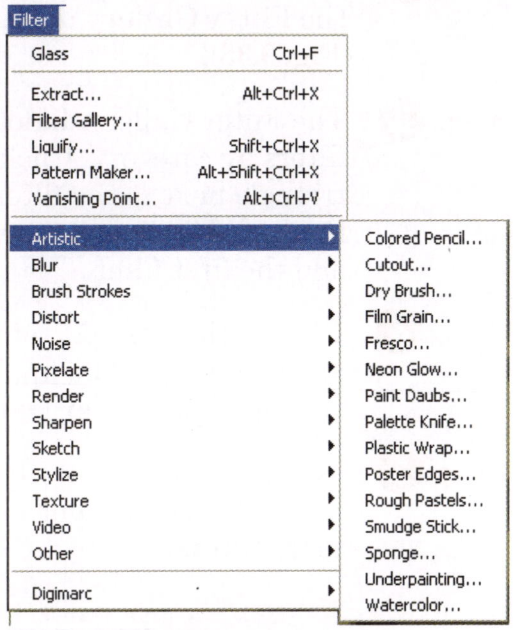

Fig 9.34 *Filter menu*

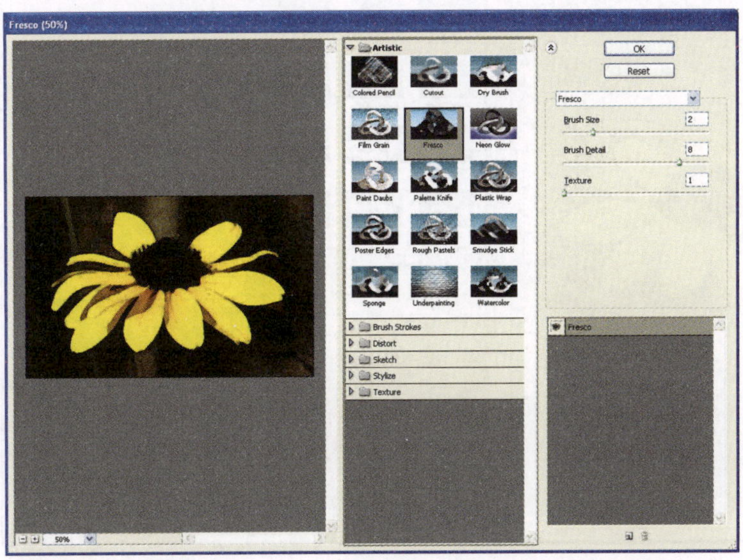

Fig 9.35 *Dialog box associated with Artistic▶Fresco filter*

Fig 9.36 *Fresco filter applied to the image*

➤ Filter Gallery

Filter Gallery offers a convenient way of applying multiple filters on the image or applying individual filters more than once on an image. To apply a filter or multiple filters on an image using the Filter Gallery, follow the given steps.

Step 1 Select the entire image layer or a particular portion of a layer to which the filter needs to be applied.

Step 2 Choose **Filter ▶ Filter Gallery** (Fig. 9.37). The **Filter Gallery** dialog box gets displayed (Fig. 9.38).

Step 3 The Filter Gallery dialog box arranges filters by category. Click the inverted triangle next to the filter category to display the list of filters. Choose a filter name to add the first filter.

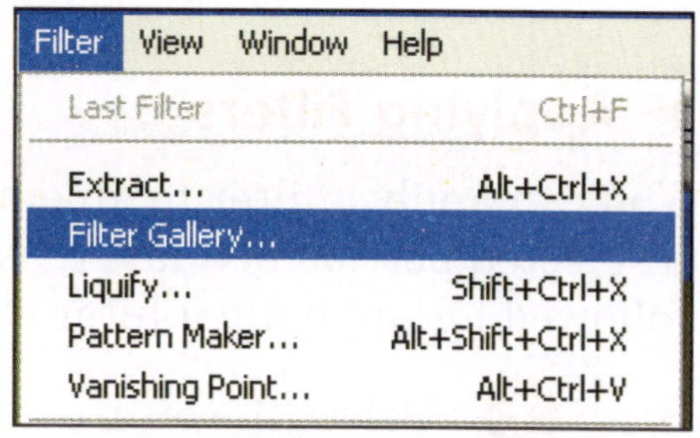

Fig 9.37 *Choosing Filter Gallery option*

Step 4 Choose the desired settings for the selected filter. The applied filter gets added to the list at the lower right corner of the Filter Gallery dialog box.

Step 5 To apply additional filters to the image, click the **New Effect Layer** icon. Choose another filter to apply. Repeat this procedure to add more filters.

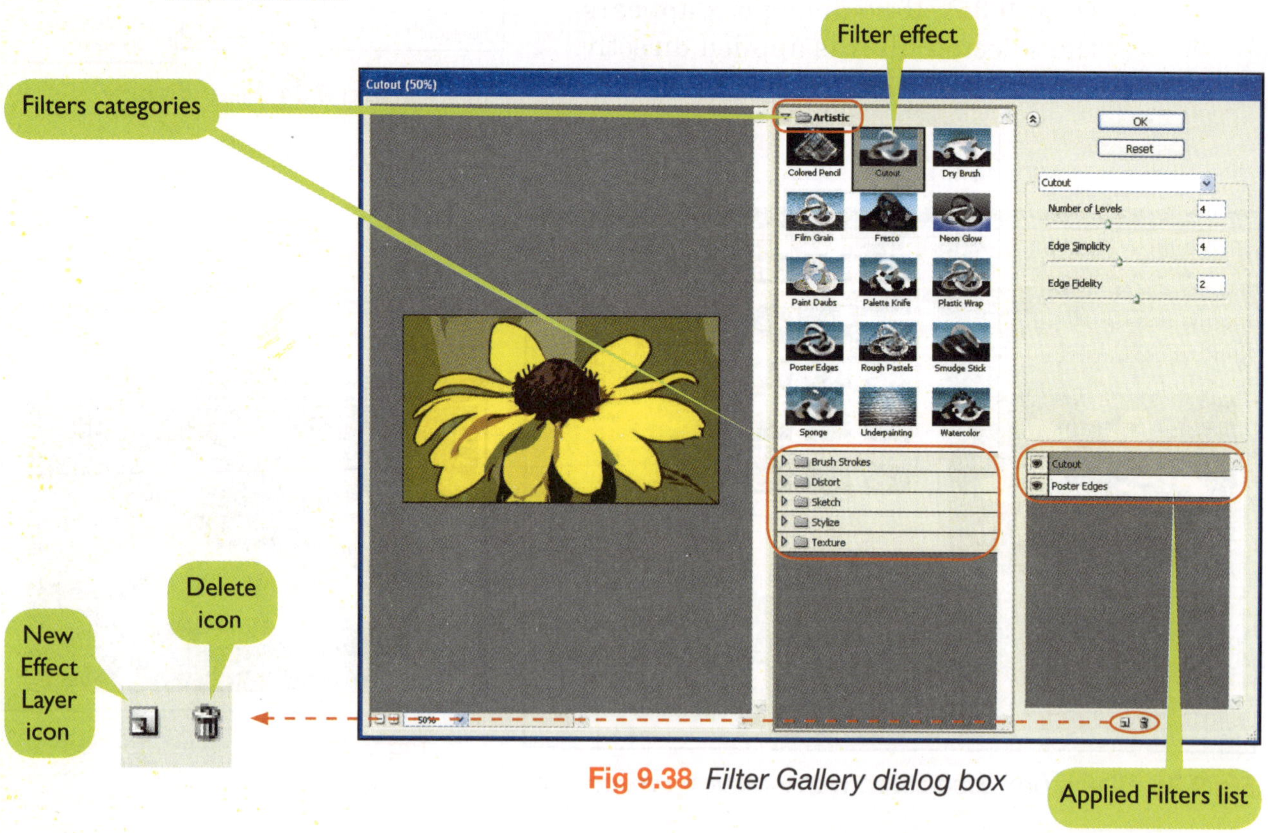

Fig 9.38 *Filter Gallery dialog box*

Step 6 To remove the already applied filters, select a filter in the applied filter list and click the **Delete** icon.

Step 7 If you are satisfied with the current image settings, click **OK**.

Fig 9.39 *Image after applying cutout and poster edges filters*

Recap Time

- Retouching tools let you repair damaged images, apply repeated patterns or enhance the look of an image by using various effects.
- The Healing Brush Tool allows you to repair imperfections such as scratches, blemishes, marks, etc in an image by setting a sampling point.
- The Spot Healing Brush Tool can be used to quickly remove blemishes and other marks in your photos without setting a sampling point.
- The Clone Stamp Tool lets you duplicate part of an image by setting a sampling point in the image to be cloned.
- The Pattern Stamp Tool lets you fill an area with a variety of preset patterns.
- The Blur Tool softens the selected portions of an image giving it a blurred effect.
- The Sharpen Tool lets you improve the clarity of the image by sharpening the edges of selected portions of an image.
- The Smudge Tool gives an effect of spreading the paint across the image as if you have dragged your finger through a wet paint.
- The Dodge Tool is used to lighten the areas of an image
- The Burn Tool is used to darken the areas of an image.
- The Eraser Tools erases pixels in an image to transparency or to the background colour as you drag it across the image. There are three variants of this tool—Eraser Tool, Background Eraser Tool and Magic Eraser Tool.
- The Type Tools are used for inserting text in Photoshop.
- Layers can be thought of transparent sheets mounted on top of each other that let you work on an individual parts of an image without affecting the other parts.
- Filters let you change the appearance of an image by adding special effects to it.

Answers to Quick Questions

1. a) Clone Stamp Tool b) Spot Healing Brush c) Magic Eraser Tool
   d) Burn Tool e) Smudge Tool f) Blur Tool
2. a) True b) False c) True
   d) False e) False f) True

Assessment Time

1 Choose the correct answer.

a) Which of the following tools let you erase all areas that share similar colour pixels?
   i) Magic Eraser Tool ii) Background Eraser Tool
   iii) Type Tool iv) Clone Stamp Tool

b) Which of the following tools can be used to repair imperfections such as scratches, blemishes and marks in an image?
   i) Blur Tool ii) Burn Tool
   iii) Sharpen Tool iv) Healing Brush Tool

c) Which of the statement holds true for filters?
   i) Filters let you change the appearance of an image by adding special effects to it.
   ii) You can apply a filter to an entire layer, or a selected portion of a layer.
   iii) You can apply multiple filters to an image using the Filter Gallery.
   iv) All of these

d) What is the use of Type Tool?
   i) It is used for inserting text in Photoshop.
   ii) It is used for filling an area with a selected pattern in Photoshop.
   iii) It is used to lighten areas of an image in Photoshop.
   iv) It is used for erasing the background colour of an image in Photoshop.

2 Fill in the blanks using the words given below.

Blur	Filter Gallery	Clone Stamp	Background	Background Eraser	Layers

a) The _______________ tool allows you to erase the background colour from an image or layer.

b) _______________ let you work on individual parts of an image without affecting others.

c) The _______________ tool lets you duplicate part of an image by setting a sampling point in the image.

d) You can use the ______________ to apply multiple filters on the image or individual filters more than once on an image.

e) To reduce focus on selected potions of an image, you use the ______________ tool.

f) The bottommost layer in the Layer palette is called ______________.

3 Answer the following questions.

a) How is Healing Brush Tool different from Spot Healing Brush Tool?

b) What is the purpose of Clone Stamp Tool?

c) Name the three variants of Eraser Tool.

d) What is the use of layers in Photoshop.

e) What is the use of filters?

f) How is Dodge Tool different from Burn Tool?

g) What do you understand by Warping text in Photoshop?

h) How will you add effects to a layer's contents?

Activity Time

1. Create a poster on School Carnival using various tools learnt in Photoshop. Add appropriate text wherever necessary.
2. Create an advertisement for a magazine on any product of your choice.
3. Try to design the logos of some famous brands in Photoshop.

Notes for the Teacher

- The teacher can demonstrate the use of various tools by taking appropriate examples.

WINDOWS MOVIE MAKER

Chapter 10

OBJECTIVES

After having studied this lesson, you will be able to:

- state the use of Windows Movie Maker.
- start Movie Maker.
- describe the elements of Windows Movie Maker interface.
- import picture, video and audio clips.
- edit video clips.
- add video effects, transition, titles and credits to a movie.
- add audio to a movie.
- save a movie.

Windows Movie Maker is a video creating and editing software program that is present on computers having Microsoft Windows Me, XP and Vista Operating System.

Windows Movie Maker is software that lets you capture, edit and arrange audio and video content to create movies or presentations. It includes features such as video effects, transitions, titles and credits and narration that can be used to easily create home movies, photo albums or any other type of presentations.

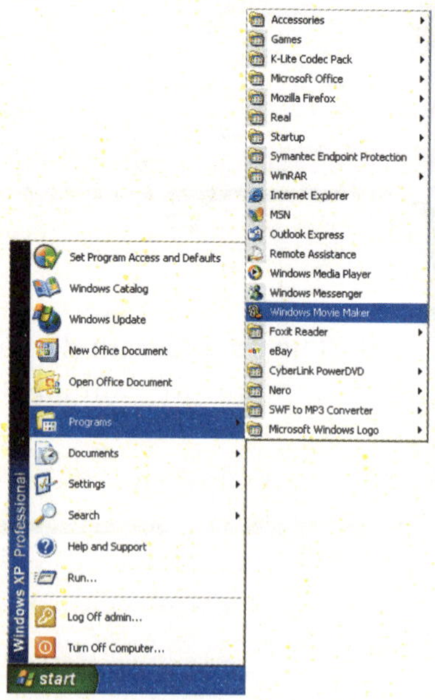

Fig 10.1 *Starting Movie Maker*

STARTING MOVIE MAKER

To start Movie Maker, click on **Start ▶ Programs ▶ Windows Movie Maker** (**Fig.10.1**).

The Movie Maker window appears (**Fig. 10.2**).

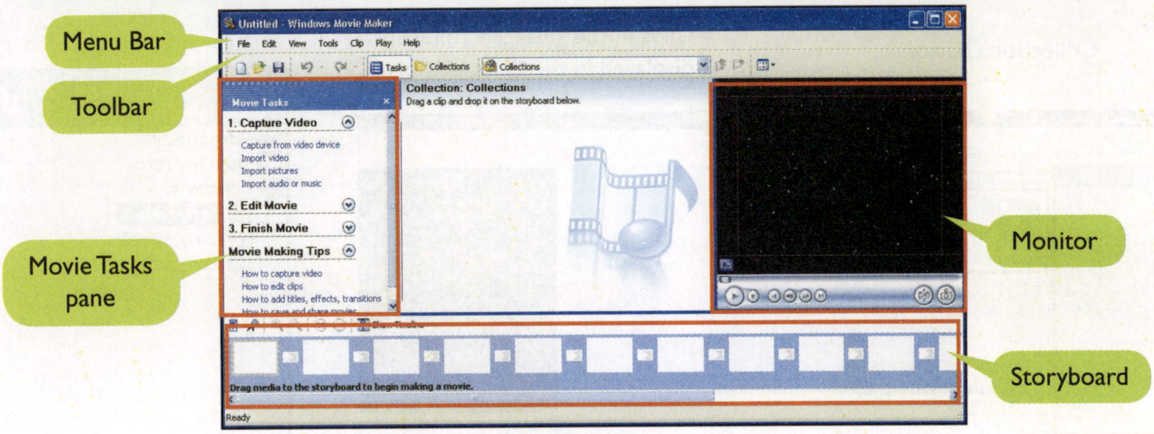

Fig 10.2 *Movie Maker window*

Let us first get familiar with the Movie Maker interface.

MOVIE MAKER INTERFACE

The interface of Movie Maker consists of following elements (**Fig. 10.2**).

1. **Menu Bar.** The Menu bar of Movie Maker consists of seven menus (**Fig. 10.3**). You can use the commands in the Menu bar to perform various tasks in Movie Maker.

Fig 10.3 *Menu bar*

2. **Toolbar.** The toolbar contains buttons that help in performing some common tasks quickly (**Fig. 10.4**). These tasks include—opening a new project, saving a project, etc.

Fig 10.4 *Toolbar*

3. **Movie Tasks Pane.** The Movie Tasks pane provides options for performing various tasks like importing or adding videos and pictures to the project, editing movies, adding effects to a movie, etc (**Fig. 10.2**).
4. **Collections Pane.** The Collections pane appears when you click on the Collections button on the Toolbar, (**Fig.10.5**). The Collections pane displays the list of collections containing clips on the left. The clips in the selected collection are displayed in the Contents pane on the right.
5. **Monitor.** Monitor is used to view individual pictures, video clips or an entire project. You can use the monitor to preview the movie made by you (**Fig. 10.7**).

   You can use the buttons on the left side of the monitor to play, stop, forward or rewind an individual clip or an entire project. The buttons on the right side of the monitor are used to perform functions such as splitting a video or an audio clip into two smaller clips or taking a picture of the current frame that is displayed in the monitor.

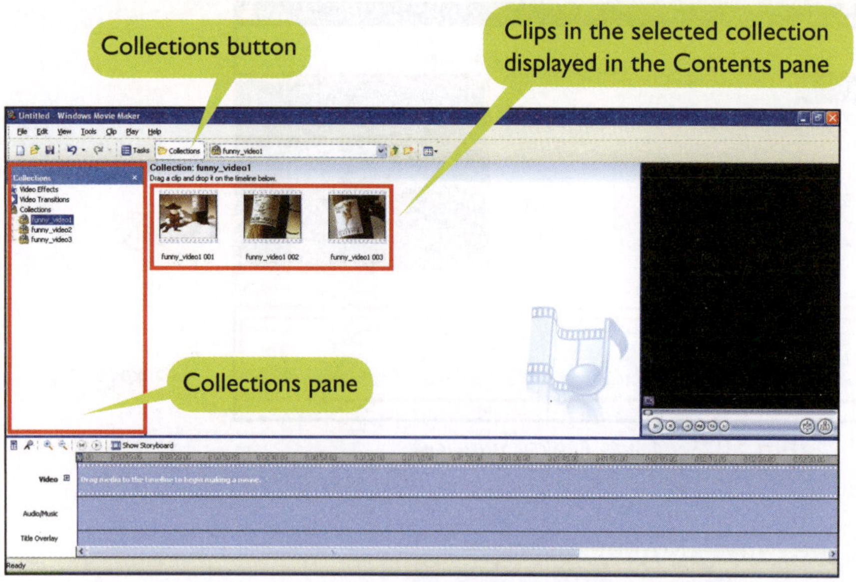

Fig 10.5 *Movie Maker window displaying Collections pane*

Fig 10.6 *Collections pane*

Fig 10.7 *Monitor*

6. **Storyboard and Timeline.** There are two important views in Movie Maker—Storyboard view and Timeline view. You can switch between the two views by making use of the View menu.

a) **Storyboard.** The Storyboard is the default view in Movie Maker. It is present at the bottom of the screen. It displays the sequence of video clips or pictures in your project. You can use this view to rearrange the order of clips in your movie.

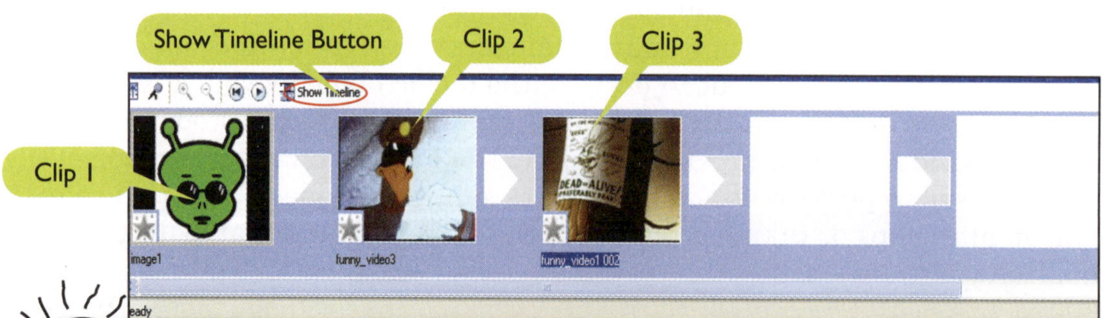

Fig 10.8 *Storyboard*

b) **Timeline.** Clicking the **Show Timeline** button located above the Storyboard (**Fig.10.8**) displays the Timeline view. You can use the timeline to review or modify the timings of clips in your movie, **Fig. 10.9**.

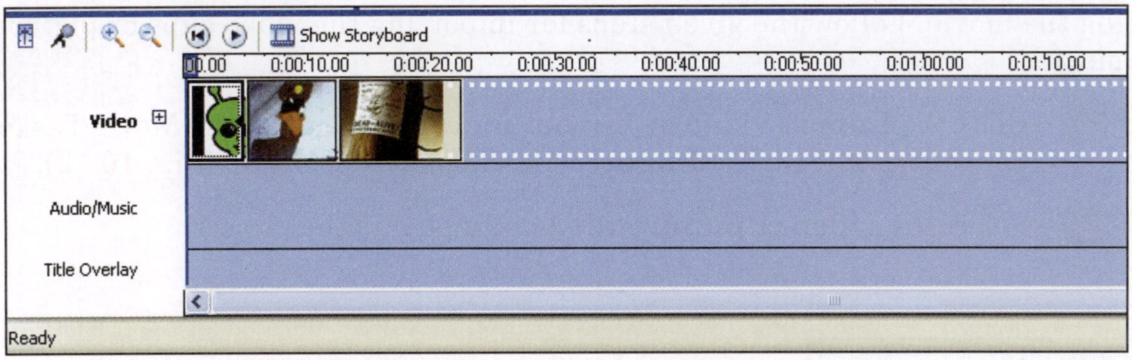

Fig 10.9 *Timeline showing timings for various clips*

QUICK QUESTION

1. **Match the following:**

Interface Element	Use
a) Storyboard	i) lets you preview the movie
b) Timeline	ii) provides a thumbnail view of the pictures, video clips, an audio files imported in Movie Maker
c) Movie Tasks pane	iii) lets you rearrange the order of clips in your movie
d) Collections pane	iv) provides options for performing common tasks such as importing videos in the Movie Maker
e) Monitor	v) lets you review or modify the timings of clips in your movie.

WORKING IN MOVIE MAKER

You create a movie by starting a new project in Movie Maker. A project is a file that contains information about the arrangement of various pictures, video/audio clips and effects used to make a movie. The File menu has options for creating, saving and opening projects (**Fig. 10.10**).

- Click **File ▶ New Project** option to start a new project.
- Click **File ▶ Save Project** to save a project. Projects are saved with *.mswmm file extension.
- Click **File ▶ Open Project** to open an already saved project.

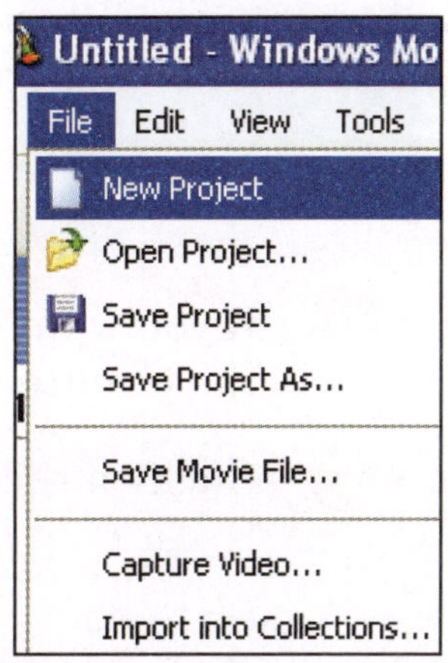

Fig 10.10 *File menu with options for creating, opening and saving a project*

➤ Importing Video Clips and Pictures

Before you start making a movie, you need to import the video clips and pictures that will be a part of your movie. These video clips and images will be used for making the movie. Follow the given steps for importing the video clips or pictures in a movie.

Step 1 Click the **Import video** or **Import pictures** option in the Movie Tasks pane (Fig. 10.11). The **Import File** dialog box opens up (Fig. 10.12).

Step 2 Select the **video** or **picture file** to be added to the project.

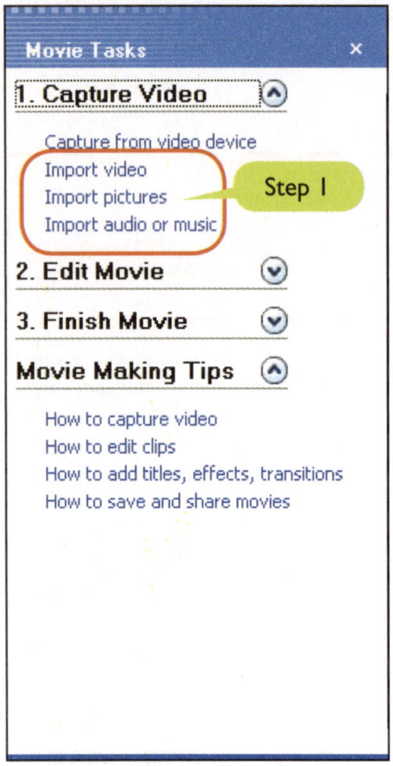

Fig 10.11 *Movie Tasks pane*

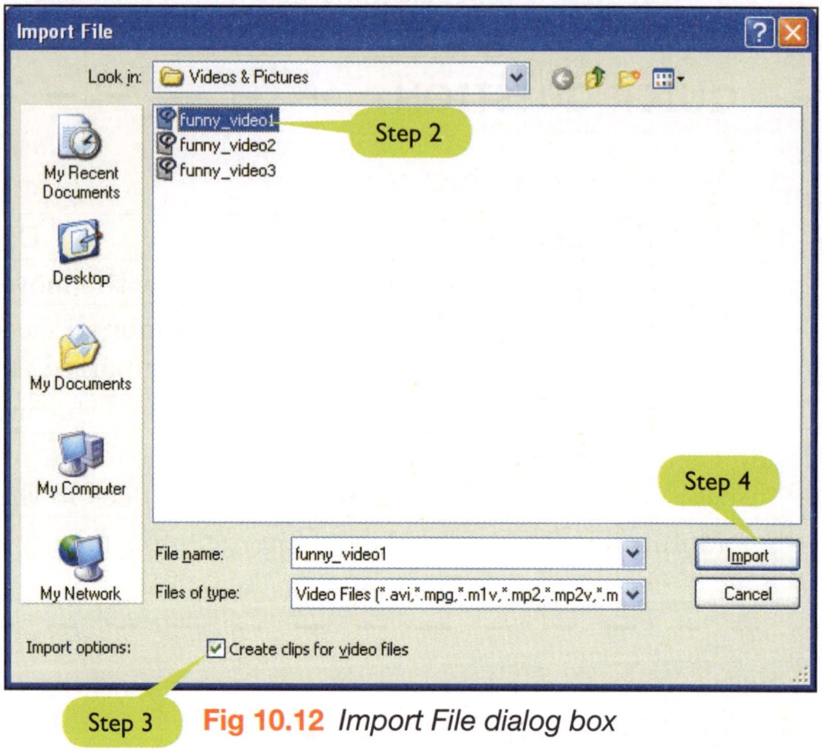

Fig 10.12 *Import File dialog box*

Step 3 If you want the selected video files to be separated into smaller clips, select the **Create clips for video files** check box.

Step 4 Click on the **Import** button.

The selected clips or pictures are added in the Collections pane.

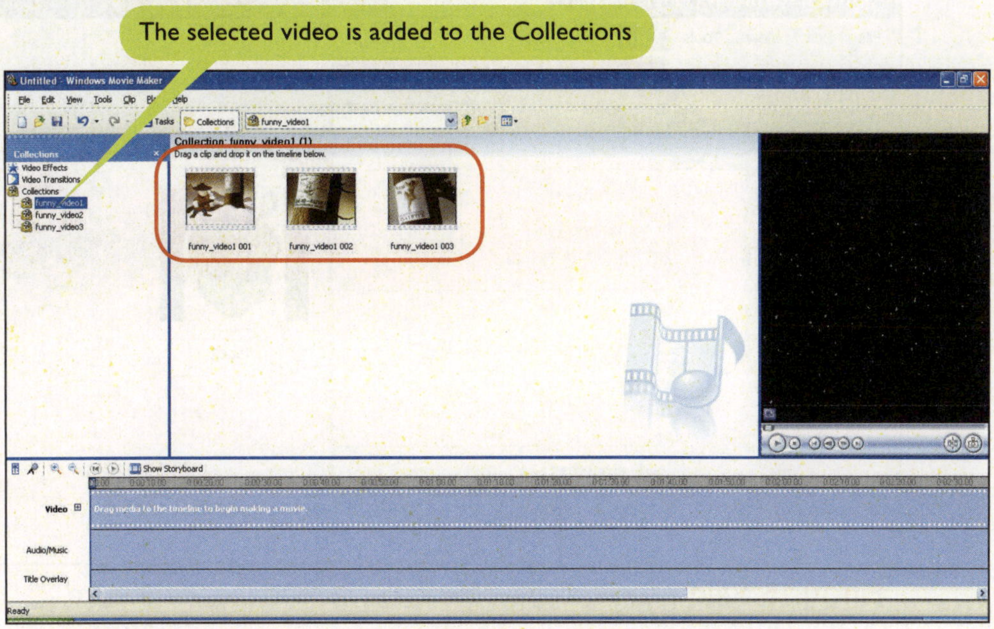

Fig 10.13 *Movie Maker window with the imported files*

➤ Working with Video Clips and Pictures

The imported clips and pictures can be used for making a movie by placing them in the required order in the Storyboard.

Adding a clip or a picture to the Storyboard

Follow the given steps to add a clip or a picture to the Storyboard.

Step 1 In the Collections pane, choose the collection that contains the clips or pictures to be used in the movie (**Fig. 10.14**).

Step 2 Select the clip or the picture by clicking on it.

Step 3 Choose **Clip ▶ Add to Storyboard** (**Fig.10.15**).

The selected clip or picture gets added to the Storyboard (**Fig. 10.16**).

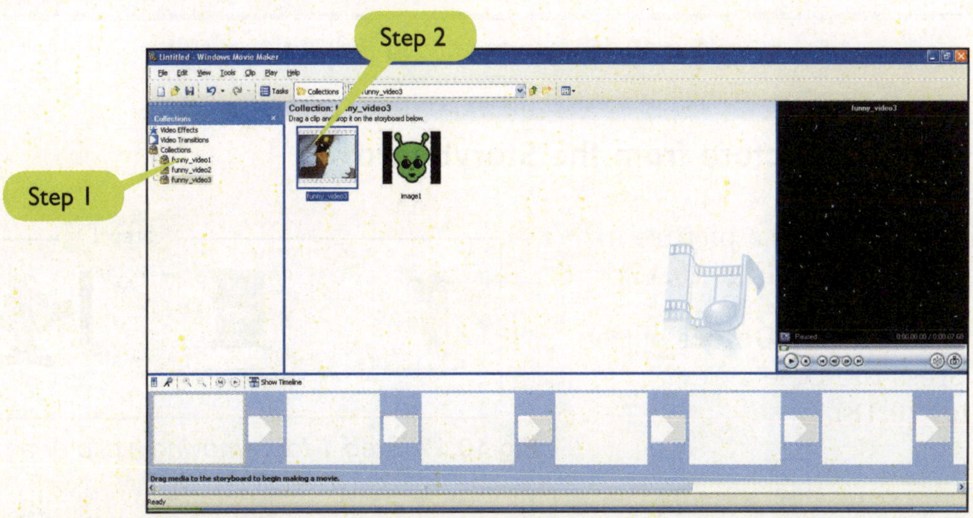

Fig 10.14 *Steps 1 and 2 for adding a clip or a picture to the Storyboard*

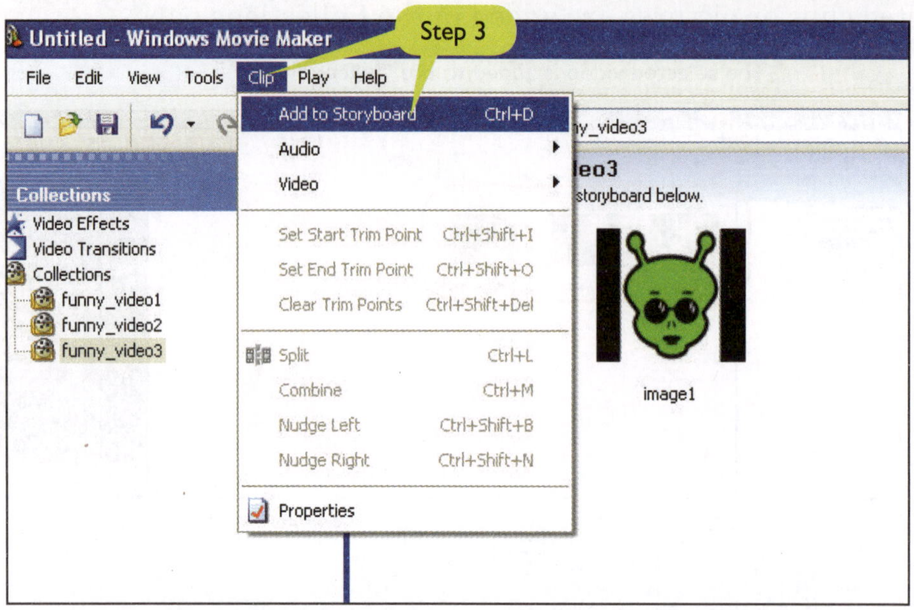

Fig 10.15 *Step 3 for adding a clip or a picture to the Storyboard*

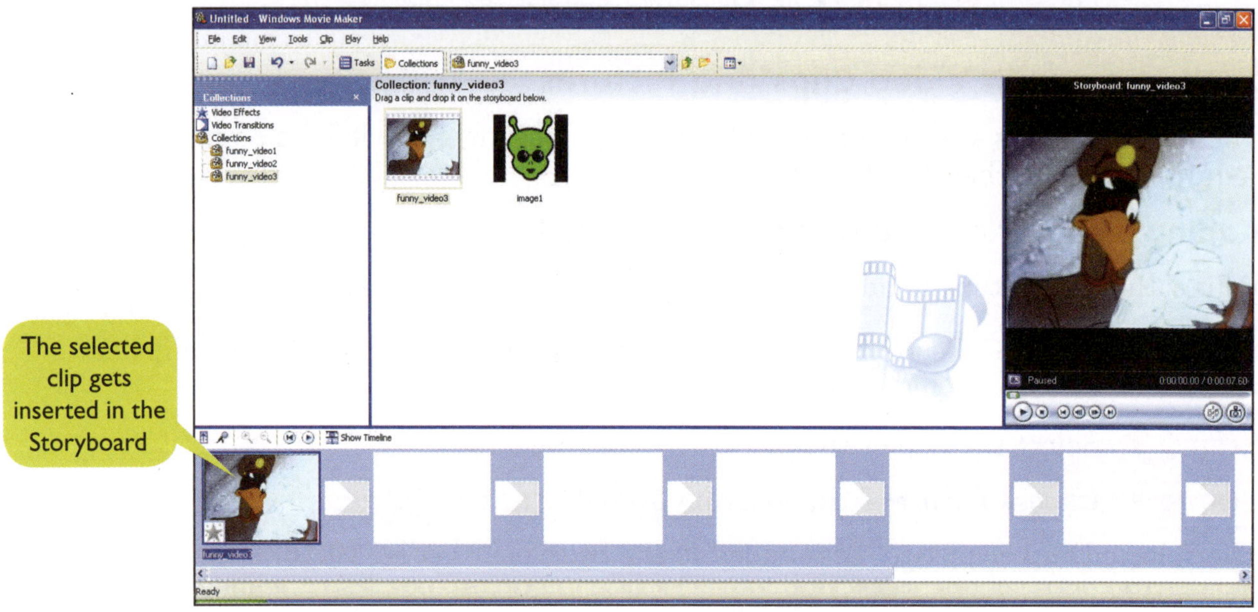

Fig 10.16 *Inserted clip in the Storyboard*

Removing a Clip or a Picture from the Storyboard

Step 1 Click on a clip or a picture in the Storyboard (**Fig. 10.17**).

Step 2 Choose **Edit ▶ Delete** option or press the Delete key (**Fig. 10.18**).

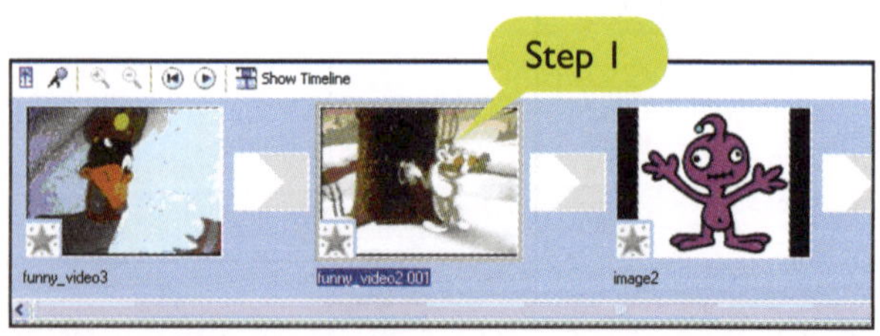

Fig 10.17 *Step 1 for removing a clip or a picture*

The selected clip is removed from the Storyboard.

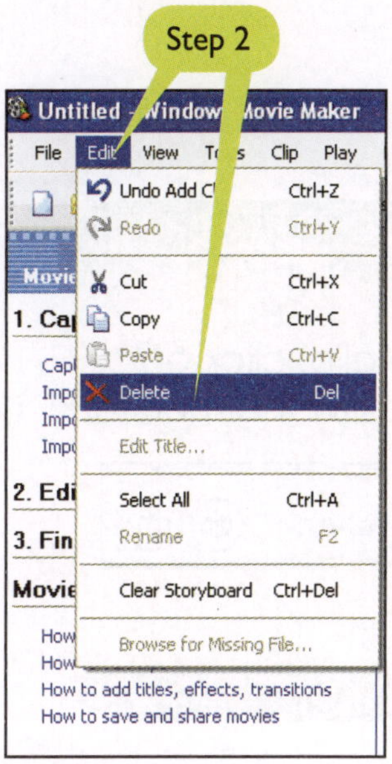

Fig 10.18 *Step 2 for removing a clip or a picture*

Quick Tip

- To quickly add a clip, click and drag the clip to the Storyboard.
- You can change the position of clips in the Storyboard by dragging or by making use of Cut and Paste option.

Quick Fact

The first version of Windows Movie Maker came with the release of the Millennium Edition of Windows or Windows Me.

Splitting a Clip

In order to divide or split a video clip into two clips, follow the given steps.

Step 1 Click the clip in the Storyboard that needs to be split (**Fig. 10.19**).

Step 2 Play the clip by clicking on the **Play** button of the monitor. Click the **Pause** button to pause the video at the point where you want to split the clip (**Fig. 10.20**).

Step 3 Choose **Clip ▶ Split** (**Fig. 10.21**).

The video clip splits into two parts.

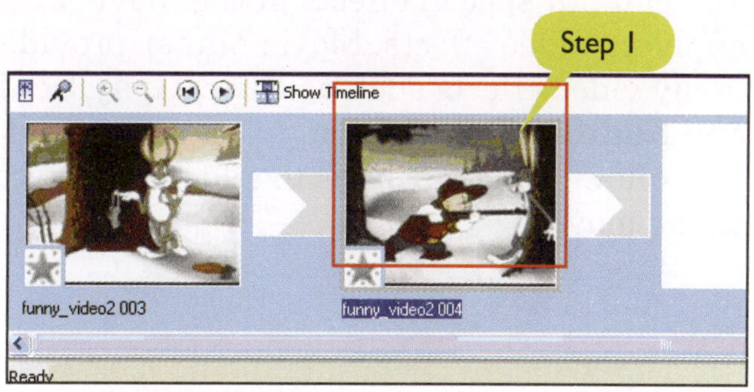

Fig 10.19 *Step 1 for splitting a clip*

Fig 10.20 *Step 2 for splitting a clip*

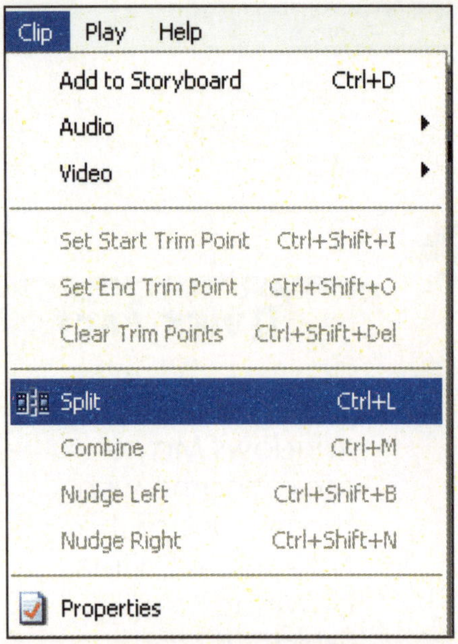

Fig 10.21 *Step 3 for splitting a clip*

Quick Tip

To quickly split a video clip, click on the Split Clip button below the monitor.

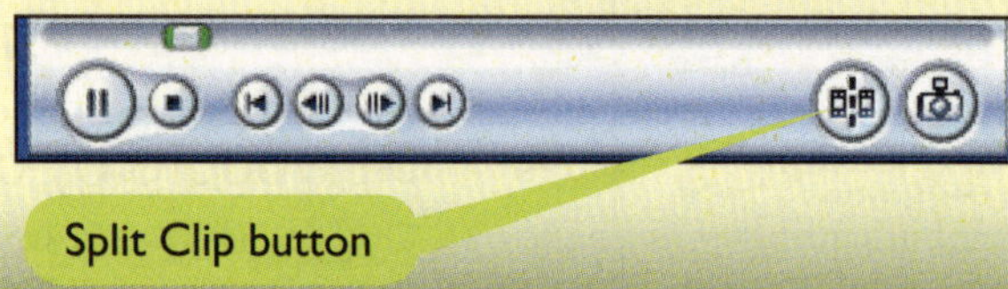

➤ Adding Effects in the Movie

After adding the desired clips or pictures in a movie, you can enhance the movie by adding different elements such as video effects, titles and credits, transitions, audio.

Let us discuss how these elements are added to a movie.

Adding Video Effects

You can put special effects in the movie by applying video effects. Movie Maker provides many video effects such as **Blur**, **Gray Scale**, and **Fade in from white**.

Follow the given steps to add video effects to the movie.

Fig 10.22 *Step 1 for adding video effects*

Step 1 Click the video clip or the picture on the Storyboard to which the video effect is to be applied.

Step 2 Choose **Tools ▶ Video Effects.** A number of video effects appear in the Contents pane.

Step 3 Click the desired video effect (Fig. 10.24).

Step 4 Choose **Clip ▶ Add to Storyboard** or simply drag the video effect on the video clip or the picture in the Storyboard.

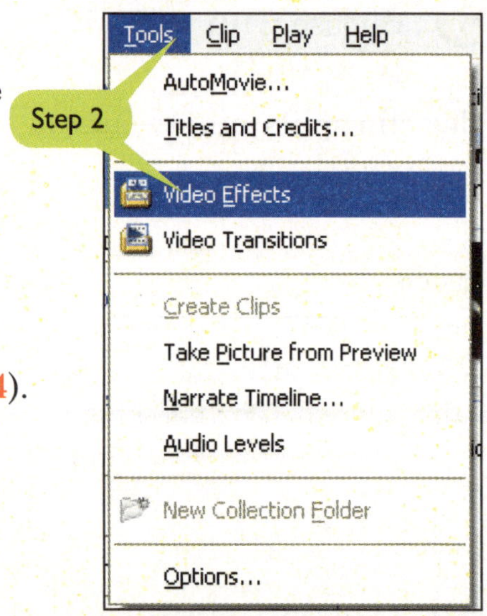

Fig 10.23 *Step 2 for adding video effects*

Fig 10.24 *Steps 3 and 4 for adding video effects*

When the video effect is applied to the video clip or picture, a small blue star appears in the lower-left corner of the video clip or picture in the Storyboard. You can preview the video effects in the Monitor.

> **QUICK TIP**
>
> Video Effects can also be accessed by choosing **Edit Movie ▶ View Video Effects** option in the Movie Tasks pane.

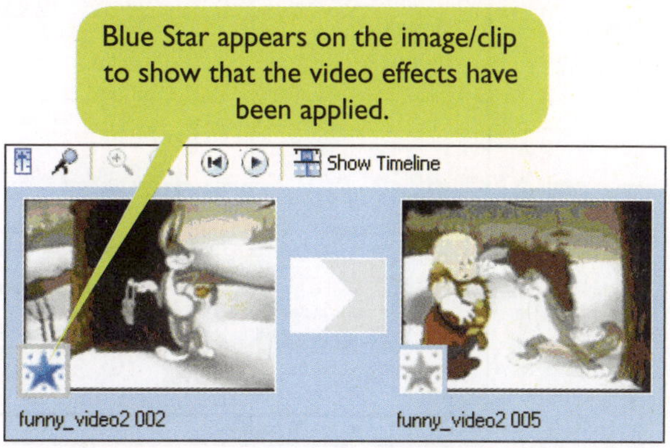

Fig 10.25 *Appearance of blue star*

➤ Adding Titles and Credits

Titles and **credits** let you add text to movies. You can add information such as the title of your movie, your name, the date, and so forth.

Titles can be added at any place in the movie—at the beginning or end of a movie, before or after a clip or overlaying a clip. However credits can be placed at the end of the movie only.

Step 1 Click **Tools ▶ Titles and Credits** (**Fig. 10.26**).

Step 2 Select the location where you want the text to appear in the movie (**Fig. 10.27**).

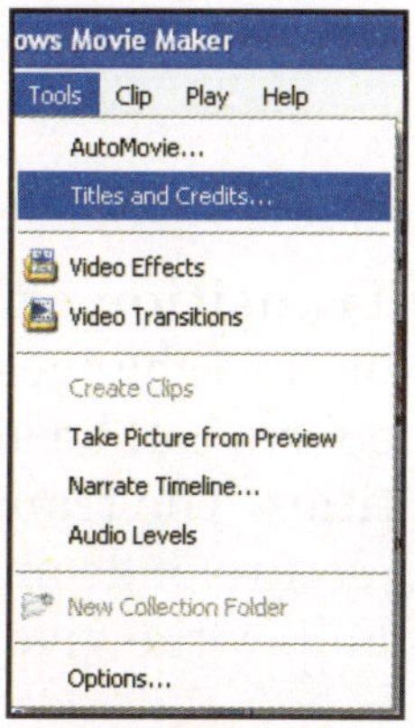

Fig 10.26 *Step 1 for adding titles and credits*

Step 3 Enter the required text (**Fig. 10.28**).

Step 4 Select an **animation style** for the text.

Step 5 Select the **font** and **color** for the text.

Step 6 Click on **Done, add title to movie** option to add the title or credits.

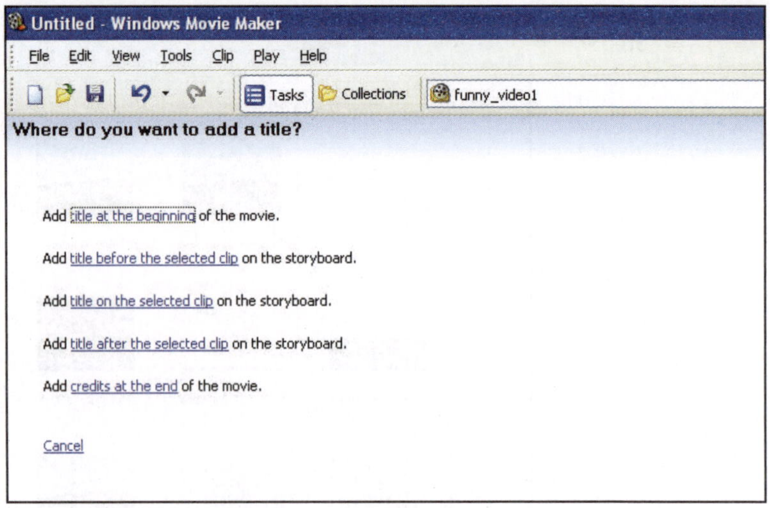

Fig 10.27 *Step 2 for adding titles and credits*

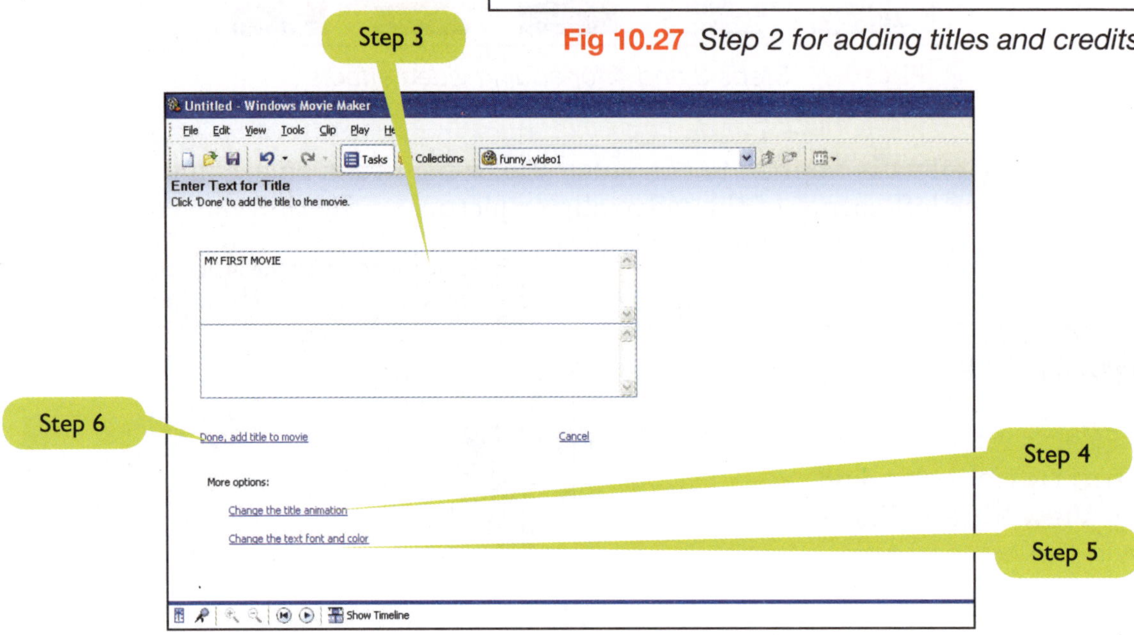

Fig 10.28 *Steps 3 to 6 for adding titles and credits*

You can preview the Titles and Credits added to the movie in the Monitor.

➤ Adding Transition Effects

Transition effects control the way how one video clip or picture changes into another video clip or picture. These effects can be added between two pictures, video clips or titles. The transition is displayed when one video clip or picture ends and the next video clip or picture is displayed. Follow the given steps to add a transition effect.

Fig 10.29 *Steps 1 for adding transition effects*

Step 1 On the Storyboard, select the **video clip** or **picture** before which you want to insert transition effect.

Step 2 Click **Tools ▶ Video Transitions** (**Fig. 10.30**). A number of transition effects appear.

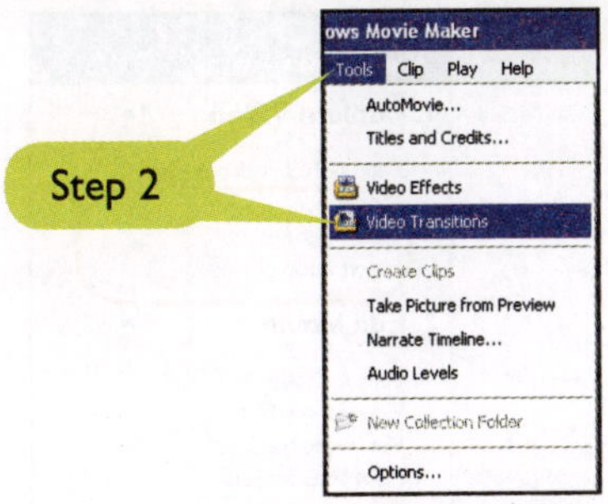

Fig 10.30 *Step 2 for adding transition effects*

Step 3 Choose a **transition effect**

Step 4 Click on **Clip ▶ Add to Storyboard** or simply drag the transition effect between the two clips.

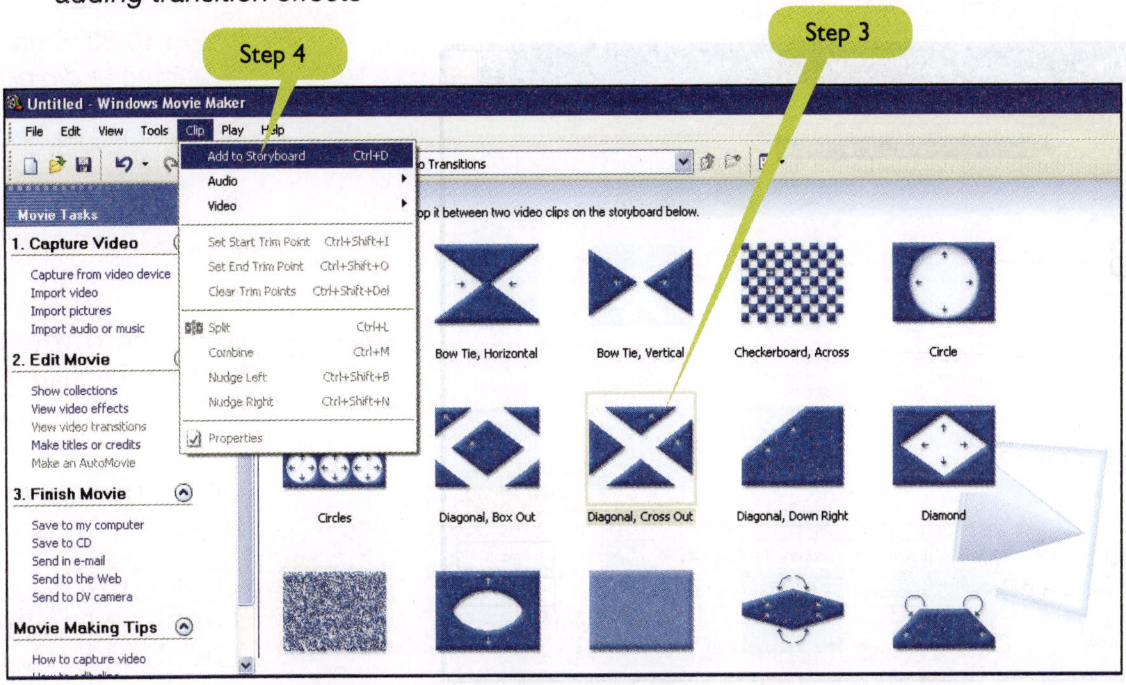

Fig 10.31 *Steps 3 and 4 for adding transition effects*

Fig 10.32 *Transition effects between two clips*

> **QUICK TIP**
>
> Transition Effects can also be accessed by choosing **Edit Movie ▶ View video transitions** option in the Movie Task pane.

The selected transition effect appears between two clips on the Storyboard. You can preview the effect on the monitor.

➤ Adding Music

Movie Maker also lets you add audio or music to the movies. Audio clips can be added in the Timeline view only. Follow the given steps to add audio or music to the movie.

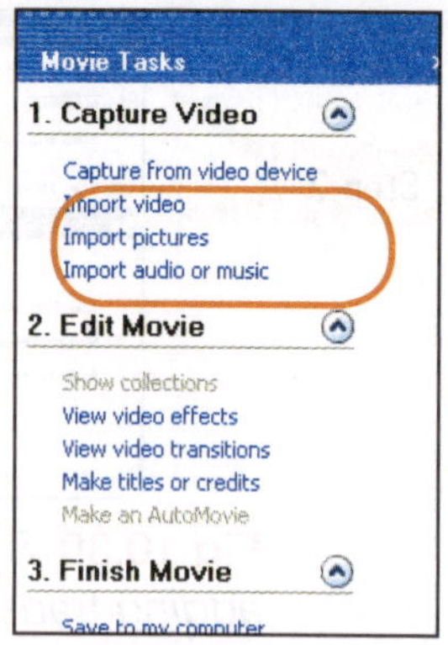

Fig 10.33 *Step 1 for adding audio clip*

Step 1 Click **Import audio or music** option on the Movie Tasks pane (**Fig. 10.33**). The **Import File** dialog box opens up (**Fig. 10.34**).

Step 2 Select the **audio file** to be added to the project.

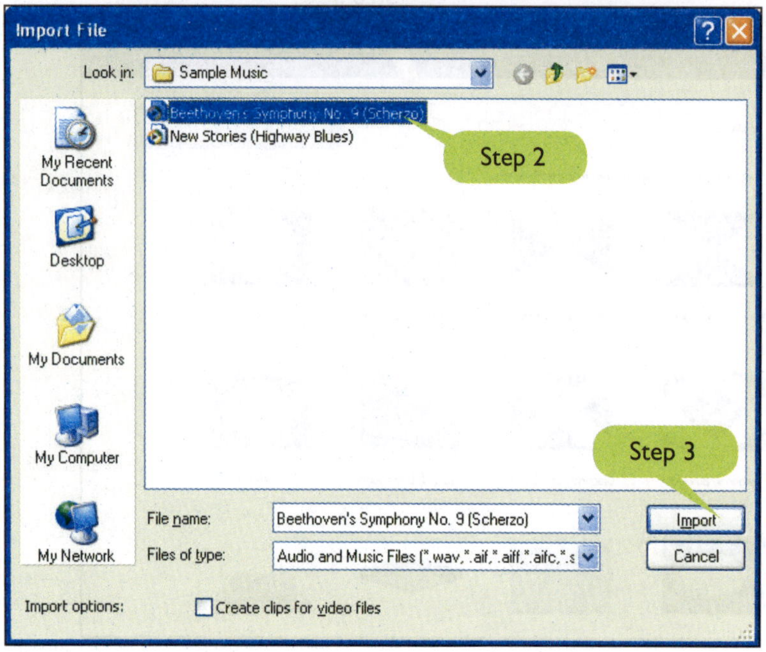

Fig 10.34 *Import File dialog box*

Step 3 Click the **Import** button. The selected audio files are added and displayed in the **Collections** pane (**Fig. 10.35**).

Step 4 Click **View ▶ Timeline** or **Show Timeline** button to switch to Timeline view, (**Fig.10. 36**).

Step 5 Choose a position in the timeline where the audio clip needs to be added (**Fig. 10.37**).

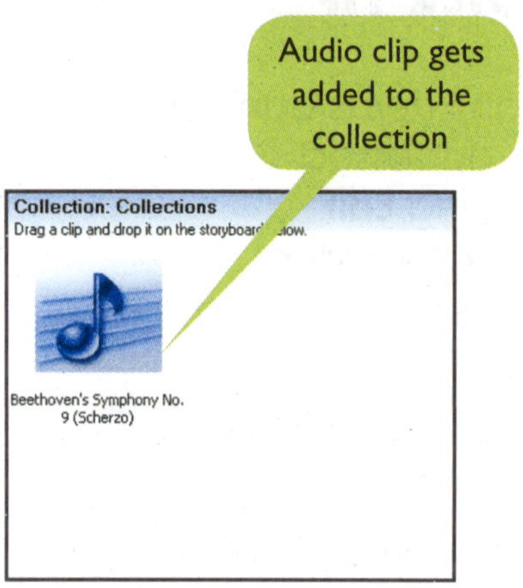

Fig 10.35 *Imported audio clip*

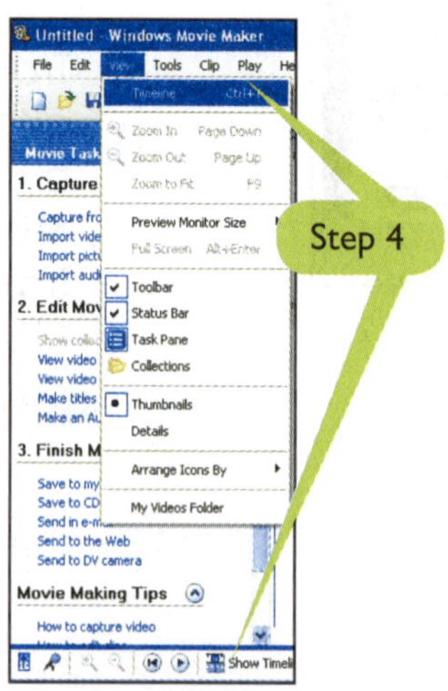

Fig 10.36 *Step 4 for adding audio clip*

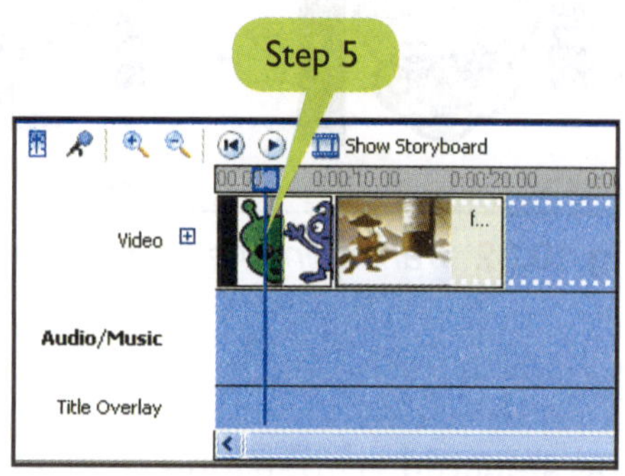

Fig 10.37 *Step 5 for adding audio clip*

Step 6 Select the imported audio clip and click **Clip ▶ Add to Timeline** (**Fig. 10.38**).

The audio clip gets inserted to the Timeline (**Fig. 10.39**).

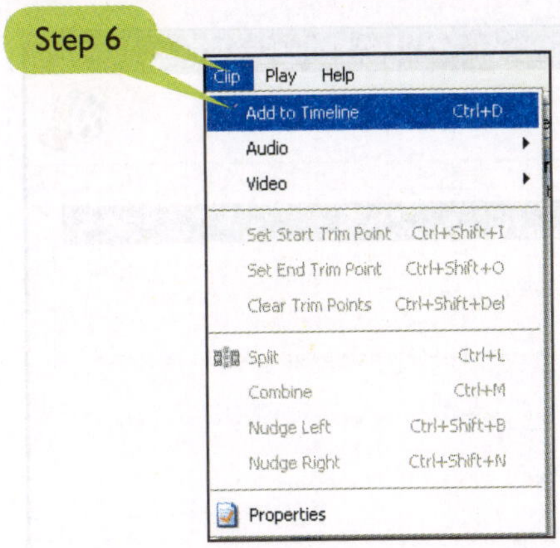

Fig 10.38 *Step 6 for adding audio clip*

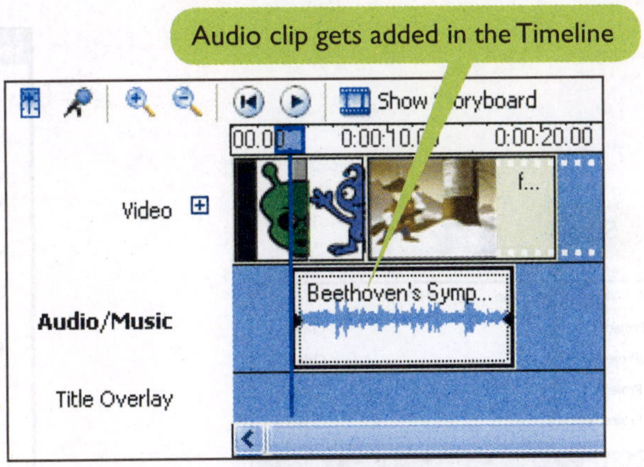

Fig 10.39 *Timeline after adding audio clip*

QUICK QUESTION

2. Fill in the blanks.

a) You can preview transition effects in the ____________.

b) Audio clips can be added only in the ____________ view.

c) Credits appear at ____________ of a movie.

d) The ____________ control the way how one video clip or picture disappears and next video clip or picture appears in a movie.

e) The extension of Movie Maker project is ____________.

➤ Saving a Movie

You can create a movie when you have completed editing and adding effects in the project. Follow the given steps to save a movie.

Step 1 Click on **File ▶ Save Movie File** option (**Fig. 10.40**). The **Save Movie Wizard** appears on screen (**Fig.10.41**).

Step 2 Choose the location where the file is to be saved. Click on the **Next** button.

Step 3 Enter the **file name** and **folder** where you want to save the movie (**Fig. 10.42**).

Step 4 Choose the setting for saving the movie. By default the movie will be saved in ***.wmv** (windows media video) format. However you can save the movie file in other file formats such as ***.avi** (audio video interleave). Click the **Next** button to complete the saving process (**Fig. 10.43–10.44**).

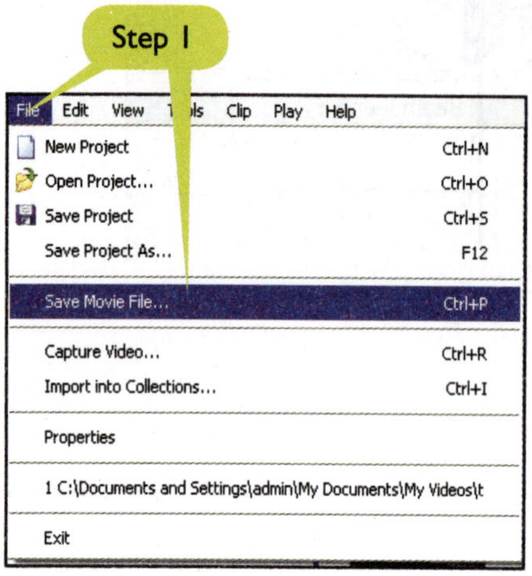

Fig 10.40 *Step 1 for saving a movie*

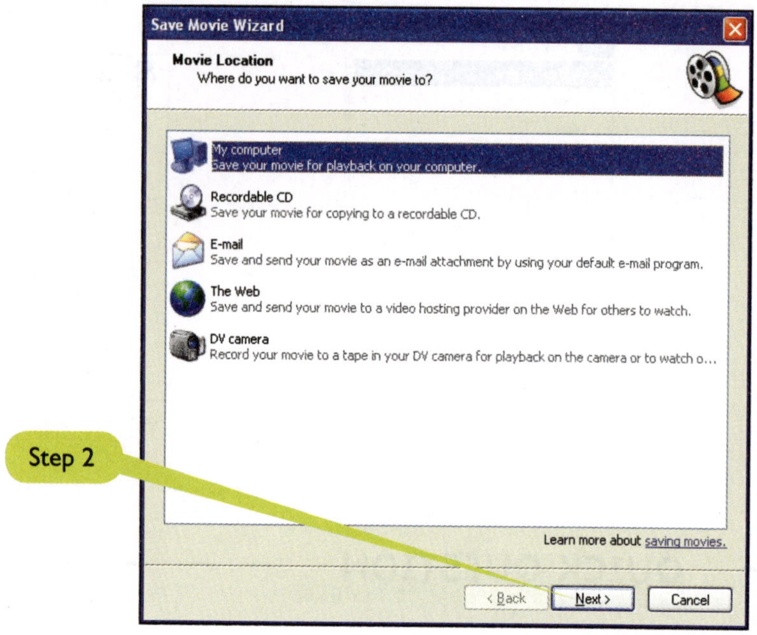

Fig 10.41 *Step 2 for saving a movie*

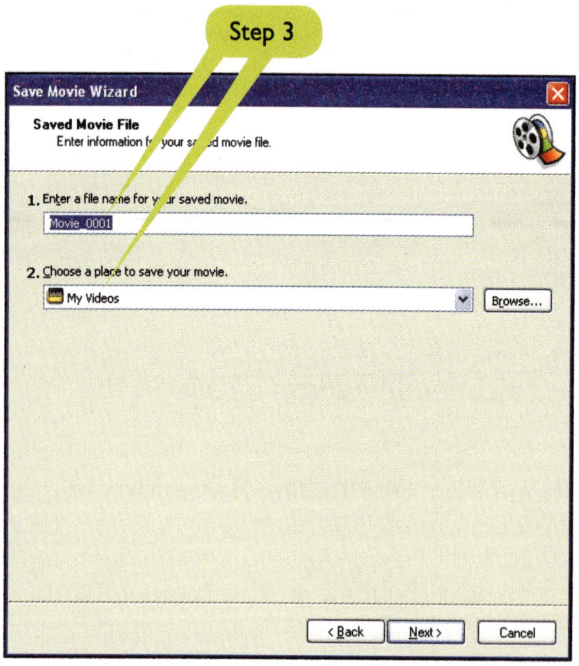

Fig 10.42 *Step 3 for saving a movie*

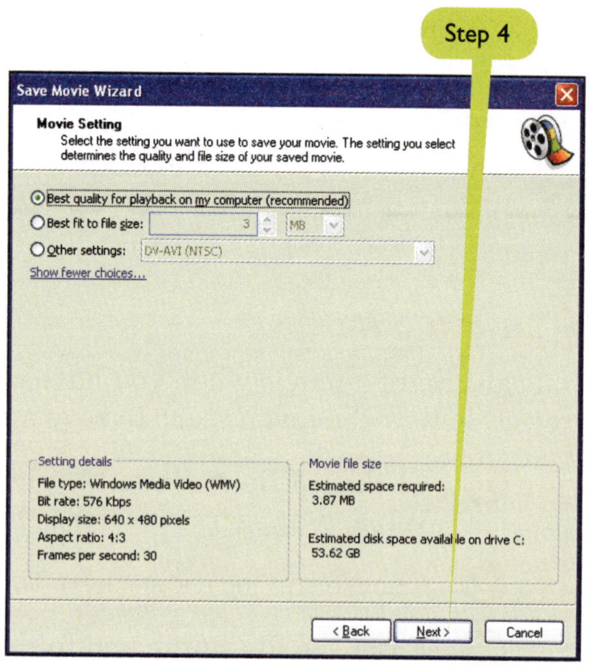

Fig 10.43 *Step 4 for saving a movie*

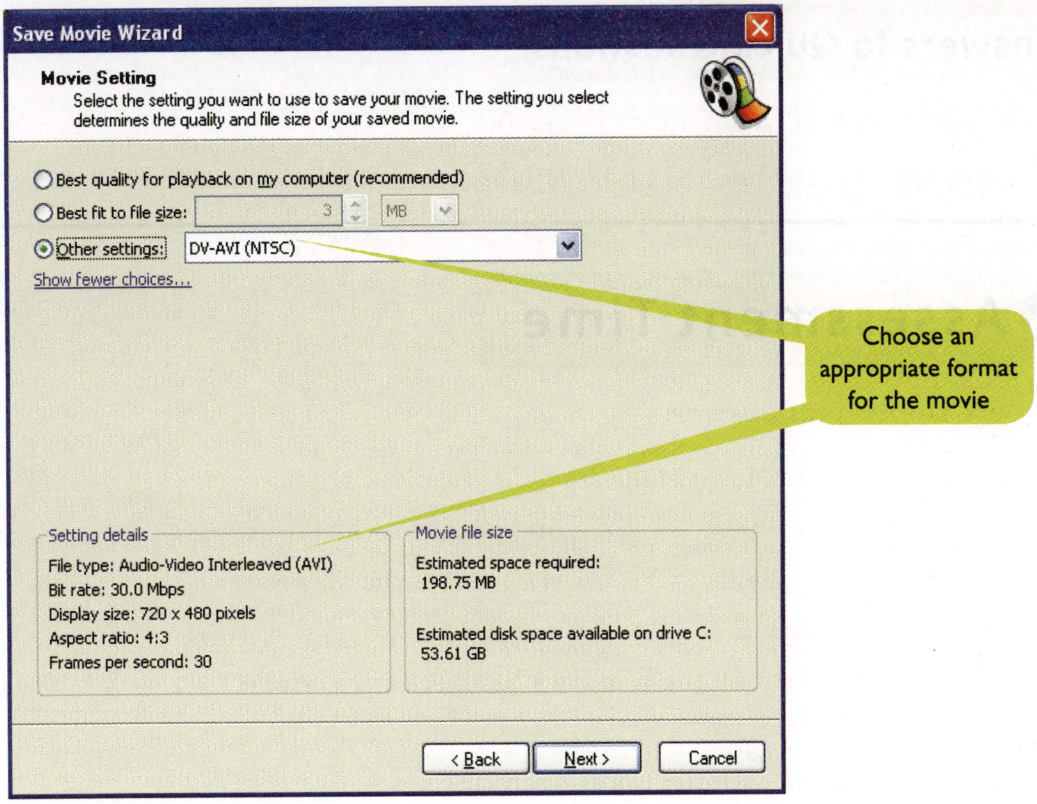

Fig 10.44 *Choosing appropriate format for the movie*

Recap Time

- Windows Movie Maker is a video creating and editing software.
- The Windows Movie Maker interface consists of various elements—Menu bar, Toolbar, Panes, Storyboard/Timeline and Monitor.
- The Movie Tasks pane has options for performing common tasks like importing or adding video clips and pictures to the project, editing movie, adding effects to movie etc.
- The Collections pane provides a Thumbnail view of videos, pictures and music imported into Movie Maker for use.
- The Monitor is used to preview the contents of the movie.
- The Storyboard displays the sequence of clips in the movie.
- The Timeline is used to review or modify the timing of video clips or pictures.
- You can add video effects, transition effects and titles and credits to enhance a movie.
- Movies created in Windows Movie Maker can be saved in different file formats such as *.wmv and *.avi.

Answers to Quick Questions

1. a) – iii) b) – v) c) – iv) d) – ii) e) – i)
2. a) Monitor b) Timeline c) End d) Transition effects e) .mswmm

Assessment Time

1 Choose the correct answer.

a) You can use Windows Movie Maker to

i) make a presentation. ii) make a video.

iii) make a photo album. iv) All of the above

b) Windows Movie Maker

i) is included free with the Windows XP operating system.

ii) is not free.

iii) is included free with the Linux operating system.

iv) None of the above

c) Identify the interface element in Movie Maker window that lets you review the timings of various clips in your movie.

i) Storyboard ii) Timeline

iii) Movie Tasks pane ii) Monitor

d) The star symbol ★ indicates that a ______________ has been applied to the clip.

i) transition ii) video effect

iii) titles and credits iv) video clip

e) Which of the following interface element lets you rearrange the order of clips in your movie?

i) Storyboard ii) Movie Tasks pane

iii) Monitor iv) Timeline

2 Fill in the blanks using the words given below.

Transition	Tools	Movie	Titles	Credits	Collections

a) You can import video clips by clicking on the Import option on the ______________ tasks pane.

b) ______________ effects appear when one clip changes to the other.

c) ________________ and ________________ let you add text to a movie.

d) The video effects and transitions options are present under the ________________ menu.

e) The ________________ tasks pane displays the video clips, pictures or audio clips that you can add to your movie.

3 Answer the following questions.

a) Give the use of the following in the Movie Maker interface.

i) Storyboard ii) Timeline

iii) Movie Tasks pane iv) Collections task pane

b) What is the difference between Video Effects and Video Transition?

c) Write the steps to add audio to your movie.

d) What is the use of Titles and Credits option in the Movie Maker?

Activity Time

1. It is the wedding anniversary of your grandparents. Collect their photographs (scan them) and make a nostalgic movie to be shown on the anniversary day.
2. Make a movie of your recent trip by combining pictures/videos and show it to your friends.
3. Collect images of your favourite story. Create an interesting movie on the story using the Movie Maker.

Notes for the Teacher

- The teacher should discuss various other software used for video editing.

PROJECT TIME

I. MS ACCESS

➤ PROJECT 1

A hospital wants to store the details of all the doctors in a database. Design the **Table: Doctor** in MS Access and insert seven records.

Table: Doctor

Field Name	Data type	Property	Description
Doc_id	Number	Primary Key Field Size: Integer	Unique Id of the Doctor
Doc_name	Text	Field Size=40 Caption="Name"	Full name of the Doctor
Doc_dob	Date/Time		Date of birth of the Doctor
Doc_fee	Number	Field Size=Double Default Value=300 Validation Rule: fee should be greater than 100 Validation Text: "Inappropriate value of fee"	Fee charged by the Doctor on a per visit basis
Doc_experience	Number	Field Size=Integer	The number of years of experience of the doctor
Doctor_category	Text	Required="Yes", Allow Zero Length="No"	Category or specialisation of the Doctor such as Cardiologist and Pediatrician
Doctor_profile	Memo		Profile of the Doctor including educational qualifications, awards, hospitals worked in, etc

➤ PROJECT 2

A Travel and Tourism company wants to store details of various buses that it operates. Design the **Table: Bus_details** in MS Access and insert six records.

Table: Bus_details

Field Name	Data type	Property	Description
Bus_no	Number	Primary Key Field Size: Integer	Bus number
Bus_origin	Text	Field Size=40 Caption="Starting Point"	Name of the starting place
Bus_dest	Text	Field Size=40 Caption="Destination Point"	Name of the destination place
Bus_Km	Number	Field Size=Single Validation Rule: value should be greater than 0 Validation Text: "Inappropriate value"	Total kilometers from origin to destination
Bus_type	Text	Default Value="Volvo" Required="Yes", Allow Zero Length="No"	Category of Bus (Volvo, Deluxe etc)
Bus_cap	Number	Field Size=Integer	Number of seats in the Bus

II. HTML

➤ PROJECT 1

Design a website using HTML that has lessons in various subjects for the school students. You may consider the layout shown alongside for the main page. Choose 4 to 6 topics from your school curriculum and design webpages on them. The main page should contain links to these pages.

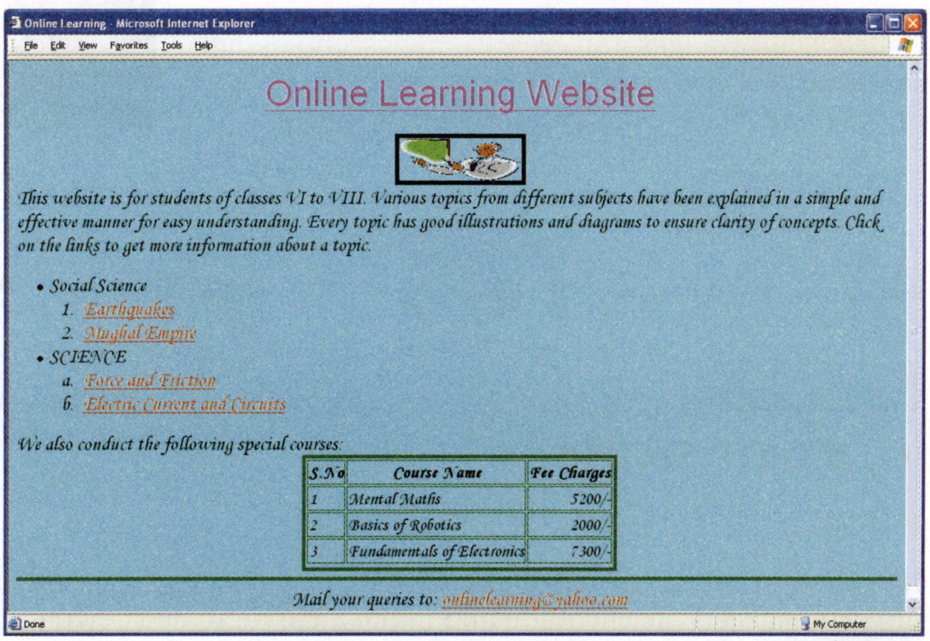

III. MICROSOFT FRONTPAGE

➤ PROJECT 1

Design a website for a 'Play School' in your area. You may consider the layout shown alongside for the main page. The other pages can contain information about the various features of the school.

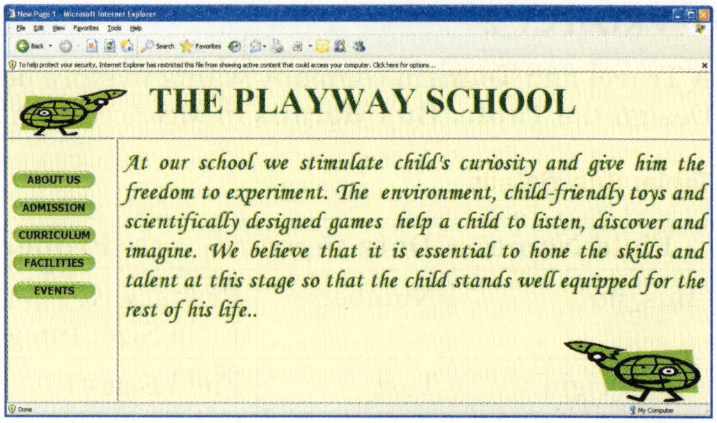

IV. VISUAL BASIC

➤ PROJECT 1

Create a Visual Basic Application that takes the Basic Salary, House Rent Allowance (HRA) and Conveyance Allowance from the user. It should then display the Salary and the Bonus. Salary is calculated as Basic Salary+House Rent Allowance+Conveyance. The Bonus is 5% of the calculated Salary.

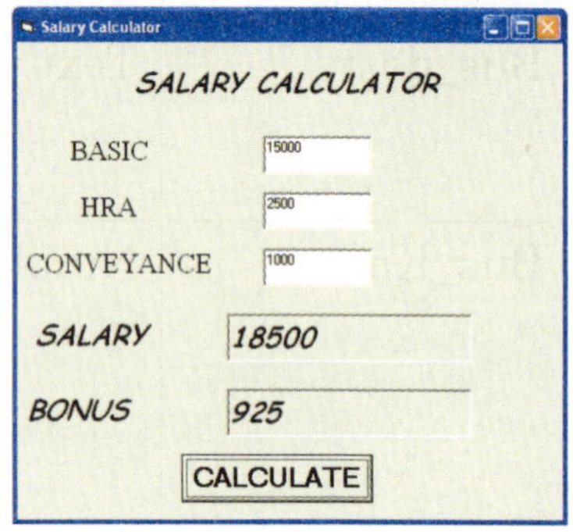

V. ADOBE PHOTOSHOP

➤ PROJECT 1: Creating a Collage

Collect pictures of some of the monuments in India and create a collage.

➤ PROJECT 2: Creating a Scene

Collect some images and create a new scene using some parts of the images. For example, three images have been used to create a new image.

 +  +  = 

VI. MOVIE MAKER

➤ PROJECT 1

It is time to bid farewell to class XII batch. Collect pictures/videos showing some of the important facets of school life and make a movie to be shown at the farewell function.

SAMPLE OLYMPIAD QUESTIONS

1. **The geographical area covered by Metropolitan Area Network is more than that of**
   a) LAN. b) WAN.
   c) Internet. d) None of these
2. **In which of the following topologies all computers are connected to one computer?**
   a) Bus b) Ring
   c) Mesh d) Star
3. **The layout or the manner in which the computers are connected to one another in a network is referred to as the**
   a) protocol. b) topology.
   c) bus. d) node.
4. **Find the odd one out.**
   a) UTP cable
   b) Coaxial cable
   c) Fibre Optic cable
   d) Microwave communication
5. **A device that has the hardware or MAC address and is attached to a computer to enable it to communicate over the network.**
   a) NIC b) Router
   c) Hub d) Switch
6. **Internet is an example of**
   a) LAN. b) MAN.
   c) WAN. d) None of these
7. **The advantages of a network is/are:**
   a) Resource Sharing
   b) File Sharing
   c) Ease of communication
   d) All of these
8. **The transmission medium that offers the maximum speed of transmission is**
   a) optical fibre cable.
   b) unshielded twisted pair cable.
   c) shielded twisted pair cable.
   d) coaxial cable.
9. **Which hardware device or software is used to prevent unauthorised access to the network?**
   a) Hub b) Switch
   c) Firewall d) None of these
10. **A device used to connect computers in a network is**
    a) hub. b) switch.
    c) firewall. d) None of these
11. **A DBMS that stores data in the form of tables.**
    a) Relational Database Management System
    b) Network Database Management System
    c) Hierarchical Database Management System
    d) None of these
12. **A Primary key**
    a) can have repetitive values and can be left blank.
    b) cannot have repetitive values and can be left blank.
    c) cannot have repetitive values and cannot be left blank.
    d) None of these

13 **The extension of MS Access files is:**

a) .mdb b) .xls
c) .vbp d) .doc

14 **Vertical columns in a table are known as**

a) fields. b) attributes.
c) records. d) both a) and b).

15 **Field properties can be set in**

a) Design View.
b) Datasheet View
c) Both a) and b).
d) None of these

16 **In MS Access, the data type that can store more characters than text data type is**

a) Date/Time. b) Number.
c) AutoNumber. d) Memo.

17 **Find the odd one out.**

a) .jpg b) .gif
c) .tiff d) .doc

18 **The field property in MS Access that is used to put conditions on the data that can be entered in a field is**

a) Default value.
b) Validation Rule.
c) Validation Text.
d) Caption.

19 **In MS Access, values in the fields with this data type are incremented automatically when a new record is inserted.**

a) AutoNumber b) Text
c) Memo d) Number

20 **In MS Access, this property is used to give an alternate, more descriptive name to a field.**

a) Format
b) Field Size
c) Caption
d) Required

21 **The number of allowed primary keys in a table is/are**

a) one.
b) two.
c) three.
d) as many as the user wants.

22 **Visual Basic projects are saved with an extension of:**

a) .vbp b) .vba
c) .frm d) .xls

23 **This control in Visual Basic is used for accepting text or numeric values.**

a) Text control
b) Command Button control
c) Label control
d) None of these

24 **The method to display message on the form window is**

a) Show. b) Hide.
c) Print. d) None of these

25 **Microsoft FrontPage is a/an**

a) HTML editor.
b) programming language.
c) operating system.
d) None of these

26 **A picture with one or more clickable areas or links is known as the**

a) Image Map. b) Frame.
c) Clip Art. d) None of these

27 **In Microsoft FrontPage, the Page view that lets you design the webpage as well as view the HTML code is**

a) Design View. b) Code View.
c) Split View. d) Preview View.

28 **Which of the following is not an attribute of `<IMG>` tag?**

a) alt b) src
c) background d) height

29 **Which attribute of TABLE tag to specify the spacing between the cells?**

a) border
b) cellspacing
c) cellpadding
d) None of these

30 **The attribute of TABLE tag allows you to specify the spacing between the content and the wall of the cell is referred to as:**

a) border.
b) cellspacing.
c) cellpadding.
d) None of these

31 **Which of the following is not a container tag?**

a) <IMG> b) <A>
c) <TABLE> d) <HEAD>

32 **The attribute of <IMG> tag used to specify text that appears in case there are problems loading the image.**

a) src b) alt
c) text d) None of these

33 **<OL> tag is used to create a**

a) bulleted list.
b) numbered or ordered list.
c) unnumbered list.
d) none of these

34 **The attribute of anchor tag that is used to identify different sections of the page by assigning them unique names is**

a) name. b) href.
c) section. d) None of these

35 **The tool(s) in Adobe Photoshop that lets you select parts of an image is/are:**

a) Lasso tools
b) Marquee tools
c) Magic Wand Tool
d) All of the above

36 **The tool in Adobe Photoshop that lets you select those areas of an image which have a similar colour.**

a) Crop Tool
b) Dodge Tool
c) Move Tool
d) Magic Wand Tool

37 **The tool used to darken the pixels in Adobe Photoshop is**

a) Dodge Tool.
b) Burn Tool.
c) Smudge Tool.
d) Clone Stamp Tool.

38 **Find the odd one out.**

a) Crop Tool b) Brush Tool
c) Pencil Tool d) Gradient Tool

39 **You can view more than one webpage in the same browser window by making use of**

a) Marquee.
b) Frames.
c) Interactive buttons.
d) None of these

40 **The colour of links can be controlled with the help of attributes like link, alink and vlink. They are attributes of**

a) <BODY> tag b) <A> tag
c) <IMG> tag d) <OL> tag

TECH TERMS

A

Antivirus software: A software used to protect the computer from different types of malware such as virus and worms.

Attribute (or Field): A vertical column in a table that stores one type of information about an item or an object.

B

Blur Tool: A tool in Photoshop that softens the selected portions of an image giving it a blurred effect.

Brush Tool: A tool in Photoshop used for creating soft strokes of colour in an image.

Burn Tool: A tool in Photoshop used for darkening the areas of an image.

Bus topology: A type of topology in which all computers are connected to a single cable called bus.

C

Clone Stamp Tool: A tool in Photoshop that allows duplicating part of an image by setting a sampling point in the image to be cloned.

Coaxial cable: An electrical cable with a conductor at its centre. The inner conductor is surrounded by a tubular insulating layer. The insulating layer is surrounded by a conductive layer called the shield which is finally covered with a thin insulating layer on the outside.

Color Replacement Tool: A tool in Photoshop used for quickly replacing a selected colour with the currently selected foreground colour.

Crop Tool: A tool in Photoshop used for removing unwanted portions of an image.

Custom Shape Tool: A tool in Photoshop used for drawing a variety of preset shapes like flowers and grids.

D

Database: An organised collection of related data.

Database Management System (DBMS): A software program that enables creation and management of databases.

Definition list: A list of terms and definitions of terms in HTML created using the <DL>, <DT> and <DD> tag.

Dodge Tool: A tool in Photoshop used for lightening the areas of an image.

E

Eraser Tool: A tool in Photoshop that erases pixels in an image to transparency or to the background colour as you drag it across the image.

External linking: Linking two different webpages in HTML.

F

Fiber Optic cable: A cable that consists of a center glass core surrounded by several layers of protective material. It transmits data in the form of light rather than electronic signals.

Filters: Filters let you change the appearance of an image by adding special effects to it.

Firewall: It can be implemented as hardware device or software that prevents unauthorised access to the network.

Frame: It lets you display more than one HTML document in the same browser window.

G

Gradient Tool: A tool in Photoshop used for filling selected areas of an image with a blend of multiple colours.

H

Healing Brush tool: A tool in Photoshop that allows repairing of imperfections such as scratches, blemishes and marks in an image.

Hotspot: A text, image or any other object that acts as a hyperlink.

I

Image map: An image in which multiple areas within the image act as hyperlinks.

Integrated Development Environment: A common environment offered by programming languages such as Visual Basic that let users to design, edit and remove errors in the programs easily.

Internal Linking: Linking different sections of the same webpage.

L

Lasso tools: A collection of tools in Photoshop used for selecting different portions of the image by drawing a freehand or a straight-edged area.

Layers: It can be thought of transparent sheets mounted on top of each other. Layers let you work on individual parts of an image without affecting others in Photoshop.

Local Area Network (LAN): A computer network that is limited to a small area such as a lab, a school and an office building.

M

Magic Wand Tool: A tool in Photoshop used for selecting areas of an image that share a similar colour.

Marquee effect: An effect that makes the text scroll or move in an HTML page.

Marquee tools: A collection of tools in Photoshop used for selecting different portions of the image in rectangular, elliptical, single row or single column shape.

Mesh topology: A type of topology in which every computer is connected to every other computer in the network.

Metropolitan Area Network (MAN): A computer network that spans a larger area than a LAN such as a network that connects two offices in a city or a neighborhood area, etc.

Modem (short for modulator-demodulator): An electronic device that converts the digital signals of a computer into analog form and vice versa so that the signals can travel over a telephone wire.

Move Tool: A tool in Photoshop used for dragging a selected part of the image to a new location in the image.

N

Network: A group of computers connected to ecah other in order to share resources such as printers and exchange files. It allows electronic communication in a network

Network Interface Card (NIC): A hardware device that stores the hardware address of a computer and enables it to communicate over the network.

O

Ordered list: A numbered list of items in HTML created using <OL> tag.

P

Pattern Stamp Tool: A tool in Photoshop that allows filling an area with a selected pattern.

Primary Key: A primary key is a field or combination of fields that uniquely identifies the records in the table.

Protocol: A set of rules used by computers on the network to communicate with each other.

R

Record: A horizontal row in a table that stores complete information about an item or object

Relation (or Table): A container in a database that stores data in row and column format.

Relational Database Management System (RDBMS): A DBMS that stores data in the form of tables.

Ring topology: A type of topology in which every computer is connected to two other computers in the network so as to form a closed ring-like structure.

S

Sharpen Tool: A tool in Photoshop that lets you improve the clarity of an image by sharpening the edges of selected portions of an image.

Smudge Tool: A tool in Photoshop that gives an effect of spreading the paint across the image as if you have dragged your finger through a wet paint.

Spot Healing Brush Tool: A tool in Photoshop that allows repairing of imperfections such as blemishes and other marks in your photos quickly.

Star topology: A type of topology in which all computers in the network are connected to a central computer.

Storyboard View: A view in Windows Movie Maker that displays the sequence of clips in the movie.

Switch: A device used to connnect computers in a network.

T

Timeline View: A view pattern in Windows Movie Maker to review or modify the timings of video clips or pictures.

Topology: The layout pattern in which computers are connected to one another to form a network.

Trojan horse: A computer program that appears to be useful software but will actually do damage once installed or run on your computer.

Twisted pair cable: A type of cable that consists of a pair of insulated wires twisted together.

Type tools: A tool in Photoshop used for inserting text.

U

Unordered list: A bulleted list of items in HTML created using the <UL> tag.

V

Virus: A computer program that can spread itself from one computer to another and interferes with the normal operations of the computer.

W

Wide Area Network (WAN): A computer network that spans a very large area. A WAN may be spread across cities, countries and continents.

Worm: A computer program that uses computer networks to send copies of itself to other computers on the network.